D0468768

# CREATED
## *in*
# GOD'S IMAGE

Anthony A. Hoekema

WILLIAM B. EERDMANS PUBLISHING COMPANY
GRAND RAPIDS, MICHIGAN

THE PATERNOSTER PRESS
CARLISLE, UK

Copyright © 1986 by Wm. B. Eerdmans Publishing Co.
First edition 1986

First paperback edition published jointly 1994
in the United States by
Wm. B. Eerdmans Publishing Co.
255 Jefferson Ave. S.E., Grand Rapids, Michigan 49503
and in the UK by
The Paternoster Press
P.O. Box 300, Carlisle, Cumbria, CA3 0QS, UK

All rights reserved.
No part of this publication may be reproduced, stored in a retrieval system,
or transmitted in any form or by any means, electronic, mechanical, photocopying,
recording, or otherwise, without the prior permission of the publishers.

Printed in the United States of America

00 99 98 97          7 6 5 4 3

**Library of Congress Cataloging-in-Publication Data**

Hoekema, Anthony A., 1913-1988.
Created in God's image.
Bibliography: p.
Includes index.
1. Man (Christian theology). 2. Reformed Church — Doctrines.
I. Title.
BT701.2.H623     1986     233     85-29380
ISBN 0-8028-0850-6

**British Library Cataloguing in Publication Data**

Hoekema, Anthony A
Created in God's image
1. Man (Christian Theology)
I. Title
233   BT 701.2
ISBN 0-85364-626-0

Unless otherwise noted, Scripture quotations are from the Holy Bible, New International
Version. Copyright © 1973, 1978, 1984 International Bible Society. Used by permission of
Zondervan Bible Publishers.

*To our dear children:*
*Dorothy*
*James*
*David*
*Helen*

# Contents

# Preface

This is the second in a series of doctrinal studies. An earlier volume, *The Bible and the Future*, dealt with Christian eschatology, or the doctrine of the last things. The present study will concern itself with theological anthropology, or the Christian doctrine of man.

In this book I will attempt to set forth what the Bible teaches about the nature and destiny of human beings. Central to the biblical understanding of man is the teaching that men and women were created in the image of God. I will present the image of God as having both a structural and a functional aspect, as involving man in his threefold relationship—to God, to others, and to nature—and as going through four stages—the original image, the perverted image, the renewed image, and the perfected image. I have based my study on a close examination of the relevant scriptural material. The theological standpoint represented here is that of evangelical Christianity from a Reformed or Calvinistic perspective.

I should like to express appreciation to my students over the years at Calvin Theological Seminary, to whom this material was originally presented, and whose responses and comments helped to sharpen my thinking on this topic. I particularly wish to thank Professors John Cooper, Cornelius Plantinga, Jr., and Louis Vos, who read parts of the manuscript and offered helpful suggestions.

I am grateful to the Calvin Theological Library for the use of its facilities and, particularly, for letting me occupy an office in the library after my retirement. I wish especially to thank the theological librarian, Peter De Klerk, for his exceptional helpfulness.

Thanks are due to the editorial staff at Eerdmans Publishing Company for their helpful advice at various stages of the writing, particularly to Jon Pott and Sandra Nowlin.

I also owe thanks to my wife, Ruth, for her constant encouragement, for her perceptive comments on the manuscript, and for her help in putting the bibliography together.

Above all, I want to thank the God who created us in his image, and who continues to make us more like himself. We look forward eagerly to the day when we shall be totally like him, since we shall see him as he is.

*Grand Rapids, Michigan*                    —ANTHONY A. HOEKEMA

# *Abbreviations*

| | |
|---|---|
| ASV | American Standard Version |
| Bavinck, *Dogmatiek* | H. Bavinck, *Gereformeerde Dogmatiek*, 3rd ed. |
| Berkouwer, *Man* | G. C. Berkouwer, *Man: The Image of God* |
| *Inst.* | J. Calvin, *Institutes of the Christian Religion* |
| ISBE | *International Standard Bible Encyclopedia*, rev. ed. |
| JB | Jerusalem Bible |
| KJV | King James Version |
| NASB | New American Standard Bible |
| NEB | New English Bible |
| NIV | New International Version |
| RSV | Revised Standard Version |
| TDNT | *Theological Dictionary of the New Testament* |

(See Bibliography for full publishing information.)

# CREATED
# IN GOD'S IMAGE

# CHAPTER 1

# *The Importance of the Doctrine of Man*

It is difficult to exaggerate the importance of the doctrine of man.[1] It has, of course, always been true that one of the most important questions to which the philosopher addresses himself is, What is man? In one of his dialogues Plato pictures his master, Socrates, as a man obsessed with one central aim in his search for wisdom: namely, to know himself. Various thinkers have given various answers to the question "What is man?", each one with far-reaching implications for thought and life.

Today, however, this question about man is being asked with a new urgency. Some have observed that people today are no longer much interested in questions about ultimate reality or ontology, but they are vitally interested in questions about man. There are many reasons for this. One is that since Immanuel Kant the problem of epistemology (how do we know?) has become primary, whereas the problem of ontology (what is ultimate being?) has become secondary. The rise of existentialism as a philosophical, theological, and literary way of thinking has brought a new emphasis: namely, that man's existence is more important than his essence—that what is unique and unrepeatable about a person is more important for understanding him or her than what he or she has in common with all other persons. Existentialism, therefore, is a new way of asking the question "What is man?" As belief in God becomes more rare, belief in man is taking its place; and so we are witnessing the rise of a new humanism.

---

1. I use the word *man* here and frequently in what follows as meaning "human being," whether male or female. When the word *man* is used in this generic sense, pronouns referring to man (he, his, or him) must also be understood as having this generic sense; the same is true of the use of such masculine pronouns with the word *person*. It is a pity that the English language has no word corresponding to the German word *Mensch*, which means human being as such, regardless of gender. *Man* in English may have this meaning, though it may also mean "male human being." It will usually be clear from the context in which sense the word *man* is being used.

1

But even humanism is in trouble. Two world wars and the unmentionable atrocities of the Nazi regime have shaken many people's faith in man's basic goodness and in the significance of human values. Hence there has appeared a new wave of nihilism, which denies all human values and speaks of the meaninglessness of life. Among the factors that threaten human values today are the following: the growing supremacy of technology; the growth of bureaucracy; the increase of mass-production methods; and the growing impact of mass media. Forces such as these tend to depersonalize humanity. New developments in biology, psychology, and sociology increase the possibility of the manipulation of the masses by the few. Practices such as artificial insemination, test-tube babies, abortion, chemical control of behavior, euthanasia, genetic engineering, and the like raise questions about the dignity of human life. Add to this such burning issues as racism, the problem of alienation (old versus young, conservative versus progressive, majority versus minority groups), the problem of equality between women and men, and the problem of decreasing respect for authority, and one can see why the question "What is man?" has acquired new urgency today.

The problem of man has therefore become one of the most crucial problems of our day. Philosophers are wrestling with it; sociologists are trying to answer it; psychologists and psychiatrists are facing it; ethicists and social activists are attempting to solve it. Novelists and dramatists also concern themselves with this question. Dostoyevski's penetrating novels are attempts to answer it, along with the related question, "Why is man here?" Jean-Paul Sartre and Albert Camus have tried to give us their non-Christian answers to the question, whereas writers like Graham Greene and Morris West have tried to give us their Christian answers. Virtually every contemporary novel or play deals with the question, "What is man?"

What one thinks about human beings is of determinative significance for his or her program of action. The goal of the Marxist is rooted in his conception of man. The same can be said for the program of the political revolutionary who may not be a Marxist. The recent feminist movement is also rooted in a certain understanding of the human person, particularly of the relation between man and woman.

We can distinguish different types of non-Christian anthropologies. *Idealistic* anthropologies consider the human being to be basically spirit, his physical body foreign to his real nature. We find this view in ancient Greek philosophy; according to Plato, for example, what is real about man is his or her intellect or reason, which is actually a spark of the divine within the person that continues to exist after the body dies. The human body, however, partakes of matter, which is of a lower order of reality; it is a hindrance to the spirit, and one is really better off without it. Those who hold this view teach the immortality of the soul but deny the resurrection of the body.

More common today is the opposite type of non-Christian anthropology, the *materialistic* type. According to this view, man is a being composed of material elements, his mental, emotional, and spiritual life being simply by-products of his material structure. For example, the Marxist view of the economic determination of history rests on a materialistic or naturalistic view of human nature. For the Marxist, man is simply a product of nature. Human beings have not been created in the image of God—in fact, the very existence of the Creator is denied. Foreign to Marxism are such concepts as an ethical imperative or one's moral responsibility to God. Humans are part of a social structure; evil arises from that structure and can be eliminated only by changes in it. The individual is not primarily responsible for the evil that he may do; society is. In Marxism, therefore, the human being is not important as an individual; he is important only as a member of society. Thus, the goal of Marxism is not individual salvation but the future attainment of the perfect society, in which the class struggle between the "haves" and the "have-nots" will have been eliminated. Violent revolutionary action may be necessary for the attainment of that future society.

Another type of materialistic anthropology influential today is the view of man that underlies the writings of B. F. Skinner. In *Beyond Freedom and Dignity*[2] Skinner maintains that the idea that the human being is responsible for his or her behavior is rooted in a tradition that is no longer scientifically acceptable. The determination of behavior must be shifted from what Skinner calls "autonomous man" to the environment.[3] The idea that the human person has freedom to act as he "wills" is a myth; one's conduct is totally determined by his or her environment. There is in man no decision-making "mind"; there is in him or her neither freedom nor dignity. Human activity is totally determined by the environment; if that environment were perfectly known, human behavior would be completely predictable.

One way of evaluating these views would be to say that they are one-sided; that is, they emphasize one aspect of the human being at the expense of others. Idealistic anthropologies lay all the emphasis on one's "soul" or "reason," while denying full reality to his or her material structure. Materialistic anthropologies, like those of Marx and Skinner, absolutize the physical side of man while denying the reality of what we might call his or her "mental" or "spiritual" side.

We must go beyond this kind of judgment, however, and enter

2. New York: Alfred A. Knopf, 1972.
3. Ibid., pp. 195, 214.

into the heart of the matter. Since each of the above-named views of man considers one aspect of the human being to be ultimate, apart from any dependence on or responsibility to God the Creator, each of these anthropologies is guilty of idolatry: of worshiping an aspect of creation in the place of God. If, as the Bible teaches, the most important thing about man is that he is inescapably related to God, we must judge as deficient any anthropology which denies that relatedness.

We must therefore make a sharp distinction between idealistic and materialistic anthropologies on the one hand, and a Christian anthropology on the other. In this book our purpose will be to explore the Christian view of man—what it is, how it differs from non-Christian views, and what are its implications for our thinking and living. We shall be trying to identify the uniqueness of the Christian view of man, that which makes Christian anthropology different from all other anthropologies.

We must remember, however, that often non-Christian notions have crept into so-called Christian anthropologies. For example, the scholastic view of man prominent during the Middle Ages, though accepted as Christian, was actually more of a hybrid anthropology. It attempted to synthesize the idealistic view of man found in Aristotelian philosophy with the Christian view. The results of this mismating of two diverse anthropologies are, unfortunately, with us to this day. For example, the common notion among Christians that "sins of the flesh" (like adultery) are far more serious than "sins of the spirit" (such as pride, jealousy, self-centeredness, racism, and the like) stems from the view, implicit in scholastic anthropology, that evil has its roots chiefly in the body.

It is therefore important for us to have the right understanding of man. As we try to arrive at a proper Christian understanding, we should keep in mind such questions as these: Are there still remnants of non-Christian anthropology in our thinking about man? How does our view of the human person help us better to understand God (e.g., does the truth that man has been made in the image of God teach us something about God as well as something about man?)? What light does our anthropology shed on the work of Christ? What light does our view of man shed on soteriology (the way in which the benefits of Christ are applied to us by the Holy Spirit)? What light does our view of human nature shed on the doctrine of the church and the doctrine of the last things? What relevance does a Christian anthropology have for our daily life? How does the Christian view of man help us better to face the pressing problems of today's world?

# CHAPTER 2

# *Man as a Created Person*

**O**ne of the basic presuppositions of the Christian view of man is belief in God as the Creator, which leads to the view that the human person does not exist autonomously or independently, but as a creature of God. "In the beginning God created the heavens and the earth. . . . So God created man" (Gen. 1:1, 27).

An obvious implication of the fact of creation is that all created reality is completely dependent on God. Werner Foerster puts it this way: "Thus in becoming, being, and perishing, all creation is wholly dependent on the will of the Creator."[1]

The Scriptures make it very clear that all created things and all created beings are totally dependent on God. "Thou [God] hast made heaven, the heaven of heavens, with all their host, the earth and all that is on it, the seas with all that is in them; and thou preservest all of them" (Neh. 9:6, RSV). That God preserves all his creatures, including human beings, implies that they are dependent on him for their continued existence. In his address to the Athenians Paul affirms that God "gives all men life and breath and everything else," and that "in him we live and move and have our being" (Acts 17:25, 28). We owe, Paul is saying, our very breath to God; we exist only in him; in every move we make we are dependent on him. We cannot lift a finger apart from God's will.

Man is not only a creature, however; he is also a person. And to be a person means to have a kind of independence—not absolute but relative. To be a person means to be able to make decisions, to set goals, and to move in the direction of those goals. It means to possess freedom[2]—at least in the sense of being able to make one's own choices. The human being is not a robot whose course is totally determined

1. *"Ktizō,"* TDNT, 3:1011.
2. More will be said in Chap. 12 about the meaning of the concept of freedom when applied to human beings.

by forces outside of him; he has the power of self-determination and self-direction. To be a person means, to use Leonard Verduin's picturesque expression, to be a "creature of option."[3]

In sum, the human being is both a creature and a person; he or she is a *created person*. This, now, is the central mystery of man: how can man be both a creature and a person at the same time? To be a creature, as we have seen, means absolute dependence on God; to be a person means relative independence. To be a creature means that I cannot move a finger or utter a word apart from God; to be a person means that when my fingers are moved, I move them, and that when words are uttered by my lips, I utter them. To be creatures means that God is the potter and we are the clay (Rom. 9:21); to be persons means that we are the ones who fashion our lives by our own decisions (Gal. 6:7-8).

I have called this the central mystery of man because to us it seems deeply mysterious that man can be both a creature and a person at the same time. Dependence and freedom seem to us to be incompatible concepts. We grant that a child is completely dependent on his or her parents in infancy, but we note that as that child develops in the direction of greater freedom and maturity, the child becomes less dependent on his or her parents. This we can understand. But how are we to conceive of a relationship in which complete dependence on God and personal freedom to make our own decisions continue to go hand in hand?

Though we cannot rationally comprehend how it is possible for the human being to be a creature and a person at the same time, clearly this is what we must think. Denial of either side of this paradox will fail to do justice to the biblical picture. The Bible teaches both man's creatureliness and man's personhood. Sometimes it addresses the human being as a creature: for example, when it speaks of God as the potter and man as the clay (Rom. 9:21). More often, however, it addresses him or her as a person: "Choose for yourselves this day whom you will serve" (Josh. 24:15); "We implore you on Christ's behalf: Be reconciled to God" (2 Cor. 5:20).

Our theological understanding of man must, therefore, keep both of these truths clearly in focus. All secular anthropologies fail to take into account human creatureliness and therefore give a distorted view of man. Any view of the human being that fails to see him or her as centrally related to, totally dependent on, and primarily responsible to God falls short of the truth. On the other hand, all deterministic an-

---

3. Verduin develops this thought extensively in Chap. 5 of his *Somewhat less than God* (Grand Rapids: Eerdmans, 1970).

terministic anthropologies, which treat humans as if they were puppets or robots, perhaps with God pulling the strings or pushing the buttons, fail to do justice to human personhood, and therefore give an equally distorted view of man. Robert D. Brinsmead stated this point well:

> The creaturehood and the personhood of man must be held both together and in tension. When theology stresses creaturehood and subordinates personhood, a hard-faced determinism surfaces and man is dehumanized. . . . When personhood is stressed to the exclusion of creaturehood, man is deified and God's sovereignty is compromised. The Lord is left standing helplessly in the wings as if man had the power to veto the plans and purposes of God.[4]

The fact that man is a created person has implications for other aspects of our theology. First, what light does this concept shed on the question of the origin of sin? While granting that the reason man sinned will always remain an unfathomable mystery, we shall have to say that man could fall into sin precisely because he was a person, able to make choices—even choices that would be contrary to the will of God. Yet we shall also have to add that even in sinning the human being remains a creature, dependent on God. God, so to speak, had to furnish man with the strength with which he sinned; the magnitude of man's sin consists in the fact that he used God-given powers in the service of Satan. Because our first parents fell into sin as created persons, we speak of God's "permissive will" with respect to man's first sin, and affirm that this first sin did not come as a surprise to God, though he held those who committed it wholly responsible for it.

Second, what light does the concept of the created person shed on the way in which God redeems man? The fact that man is a creature implies that after he has fallen into sin (through his own fault), he can be redeemed from sin and rescued from his fallen state only through God's sovereign intervention on his behalf. Since he is a creature, man can only be saved by grace—that is, in utter dependence on the mercy of God. But the fact that man is also a person implies that he or she has an important part to play in the process of being redeemed. Man is not saved like a robot whose activities have been programmed by some celestial computer, but like a person. Therefore human beings have a responsibility in the process of their salvation. They must choose freely, in the strength of the Holy Spirit, to repent of sin and to believe in the Lord Jesus Christ. They cannot be saved apart from such personal choices (though exceptions must be made for cases in which the individuals involved are not capable of making personal choices).

4. "Man as Creature and Person," *Verdict* (Aug. 1978):21-22.

After a person has made such a choice, he or she must continue to live in fellowship with God and in the obedience of faith. The fact that we can live in this way only through God's strength does not take away our responsibility to live such a life.

As an illustration of this point, let us consider how regeneration is related to faith. Regeneration can be defined as that act of the Holy Spirit, not to be separated from the preaching of the Word, whereby he initially brings a person into living union with Christ and changes his heart so that he who was spiritually dead becomes spiritually alive. Such a radical change cannot be the work of man but must be the work of God. Those who are regenerate are described as having been "born, not of blood, nor of the will of the flesh, nor of the will of man, but of God" (John 1:13, RSV). Further, apart from regeneration man is spiritually dead (Eph. 2:5), and a dead person cannot make himself or herself alive. Since man has gotten himself into a state of spiritual deadness, and since he is a creature, he can receive new life only through a miraculous act of God—so miraculous that Paul can call a person so regenerated a new creation (2 Cor. 5:17).

Since man is a creature, God must regenerate him—give him new spiritual life. Since man is also a person, however, he or she must also believe—that is, in response to the gospel, he or she must make a conscious, personal choice to accept Christ and follow him. These two, regeneration and faith, must always be seen together. It is significant that John in his Gospel keeps these two together. After Jesus told Nicodemus that unless one has been born again he cannot see the kingdom of God (John 3:3), he also told him that God so loved the world that he gave his only Son, that whoever believes in him should not perish but have eternal life (v. 16). Regeneration, which is the work of the Holy Spirit, is absolutely necessary if one is to see the kingdom of God—but at the point where the gospel call makes its appeal to the hearer, it calls for faith, which involves a personal decision. God must regenerate and man must believe: these two must always be kept together.

As a further illustration of this point, let us look at the process of sanctification. Sanctification may be defined as that operation of the Holy Spirit, involving man's responsible participation, by which he renews man's nature and enables him to live to the praise of God. Sanctification, therefore, is both the work of God and the task of man. Since human beings are creatures, God in the person of the Holy Spirit must sanctify them; since they are also persons, they must themselves be responsibly involved in their sanctification, "perfecting holiness out of reverence for God" (2 Cor. 7:1).

In this connection, note Paul's striking words in Philippians

2:12-13: "Continue to work out your salvation with fear and trembling, for it is God who works in you to will and to act according to his good purpose." The word translated "work out," *katergazesthe*, is commonly used in the papyri of the early Christian centuries to describe what a farmer does when he cultivates his land.[5] "Work out your salvation," therefore, means: "cultivate" the salvation God has given you; "work out" what God has "worked in"; apply the salvation you have received to every area of your lives—work, recreation, family life, culture, art, science, and the like. In other words, Paul is telling his readers to take an active part in the advancement of their sanctification. "For," he goes on to say, "it is God who works in you to will and to act." Willing and acting (or "working," ASV, RSV) designate everything we think or do. It is God, therefore, who is continually working in us the entire process of sanctification: both the willing of it and the doing of it. The harder we work, the more sure we may be that God is working in us. In sanctifying us God deals with us both as persons and as creatures.

The same principle holds for the doctrine of the perseverance of the saints. Since we are creatures, God must preserve us and keep us true to him. The Bible clearly teaches this (see, e.g., John 10:27-28; Rom. 8:38-39; Heb. 7:25; 1 Pet. 1:3-5; Jude 24). But we must not lose sight of the other side of the paradox: believers must persevere in the faith (Matt. 10:22; 1 Cor. 16:13; Heb. 3:14; Rev. 3:11). It is not a question of preservation *or* perseverance. Because we are creatures, God must preserve us or we shall surely fall. But because we are also persons, God preserves us by enabling us to persevere.

There are yet more implications for our theology of the creature-person concept. Scripture teaches that God saves man by placing him into a covenant relationship with him. Since God is the Creator and man is a creature, it is obvious that God must take the initiative in placing his people into such a covenantal relationship—hence we say that the covenant of grace is unilateral in its origin. But since man is a person, he has responsibilities in this covenant, and must fulfill his covenant obligations—hence we say that the covenant of grace is bilateral in its fulfillment.

Further, the understanding of man as a created person helps us to answer the much-debated question of whether the covenant of grace is conditional or unconditional. Because man is a creature, the covenant is unconditional in its origin; God graciously establishes his covenant with his people apart from any conditions they must fulfill.

---

5. J. H. Moulton and G. Milligan, *The Vocabulary of the Greek Testament Illustrated from the Papyri* (Grand Rapids: Eerdmans, 1957), pp. 335-36.

But since man is also a person, God requires that his people fulfill certain conditions in order to enjoy the blessings of the covenant. But people can only fulfill these conditions through the enabling power of God. In the covenant of grace, therefore, both God's sovereign grace and man's serious responsibility come into focus. Hence the Bible contains both covenant promises and covenant threats, and we must do full justice to both.

Another important theological concept is that of the image of God. In later chapters I will develop this concept in much greater detail. Here I can be brief. Because of his fall into sin, man has in one sense lost the image of God (some theologians call this the narrower or functional sense). Instead of serving and obeying God, man is now turned away from God; he is "man in revolt." In the work of redemption God graciously restores his image in man, making him once again like God in his love, faithfulness, and willingness to serve others. Because human beings are creatures, God must restore them to his image—this is a work of sovereign grace. But because they are also persons, they have a responsibility in this restoration—hence Paul can say to the Ephesians, "Be imitators of God" (5:1).

Enough has been said to show that the understanding of man as a created person is both important and relevant. Theologians like myself who stand in the Reformed or Calvinistic tradition have commonly emphasized the creaturely aspect of man (his total dependence on God), and therefore the ultimate sovereignty of God in every area of life, particularly in the work of saving his people from their sins. Arminian theologians, on the other hand, usually lay all the stress on man's personhood. Hence when they speak of the process of salvation they will emphasize the importance of man's voluntary decision and continuing faithfulness to God. Keeping in mind the paradox that man is both a creature and a person will help us do full justice to both the sovereignty of God and the responsibility of man. Those of us who stand in the Reformed tradition must not neglect or deny the responsibility of man; those who stand in the Arminian tradition should not neglect or deny the ultimate sovereignty of God.

## CHAPTER 3

# The Image of God:
# Biblical Teaching

The most distinctive feature of the biblical understanding of man is the teaching that man has been created in the image of God. We will explore this concept in this and the following two chapters. Our first task is to examine the biblical teaching on the image of God, as found first in the Old Testament and then in the New.

## OLD TESTAMENT TEACHING

The Old Testament does not say much about the image of God. In fact, the concept is dealt with explicitly in only three passages, all of them from the Book of Genesis: 1:26-28; 5:1-3; and 9:6. One could also think of Psalm 8 as describing what man's creation in God's image means, but the phrase "image of God" is not found there. We will look at all four of these passages in turn.

Genesis 1:26-28 reads:

> (26) Then God said, "Let us make man in our image, after our likeness; and let them have dominion over the fish of the sea, and over the birds of the air, and over the cattle, and over all the earth, and over every creeping thing that creeps upon the earth." (27) So God created man in his own image, in the image of God he created him; male and female he created them. (28) And God blessed them, and God said to them, "Be fruitful and multiply, and fill the earth and subdue it; and have dominion over the fish of the sea and over the birds of the air and over every living thing that moves upon the earth." (RSV)

The first chapter of Genesis teaches the uniqueness of the creation of man. Here we read that, while God created each animal "according to his kind" (vv. 21, 24, 25), only man was created in God's image and after God's likeness (vv. 26-27). Herman Bavinck puts it this way:

> The entire world is a revelation of God, a mirror of his virtues and perfections; every creature is in his own way and according to his own

**11**

measure an embodiment of a divine thought. But among all creatures only man is the image of God, the highest and richest revelation of God, and therefore head and crown of the entire creation.[1]

The first thing that strikes us as we look at Genesis 1:26 is that the main verb is in the plural: "Then God said, 'Let us make man. . . .' " This indicates that the creation of man is in a class by itself, since this type of expression is used of no other creature. Many scholars have attempted to explain this plural. Some call it a "plural of majesty," an unlikely possibility since such a plural is not found elsewhere in Scripture. Others have suggested that God is here addressing the angels. We must also reject this interpretation, since God is never said to take counsel with angels, who—themselves creatures—cannot create man, and since man is not made in the likeness of angels.[2] Rather, we should interpret the plural as indicating that God does not exist as a solitary being, but as a being in fellowship with "others." Though we cannot say that we have here clear teaching about the Trinity, we do learn that God exists as a "plurality." What is here merely hinted at is further developed in the New Testament into the doctrine of the Trinity.

It should also be noted that a divine counsel or deliberation preceded the creation of man: "Let us make man. . . ." This again brings out the uniqueness of man's creation. In connection with no other creature is such a divine counsel mentioned.

The word translated as *man* in these verses is the Hebrew word *'ādām*. This word is sometimes used as a proper name, *Adam* (see, e.g., Gen. 5:1, "This is the book of the generations of Adam," RSV). The Hebrew word *'ādām*, however, may also mean *man* in the generic sense: man as a human being. In this sense, the word has the same meaning as the German word *Mensch*: not man in distinction from woman, but man in distinction from nonhuman creatures, that is, man as either male *or* female, or man as both male *and* female. It is in this sense that the word is used in Genesis 1:26 and 27. The word *'ādām* may also occasionally mean *humankind* (see, e.g., Gen. 6:5, "The Lord saw that the wickedness of man was great in the earth," RSV). Since

1. Herman Bavinck, *Dogmatiek*, 2:566 [trans. mine].
2. Note, e.g., what is said about God in Isa. 40:14, "With whom took he counsel. . . ?" (ASV). Note, too, that Gen. 3:21 also refers to God in the plural, where angels are obviously excluded: "The man has now become like one of us." On this point see Calvin, *Comm. on Genesis*, trans. John King (Grand Rapids: Eerdmans, 1948), *ad loc.*; G. Ch. Aalders, *Genesis*, trans. W. Heynen (Grand Rapids: Zondervan, 1981), *ad loc.*; H. C. Leupold, *Exposition of Genesis* (Grand Rapids: Baker, 1953), *ad loc.*; and L. Berkhof, *Systematic Theology* rev. and enl. ed. (Grand Rapids: Eerdmans, 1941), p. 182.

the blessing found in Genesis 1:28 applies to all of humankind, we could even say that verses 26 and 27 describe the creation of humankind, but then we shall have to qualify the statement in some such way as this: God created the man and the woman from whom all humankind would descend.

We come now to the significant words: "in our image, after our likeness." The word translated as *image* is *tselem*; the word rendered as *likeness* is *demûth*. In the Hebrew there is no conjunction between the two expressions; the text says simply "let us make man in our image, after our likeness." Both the Septuagint[3] and the Vulgate[4] insert an *and* between the two expressions, giving the impression that "image" and "likeness" refer to different things. The Hebrew text, however, makes it clear that there is no essential difference between the two: "after our likeness" is only a different way of saying "in our image." This is borne out by examining the usage of these words in this passage and in the two other passages in Genesis. In Genesis 1:26 both *image* and *likeness* are used; in 1:27 only *image* is used, while in 5:1 only the word *likeness* is used. In 5:3 the two words are used again but this time in a different order: *in his own likeness, after his image*. And again in 9:6 only the word *image* is used. If these words were intended to describe different aspects of the human being, they would not be used as we have seen them used, that is, almost interchangeably.

Although these words are used generally as synonyms, we may recognize a slight difference between the two. The Hebrew word for image, *tselem*, is derived from a root that means "to carve" or "to cut."[5] It could therefore be used to describe a carved likeness of an animal or a person. When it is applied to the creation of man in Genesis 1, the word *tselem* indicates that man images God, that is, is a representation of God. The Hebrew word for likeness, *demûth*, comes from a root that means "to be like."[6] One could therefore say that the word *demûth* in Genesis 1 indicates that the image is also a likeness, "an image which is like us."[7] The two words together tell us that man is a representation of God who is like God in certain respects.

In what way man is like God is not specifically and explicitly

---

3. The Greek version of the Old Testament, produced in the third century B.C.

4. The Latin translation of the Bible, produced by Jerome from 382 to 404 A.D.

5. Francis Brown, S. R. Driver, and Charles Briggs, *Hebrew and English Lexicon of the Old Testament* (New York: Houghton Mifflin, 1907), p. 853.

6. Ibid., pp. 197-98.

7. Ascribed to Luther in Keil and Delitzsch, *Biblical Commentary on the Old Testament*, vol. 1, *The Pentateuch*, trans. James Martin (Edinburgh: T. & T. Clark, 1861), p. 63.

stated in the creation account, although one may note that certain resemblances to God are implied there. For example, from Genesis 1:26 we may infer that dominion over the animals and over all the earth is one aspect of the image of God. In exercising this dominion man is like God, since God has supreme and ultimate dominion over the earth. From verse 27 we may infer that another aspect of the image of God is man's having been created male and female. Since God is spirit (John 4:24), we may not conclude that the resemblance to God in this instance is found in the physical difference between men and women. Rather, the resemblance must be found in the fact that man needs the companionship of woman, that the human person is a social being, that woman complements man and that man complements woman. In this way human beings reflect God, who exists not as a solitary being but as a being in fellowship—a fellowship that is described at a later stage of divine revelation as that between the Father, the Son, and the Holy Spirit. From the fact that God blessed human beings and gave them a mandate (v. 28), we may infer that humans also resemble God in that they are persons, responsible beings, who can be addressed by God and who are ultimately responsible to God as their Creator and Ruler. As God is here revealed as a person (later in the history of revelation this is expanded to three persons) who is able to make decisions and to rule, so man is a person who is likewise able to make decisions and to rule.

Continuing our study of Genesis 1:26-28, we see in verse 28 God's blessing upon man (as v. 22 shows God's blessing on the animals). The last part of this blessing corresponds very closely to what was said about human beings in verse 26: "let them have dominion." Only now the verbs are in the second person plural and are addressed to our first parents. These words about man's dominion are preceded by the following words, not found in verse 26: "Be fruitful and multiply and fill the earth." The injunction to be fruitful and multiply implies the institution of marriage, the establishment of which is narrated in the second chapter of Genesis (vv. 18-24).

In giving his blessing, God promises to enable human beings to propagate and bring forth children who will fill the earth; he also promises to enable them to subdue the earth and to have dominion over the animals and over the earth itself. Though these words are called a blessing, they also contain a commandment or a mandate. God commands man to be fruitful and to have dominion. This is commonly called the *cultural mandate*: the command to rule the earth for God, and to develop a God-glorifying culture.

Before we move on to the next passage, one more thing should be noted. Verse 31 reads: "And God saw everything that he had made, and behold, it was very good" (RSV). "Everything that he had made" includes man. Man, therefore, as he came from the hands of the Creator, was not corrupt, depraved, or sinful; he was in a state of integrity, innocence, and holiness. Whatever in human beings today is evil or perverted was not part of man's original creation. At the time of his creation man was very good.

The second passage that deals with the image of God, Genesis 5:1-3, reads as follows:

> (1) This is the book of the generations of Adam. When God created man, he made him in the likeness of God. (2) Male and female he created them, and he blessed them and named them Man when they were created. (3) When Adam had lived a hundred and thirty years, he became the father of a son in his own likeness, after his image, and named him Seth. (RSV)

We have in verse 1 a reminder that God made man in his likeness. Here only one of the two words used in Genesis 1:26 is employed, the word *likeness*. The omission of the word *image* is not particularly significant, though, for as we have seen, these words are used synonymously.

Some believe that at the time of man's fall into sin he lost the image of God, and can therefore no longer be called God's image-bearer. But there is no hint of this in Genesis 5:1. This statement, occurring after the narrative of the Fall (chap. 3), still speaks of Adam as someone who was made in the likeness of God. There would be no point in saying this if by this time the divine likeness had completely disappeared. We may indeed think of the image of God as having been tarnished through man's fall into sin, but to affirm that man had by this time completely lost the image of God is to affirm something that the sacred text does not say.

In verse 3 we read that Adam became the father of a son in his likeness, after his image. Here the same two words are used as in Genesis 1:26; only the order of the words is reversed and the words are modified by different prepositions—further proof that *image* and *likeness* are used synonymously. What strikes us here is that it is not said that Adam's son Seth was made in the image and likeness *of God*. Rather, it is said that Adam became the father of a son in *his* likeness, after *his* image. But if Adam was still the image-bearer of God, as we saw, we may infer that Seth, his son, was also an image-bearer of God. Further, since the Bible teaches that Adam's nature was corrupted and polluted by the Fall,[8] we may again infer that Adam transmitted this

---

8. See below, pp. 142-43, 149-54.

corruption and pollution to his son. But again, there is no hint here that the image of God has been lost.

Genesis 9:6, the third passage dealing with the image of God, reads: "Whoever sheds the blood of man, by man shall his blood be shed; for in the image of God has God made man."

First, note the setting of these verses. The waters of the flood have abated, and Noah and his family have left the ark. After Noah built an altar and brought an offering to the Lord, the Lord promised Noah that he would never again curse the ground because of man, and that he would preserve the earth for the purpose of carrying out his redemptive purpose for mankind (8:20-22).

The first seven verses of chapter 9 contain the ordinances God now instituted in order to preserve the earth and its inhabitants. "These ordinances refer to the propagation of life, the protection of life, from animals and men both, and the sustenance of life."[9] The command to multiply and fill the earth is repeated (v. 1). It is further announced that the animals shall be afraid of human beings (v. 2). Man is now given explicit permission to eat the flesh of animals (v. 3), but the eating of flesh with blood in it is forbidden (v. 4). God will require the lifeblood of every animal that kills a man and of every human being who kills a man (v. 5). Within this context come the familiar words of verse 6.

What has been said in verse 5 about animals and human beings is now said specifically about man: whoever (that is, whatever man) sheds man's blood, by another man shall he be put to death ("shall his blood be shed"). These words do not say how this execution will take place, nor whether there are any exceptions to this rule. Neither is it specified who shall carry out such an execution. Many interpreters have suggested that these words point to the establishment of a governmental agency whereby such punishment can be carried out. Though this passage could be construed as implying the existence of such a governmental agency, the text says nothing about it.

The second half of verse 6 gives the reason for this command: "for in the image of God has God made man." The reason that murder is here said to be such a heinous crime that it must be punished by death is that the man who has been murdered is someone who imaged God, reflected God, was like God, and represented God. Therefore, when one kills a human being, not only does he take that person's life, but he hurts God himself—the God who was reflected in that individual. To touch the image of God is to touch God himself; to kill the image of God is to do violence to God himself.

9. Geerhardus Vos, *Biblical Theology* (Grand Rapids: Eerdmans, 1948), p. 64.

It seems clear, therefore, that according to this passage fallen man is still an image-bearer of God. That our first parents had fallen into sin had been recorded earlier in the Book of Genesis; that human nature had therefore become corrupt is clearly stated in the immediate context of the passage we are discussing: "Never again will I curse the ground because of man, even though every inclination of his heart is evil from childhood" (8:21). Though all this is true about man, in Genesis 9:6 murder is forbidden because man was made in the image of God—that is, he still bears that image.

Not all theologians agree with this interpretation. The Dutch theologian Klaas Schilder, in his commentary on the Heidelberg Catechism, asserts that this passage teaches only that God made man in his image at the time of creation, but does not say that God permitted man to remain in his image after the Fall.[10] Fallen man, so Schilder continues, no longer bears the image of God. It is possible, however, that in the future he may again bear that image:

> Who knows what may still happen to this washed-out world? Who knows whether, perhaps, at some time in the future, the image of God will be seen again? So interpreted, this passage [Gen. 9:6] says everything about the *past* and probably much about the *future*, but nothing about what man is *at the present time*. These words only tell us what God intended with man when he created him, what he purposed when he formed him.[11]

The trouble with this interpretation, however—an interpretation shared by G. C. Berkouwer[12]—is that it does violence to the meaning of Genesis 9:6. The reason you should not murder, the passage is saying, is that the person you are about to murder is someone who is in the image of God. If fallen man no longer bears the image of God apart from redemption, as Schilder and Berkouwer claim, these words lose their thrust. The passage would then be saying, you must not kill a man, for the man whom you are about to kill was *at one time* an image-bearer of God, though he no longer is that today. By his own sin man forfeited the privilege of remaining an image-bearer of God— so these theologians would argue—and yet, though he has lost that image, you must not put him to death. It is indeed possible that this man whom you are about to murder might, if his life were spared, at some time in the future again be an image-bearer of God, though we can never be sure of this; nevertheless you ought not to kill him. Man

10. *Heidelbergsche Catechismus*, vol. 1 (Goes: Oosterbaan & Le Cointre, 1947), pp. 296-97.
11. Ibid., pp. 297-98 [trans. mine].
12. *Man*, pp. 56-59.

was the image-bearer of God in the past, at the time of his creation, and he may possibly be an image-bearer of God in the future, but he does not bear God's image now. And this is the reason why you ought not to kill him.

This kind of argumentation, however, fails to do justice to the text. The reason no human being may shed man's blood, the passage says, is that man has unique value, a value that is not to be attributed to any other of God's creatures: namely, that he is an image-bearer of God. Precisely because he *is* such an image-bearer, not *was* one in the past, or *might be* one in the future, is it so great a sin to kill him.

The Old Testament passages we have looked at so far teach that man was created in God's image, and still exists in that image. In fact, we ought to say not only that man *has* the image of God but that man *is* the image of God. From the Old Testament standpoint, to be human is to bear the image of God.

Though the expression "image of God" is not found in Psalm 8, this psalm does picture man in a way that reaffirms his having been created in God's image. As Franz Delitzsch affirms, Psalm 8 is a "lyric echo" of Genesis 1:27-28.[13] The main purpose of this psalm is to ascribe praise to God for the works of his hands, particularly for the starry heavens above and man below.

The psalmist's contemplation of the marvels of the starry heavens makes him realize, by comparison, the smallness and insignificance of man. Yet God has assigned to man an exalted position on the earth, having given him dominion over the rest of creation. And this is even more to be wondered at than the heavens themselves.

Verse 5 describes man's exalted state: "Yet thou [Lord] hast made him [man] little less than God, and dost crown him with glory and honor" (RSV). Translators and commentators differ on the question of how the word *'elōhim* is to be rendered. Some translations, like the RSV just quoted, render this word as *God* (ASV, NASB, Amplified Bible, Today's English Version); other versions have *angels* (LXX, Vulgate, KJV), *heavenly beings* (NIV), or *a god* (NEB, JB). Though *'elōhim* may sometimes mean "heavenly beings" or "angels," the most common meaning of the word is "God." I favor the rendering "God" in Psalm 8:5 for the following reasons: (1) it is the most common meaning of *'elōhim*; (2) angels have not been given dominion over the works of God's hands, as human beings have; and (3) it is never said of angels that they have been created in the image of God; so why

13. Quoted in John Laidlaw, *The Bible Doctrine of Man* (Edinburgh: T. & T. Clark, 1905), p. 147.

should they be thought of as higher than human beings, who have been created in God's image?[14]

Man, so says the inspired author of Psalm 8, was made only a little lower than God—a statement that strongly reminds us of the words of Genesis 1 about man's having been created in the image and likeness of God. Similarly echoing Genesis 1, verses 6-8 of the psalm affirm that God has given man dominion over the works of the Creator's hands and has put all things under man's feet.

The picture of man that emerges from this psalm is similar to that sketched in Genesis 1:27-28. Man is the highest creature God has made, an image-bearer of God, who is only a little lower than God, and under whose feet all of creation has been placed. All this is true despite man's fall into sin. Thus, according to the Old Testament fallen man still bears the image of God.

## New Testament Teaching

What, now, is the teaching of the New Testament on the image of God? One passage clearly teaches that fallen man still bears the image of God and is, therefore, a New Testament echo of the Old Testament material we have just been examining. In James 3:9 we read: "With the tongue we praise our Lord and Father, and with it we curse men, who have been made in God's likeness." To understand what James is saying here, we should also take note of verses 10 through 12:

> (10) Out of the same mouth come praise and cursing. My brothers, this should not be. (11) Can both fresh water and salt water flow from the same spring? (12) My brothers, can a fig tree bear olives, or a grapevine bear figs? Neither can a salt spring produce fresh water.

The setting for James 3:9 is a discussion of the sins of the tongue—an area in which we all stumble. Animals, James said in the preceding verses, can be tamed, but no man can tame the tongue, which "is a restless evil, full of deadly poison" (v. 8).

In verse 9 James points out the inconsistency of which people are guilty when they use the same tongue to praise God and to curse men. Why is this such an inconsistency? Because the human beings whom

14. Among commentators who favor the translation "God" are the following: Helmer Ringgren, "*elōhim*," in G. Johannes Botterweck and Helmer Ringgren, *Theological Dictionary of the Old Testament*, trans. John T. Willis, vol. 1, rev. ed. (Grand Rapids: Eerdmans, 1977), p. 282; and N. H. Ridderbos, *De Psalmen* in the Korte Verklaring series (Kampen: Kok, 1962), 1:123. J. A. Alexander, in his *Commentary on the Psalms* (Philadelphia: Presbyterian Board of Publication, 1850), states: "*And remove him a little from divinity*—i.e., from a divine and heavenly, or at least a superhuman state" (p. 60).

we curse—note James's use of the first person—are creatures who have been made in the likeness of God. Therefore, to curse men means, in effect, to curse God in whose likeness they have been made. The following verse underscores this inconsistency: "Out of the same mouth come praise and cursing. My brothers, this should not be."

What is particularly significant here for our purpose is the tense of the verb translated as "have been made." The Greek verb is *gegonotas*, the perfect participle of the verb *ginomai*, meaning "to become" or "to be made." The force of the perfect tense in Greek is to describe "past action with abiding result." Thus, the thrust of the Greek expression *kath' homoiōsin theou gegonotas* is this: human beings as here described have at some time in the past been made according to the likeness of God *and are still bearers of that likeness. For this reason* it is inconsistent to praise God and curse men with the same tongue, since the human creatures whom we curse still bear the likeness of God. *For this reason* God is offended when we curse men.

Someone might conceivably reply, But is not James writing this epistle to believers? And is he therefore not speaking of people who have been restored to the likeness of God by the renewing power of the Holy Spirit as those who still possess that likeness? The answer to the second question is No. James does not say, "with the tongue we curse brothers, fellow believers, who have been made (or remade) in God's likeness." What he says is this: "with the tongue we curse men" (*anthrōpous*)—a term designating human persons in general, whether they are believers or not. James certainly is not suggesting that cursing is a sin only when it is directed toward fellow believers. He is saying that it dishonors God when we curse any man or woman who may cross our paths. Whoever that person may be, God is displeased when we curse him, since God has made him in his own likeness—a likeness that man still reflects.

This passage does not tell us exactly in what the likeness to God consists. Neither does it tell us what man's fall into sin has done to that likeness or what happens to that likeness when God by his Spirit recreates us in his image. But what the passage does say with the utmost clarity is that, whatever the Fall has done to the image of God in man, it has not totally obliterated that image. The passage would be completely pointless if fallen man were not still, in a very important sense, a being who bears and reflects a likeness to God—a being who is still, in distinction from all other creatures, an image-bearer of God.

God made man in his image—this is clear from both Old and New Testaments. But the Bible also teaches us that Jesus Christ is the perfect man—the unsurpassed example of what God wants us to be like. It is therefore exciting to see that in the New Testament Christ is called the perfect image of God. In 2 Corinthians 4:4 Paul writes about those who "cannot see the light of the gospel of the glory of Christ, who is the image of God." The word translated here as "image" is *eikōn*, the Greek equivalent of the Hebrew word *tselem*. What is meant by the identification of Christ as the image of God is further elaborated in verse 6: "For God, who said, 'Let light shine out of darkness,' made his light shine in our hearts to give us the light of the knowledge of the glory of God in the face of Christ." God's glory, in other words, is revealed in the face of Christ; when we see Christ, we see the glory of God.

To the same effect are Paul's words in Colossians 1:15: "He [Christ] is the image of the invisible God, the firstborn over all creation." So, though God is invisible, in Christ the invisible God becomes visible; one who looks at Christ is actually looking at God.

According to John's Gospel, Christ himself made the same point when he walked on this earth. When Philip said to Jesus, "Lord, show us the Father," Jesus replied, "Don't you know me, Philip, even after I have been among you such a long time? Anyone who has seen me has seen the Father" (John 14:8-9). Jesus' words come down to this: If you look carefully at me, you will have seen the Father, since I am the Father's perfect image.[15]

A remarkable passage containing a similar thought is found in Hebrews 1:3, "The Son is the radiance of God's glory and the exact representation of his being." The glory that Christ the Son radiates, according to the author of Hebrews, is not his own but is the glory of God the Father. The word translated here as "exact representation" (*charaktēr*) is a very interesting one. According to W. E. Vine, it denotes "a stamp or impress, as on a coin or a seal, in which case the seal or die which makes an impression bears the image produced by it, and, *vice versa*, all the features of the image correspond respectively with those of the instrument producing it."[16] As one can tell by looking at a coin exactly what the original die that stamped out the coin looked like, so one can tell by looking at the Son exactly what the Father is like. It is hard to imagine a stronger figure to convey the thought that Christ is a perfect reproduction of the Father. Every trait, every characteristic, every quality found in the Father is also found in the Son, who is the Father's *exact representation*.

When we reflect on the fact that Christ is the perfect image of

15. To the same effect are the following words from the Prologue of John's Gospel: "No one has ever seen God, but God the only Son, who is at the Father's side, has made him known" (1:18).

16. *An Expository Dictionary of New Testament Words* (Old Tappan, NJ: Revell, 1940; reprint 1966), under "Image," p. 247.

God, we see an important relationship between the image of God and the Incarnation. Would it have been possible for the Second Person of the Trinity to assume the nature of an animal? This does not seem likely. The Incarnation means that the Word who was God became flesh—that is, assumed the nature of man (John 1:14). That God could become flesh is the greatest of all mysteries, which will always transcend our finite human understanding. But, presumably, it was only because man had been created in the image of God that the Second Person of the Trinity could assume human nature. That Second Person, it would seem, could not have assumed a nature that had no resemblance whatever to God. In other words, the Incarnation confirms the doctrine of the image of God.

Since Christ was totally without sin (Heb. 4:15), in Christ we see the image of God in its perfection. As a skillful teacher uses visual aids to help his or her pupils understand what is being taught, so God the Father has given us in Jesus Christ a visual example of what the image of God is. There is no better way of seeing the image of God than to look at Jesus Christ. What we see and hear in Christ is what God intended for man.

If this is so, then the best way to learn what the image of God is is not to contrast man with animals, as has often been done, and then to find the divine image to consist in those qualities, abilities, and gifts that man has in distinction from the animals. Rather, we must learn to know what the image of God is by looking at Jesus Christ. What must therefore be at the center of the image of God is not characteristics like the ability to reason or the ability to make decisions (important as such abilities may be for the proper functioning of the image of God), but rather that which was central in the life of Christ: love for God and love for man. If it is true that Christ perfectly images God, then the heart of the image of God must be love. For no man ever loved as Christ loved.[17]

A number of New Testament passages teach that there is a sense in which the image of God needs to be restored. I have in mind those

17. One could perhaps counter that other virtues graced the life of Christ as well as love (which is, of course, true). Yet love, which is called in the New Testament the fulfillment of the law (Rom. 13:10; Gal. 5:14), and is described in Col. 3:14 as that excellence which binds all the other virtues together, was revealed in the life of Christ in a way that has never been surpassed. We think, for example, of such passages as John 15:9 ("As the Father has loved me, so have I loved you") and 1 John 3:16 ("This is how we know what love is: Jesus Christ laid down his life for us"). That love is central in the image of God is, further, clearly implied in Eph. 5:1-2, "Be imitators of God, therefore, as dearly loved children and live a life of love, just as Christ loved us and gave himself up for us."

passages which describe the moral and spiritual renewal of man as a process in which he is being conformed more and more to the image of God. If human beings need so to be conformed (or reconformed) in a process that continues throughout this life, the image of God in which they were created must in some sense have been corrupted by the Fall.

We look first of all at Romans 8:29: "For those God foreknew he also predestined to be conformed to the likeness [or image, RSV] of his Son, that he might be the firstborn among many brothers." The passage speaks about certain ones who were predestined or foreordained (*proōrisen*) to be conformed to or made like (*symmorphous*) the image (*eikōn*) of God's Son, so that the Son might become the firstborn or preeminent one (*prōtotokon*) among many brothers.

Before God's people had come into existence, or before the foundation of the world (see Eph. 1:4), God foreknew (in the sense of foreloved)[18] his chosen people. Those he foreknew he foreordained or predestined to be made like the image of his Son. Since the Son, as we have just seen, is the perfect image of God the Father, we will not do violence to the text if we interpret the expression "image of his Son" as being equivalent to "image of God." According to this passage, therefore, something has happened to the image of God. That image has apparently been so corrupted or spoiled through man's fall into sin that he needs once again to be conformed to that image. Conformity to the image of the Son—and therefore to the image of God—is described here as the purpose or goal for which God has predestined his chosen people. That purpose, though it is beginning to be carried out here and now, will not be fully realized until the life to come, at which time we shall be perfectly like Christ (1 Cor. 15:49; Phil. 3:21; 1 John 3:2).

Another passage that speaks of the renewing of the image of God in man is 2 Corinthians 3:18, "And we, who with unveiled faces all reflect the Lord's glory, are being transformed into his likeness with ever-increasing glory, which comes from the Lord, who is the Spirit." In the old dispensation of the covenant of grace, Paul is saying here, Moses had to cover his face with a veil when he spoke to the Israelites after having been in the presence of God. In the present era, however, the era of the new covenant, God's people do not need to cover or veil their faces after they have communed with God. We all now reflect the glory of the Lord—that is, the glory of Christ—with unveiled faces. Though the KJV translated the word *katoptrizomenoi* with "be-

---

18. Cf. John Murray, *The Epistle to the Romans* (Grand Rapids: Eerdmans, 1959), *ad loc.*; Herman Ridderbos, *Aan de Romeinen* (Kampen: Kok, 1959), *ad loc.*

holding," most modern versions, like the NIV, render the word as "reflecting."[19] The Greek word is derived from *katoptron*, which means "mirror." Literally, therefore, *katoptrizomenoi* means "mirroring." The word could mean either "beholding as in a mirror" or "reflecting like a mirror." I prefer the second meaning, since it fits so well into the context. Moses' face was reflecting the glory of God after he had been in face-to-face communion with him. Since this glory was too bright for the Israelites to look at, and since this radiance was one that would soon fade away (v. 13), Moses had to veil his face. But today, Paul indicates, we may reflect the glory of the Lord Jesus Christ with unveiled faces. In this way we see the superiority of the new covenant to the old.

The tense of the participle *katoptrizomenoi* is present, suggesting that we who are God's people today are *continually* reflecting the glory of the Lord. As we are reflecting that glory, however, we are also being transformed into the same image (*tēn autēn eikona*)—that is, into the image of Christ—from one degree of glory to another (*apo doxēs eis doxan*). Since the verb translated "are being transformed" (*metamorphoumetha*) is in the present tense, this process of transformation is also said to be a continuing one. As we continually reflect the glory of the Lord, we are continually being transformed into the image of the one whose glory we are reflecting. This transformation, Paul goes on to say, comes from the Lord, who is the Spirit.

Both Romans 8:29 and 2 Corinthians 3:18 teach that the goal of the redemption of God's people is that they shall be fully conformed to the image of Christ. But whereas in the Romans text this conformity to the image of Christ is treated as the goal for which God predestined us, in the passage from 2 Corinthians the emphasis falls on the progressive character of this transformation throughout the present life ("from one degree of glory to another," RSV) and on the fact that this transformation is the work of the Holy Spirit. Both passages, however, clearly assert that we who are victims of the Fall need to be more and more conformed to or transformed into the image of Christ, who is the perfect image of God.

The thought that Christians need continually to grow in being conformed to the image of God is also found in two New Testament passages that speak of putting off the "old man" and putting on the "new man." Recent translations of the Bible render these expressions as "old nature" and "new nature" or "old self" and "new self." But the original Greek used the words "old man" (*palaios anthrōpos*) and

19. Both the ASV and the RSV have "beholding" in the text and "reflecting" in the margin.

"new man" (*kainos* or *neos anthrōpos*)—though we should point out that the Greek word for man used here means "human being" and not "male human being."

The first of these two passages, Colossians 3:9-10, reads as follows:

> (9) Do not lie to each other, since you have taken off your old self with its practices (10) and have put on the new self, which is being renewed in knowledge in the image of its Creator.

At the beginning of chapter 3 Paul addresses his Colossian readers as those who have been raised with Christ, and must therefore set their hearts on things above rather than on earthly things (vv. 1-2). He then urges his readers to put to death whatever belongs to their earthly nature, and goes on to utter a number of prohibitions. In verse 9 Paul tells the Colossian Christians not to lie to each other, "since you have taken off your old self with its practices. . . ."

What does Paul mean here by "old self" or "old man"? According to John Murray, " 'Old man' is a designation of the person in his unity as dominated by the flesh and sin."[20] The old self, in other words, is what we are by nature: slaves to sin. However, Paul says to the believers at Colossae, since you have become one with Christ you are no longer slaves to sin, for you have taken off the old man or old self that was enslaved to sin and have put on the new self (*neos anthrōpos*). After the analogy of what has just been said about the old man, we conclude that the new man or new self must mean the person in his unity ruled by the Holy Spirit. You ought not to lie, Paul is saying, because lying does not comport with the new self you have put on.

But even the new self is not yet perfect, for, as Paul goes on to say, it "is being renewed in knowledge in the image of its Creator" (v. 10). If something needs to be renewed it is not yet perfect. It is interesting to note the tenses of the Greek verbs used in this passage. The two main verbs, "have taken off" (*apekdusamenoi*) and "have put on" (*endusamenoi*) are in the aorist tense, suggesting momentary or snapshot action. The participle translated as "being renewed" (*anakainoumenon*) is in the present tense, which describes action in progress or continuing action. In this passage, therefore, Paul looks upon believers as those who have once and for all taken off or put off their old selves and have once and for all put on their new selves—new selves, however, that are being continually and progressively renewed. In other words, in the light of this passage believers should not look upon themselves as slaves to sin or as "old selves," nor as being partly "old selves" and partly "new selves," but as those who are new persons

20. *Principles of Conduct* (Grand Rapids: Eerdmans, 1957), p. 218.

in Christ. Yet the new selves believers have put on are not yet perfect or sinless, since these new selves must still be progressively renewed by the Holy Spirit. Christians should therefore see themselves as people who are *genuinely* new, though not yet *totally* new.[21]

This new self that the believer has put on is being "renewed in knowledge." The word used here for knowledge, *epignōsis,* suggests a rich and full knowledge, a knowledge that involves not only the mind but also the heart. The object of this knowledge is the will of God. As the believer grows in his understanding of God's will, he will trust God more and serve him better.

This new self is being renewed in knowledge "in the image of its Creator"—literally, according to the image (*kat' eikona*) of the one who created him. Here once again we find an echo of the words of Genesis 1:27, which tell us that God created man in his own image. The fact that the new self is said to be progressively renewed after the image of its Creator implies that man through his fall into sin has so corrupted the original image that it must be restored in the process of redemption. But the goal of redemption is to raise man to a higher level than he was before the Fall—a level in which sin or unbelief will be impossible.[22] The goal of redemption is that, in knowledge as well as in other aspects of their lives, God's people will be totally and flawlessly image-bearers of God.

The second New Testament passage that speaks of putting off the "old man" and putting on the "new man" is Ephesians 4:22-24:

> (22) You were taught, with regard to your former way of life, to put off your old self, which is being corrupted by its deceitful desires; (23) to be made new in the attitude of your minds; (24) and to put on the new self, created to be like God in true righteousness and holiness.

This passage contains three infinitives, both in the translation and in the Greek: "to put off" (*apothesthai,* aorist tense); "to be made new" (*ananeousthai,* present tense); and "to put on" (*endusasthai,* aorist tense). Many English translations render these infinitives as if they were imperatives, as if the apostle were saying: You *must* put off the old self, you *must* be renewed, and you *must* put on the new self. Though occasionally Greek infinitives may be used as imperatives (as, e.g., in Rom. 12:15), it is not necessary to interpret them as such

---

21. Cf. Donald MacLeod, "Paul's Use of the Term 'The Old Man,'" in *The Banner of Truth* (London), no. 92 (May 1971):13-19. On the implications of this teaching for the Christian's self-image, see my *The Christian Looks at Himself,* rev. ed. (Grand Rapids: Eerdmans, 1977).
22. On this point, see below, pp. 82-83, 92.

here. I prefer, with John Murray,[23] to think of these forms as infinitives of result or as explanatory infinitives, depending on the verb "you were taught" (*edidachthēte*, from v. 21 in the Greek), and giving the content of that teaching. This is, in fact, the way in which the NIV renders the passage (see above).[24]

Since you have come to know Christ, Paul is saying to the believers in Ephesus,[25] you have been taught once and for all to put off your old self (or "old man," *palaion anthrōpon*), to be continually made new in the attitude of your minds, and once and for all to put on the new self (or "new man," *kainon anthrōpon*). In words reminiscent of Colossians 3:9-10, Paul says that a Christian is a person who has decisively and irrevocably put off the old self and put on the new self, and who must continually and progressively be renewed (*ananeousthai*, present tense) in the spirit or attitude of his or her mind. A once-for-all change of direction is to be accompanied by daily, progressive renewal. The Christian is a new person, but he or she still has a lot of growing to do.

Notice now what is said about the new self the believer has put on: this new self has been "created to be like God in true righteousness and holiness." Though the expression "image of God" does not occur in this text, we do have the expression "created in accordance with God" (*kata theon ktisthenta*). As God was the Creator of man in the beginning, so God is also the Creator of the new self or the new man believers have put on. As man was created in the image of God to begin with, so the new self that God has created for us is "in accordance with" God, or like God. Since the believer is not yet perfect but must be progressively renewed (v. 23), we conclude that this renewal consists of a growing and ever-increasing likeness to God. Here again we see that the purpose of redemption is to restore the image of God in man.

The new self as described here is said to have been created to be "like God in true righteousness and holiness" (lit., in "righteousness and holiness of the truth".)[26] There is an obvious contrast here be-

---

23. *Conduct*, pp. 214-19.

24. This understanding of the verse would make its teaching parallel to that found in a twin epistle, Col. 3:9-10, which we have just examined. Taking off the old self and putting on the new self are not actions the believer must still be exhorted to do, but actions he or she has already done.

25. Or to believers in general, if one follows manuscripts that omit "in Ephesus" in v. 1.

26. The three words used in Col. 3:9-10 and Eph. 4:24 to describe aspects of the new self (knowledge, righteousness, and holiness) are often used to indicate what is meant by the image of God in the so-called narrower sense—the sense in which it has been lost because of the Fall and is being restored in the process of redemption. The Hei-

tween the righteousness and holiness that characterize the new self and the "deceitful desires" or "lusts of deceit" (v. 22) that mark the old self. Sinful lusts deceive us, never providing the good things they seem to promise, but the righteousness and holiness we pursue as new selves will never deceive us.

In sum, the four passages we have just looked at (Rom. 8:29; 2 Cor. 3:18; Col. 3:9-10; Eph. 4:22-24) teach that the goal of our redemption in Christ is to make us more and more like God, or more and more like Christ who is the perfect image of God. The fact that the image of God must be restored in us implies that there is a sense in which that image has been distorted. Though, as we have seen, some Bible passages teach that there is a sense in which even fallen man is still an image-bearer of God, these texts clearly imply that there is a sense in which we no longer image God properly because of our sin, and that therefore we need to be restored to that image. The image of God in this sense is not static but dynamic. It is the pattern according to which our lives are being renewed by the Holy Spirit, and the eschatological goal toward which we are moving. We should think of the image of God in this sense, therefore, not as a noun but as a verb: we no longer *image* God as we should; we are now being enabled by the Spirit to *image* God more and more adequately; some day we shall *image* God perfectly.

Not only is our renewal into greater likeness to God something that the Holy Spirit works in us in the process of redemption; it is also pictured in the New Testament as something that involves our own efforts. To be sure, this renewal is primarily the work of God—he who sanctifies us through his Spirit. But some New Testament passages indicate that renewal into greater conformity to God is also, at the same time, the responsibility of man. Renewal in the image of God, in other words, is not just an indicative; it is also an imperative.

Let us look, for example, at Ephesians 5:1: "Be imitators of God, therefore, as dearly loved children." To be imitators of God means to continue to be like God (the Greek verb is in the present tense). There are, of course, many ways in which we cannot be like God—such as in his omniscience, omnipresence, or omnipotence. But in other ways we can be like God, if not perfectly, at least in principle. Paul specifies two of these ways in the verses immediately preceding and immediately following this passage. In the verse preceding (4:32), Paul tells

---

delberg Catechism uses the words in this sense in Answer 6: "God created man good and in his own image, that is, in true righteousness and holiness, so that he might truly know God his creator, love him with all his heart, and live with him in eternal happiness for his praise and glory" (1975 trans., Christian Reformed Church). We will develop this point further in Chap. 5.

his readers that they should forgive one another "as in Christ God forgave" them. And in the verse following (5:2), Paul continues, "And live a life of love, just as Christ loved us." We must therefore continually seek to forgive as God forgave us, and to love as Christ loved us. Since forgiving others is an aspect of love, we see here again that the heart of the image of God is love. As in the verses previously considered, imaging God is presented here as a process in which we must continue to be engaged. But here the process is one in which we must not be passive but active.

In a similar passage (1 Cor. 11:1), Paul writes: "Be imitators of me, as I am of Christ" (RSV). This is not the only place in his letters where Paul urges his readers to imitate him (see also 1 Cor. 4:16 and 2 Thess. 3:9); but what is striking about this passage is that Paul here urges his readers to be (or become, *ginesthe*) imitators of him as he, in turn, is an imitator of Christ (cf. 1 Thess. 1:6). The Corinthians are told to be more and more like Paul, while Paul tries more and more to pattern himself after Christ. Since Christ is the perfect image of God, Paul is trying more and more to be like God, who is perfectly represented in Christ; for this reason he asks his readers to be more and more like himself. As his readers become more like Paul, they will also become more like God. Imaging God is again presented here as an activity in which both Paul and his readers must continually engage.[27]

In Philippians 2:5-11, Paul urges his readers to "have this mind among yourselves, which is yours in Christ Jesus" (v. 5, RSV), and then goes on to describe this so-called mind of Christ: to be willing, like Christ, to humble yourselves, even, if necessary, to the point of death. Clearly, we cannot be like Christ in every respect. But we can be like him in his humiliation, in his willingness to humble himself for the sake of his brothers and sisters. We must be ready and willing to imitate Christ, who is the perfect image of God.

Christ himself, in fact, called for such imitation of himself when he was still on earth. After he had washed the disciples' feet—a menial task that none of the disciples had offered to do—Jesus said to them, "If I then, your Lord and Teacher, have washed your feet, you also ought to wash one another's feet. For I have given you an example, that you also should do as I have done to you" (John 13:14-15, RSV). When Jesus said these words, he was not instituting a ritual of ecclesiastical footwashing. But he was directing his disciples, and thus all believers, to follow his example of lowly service. All of us, therefore,

27. Cf. Willis P. De Boer, *The Imitation of Paul: An Exegetical Study* (Kampen: Kok, 1962).

who are Christians must imitate Christ in this respect, and to imitate Christ is to imitate God.

What we learn from these four passages is that all Christians are called increasingly to imitate God and Christ, who is the perfect image of God. This is our task, our responsibility—a responsibility we can fulfill only as God enables us to do so, but our responsibility nonetheless. The very fact, however, that we are called to this task indicates that there is a sense in which the image of God has been marred by sin.

A final point. In the New Testament the image of God is sometimes described from an eschatological perspective. The final goal of our sanctification is that we shall be totally like God, that we shall perfectly image God. This is usually described in New Testament writings in terms of our becoming completely like Christ, who is the perfect image of God.

An example of this is 1 Corinthians 15:49: "Just as we have borne the image of the man of dust, we shall also bear the image of the man of heaven" (RSV). In the immediate context the contrast intended is between the first and last Adam. The first Adam was "from the earth, a man of dust" (v. 47, RSV); the second man, or the last Adam, is from heaven. The last Adam is obviously Christ. As we have borne the image of the man of dust or of the earthly man (*choïkou*), so Paul here teaches, we shall bear the image (*eikona*) of the man of heaven (or heavenly man, *epouraniou*). In keeping with the theme of this chapter, the primary reference here is to the resurrection body. During this present life we have been—and still are—bearing the image of Adam, the earthly man, the man of dust; but in the life to come we shall fully bear the image of Christ, the man from heaven. Our future existence will be glorious, because we shall then be perfectly like Christ. Though Paul is speaking primarily about the body, we shall do no violence to the text if we understand it to refer not only to the body but to our entire existence.[28]

The same thought is found in a passage that constitutes the eschatological highlight of John's first epistle, 1 John 3:2, "Beloved, we are God's children now; it does not yet appear what we shall be, but we know that when he appears we shall be like him, for we shall see him as he is" (RSV). After having expressed his amazement at the marvel of the divine love that has made us children of God (v. 1), John goes on to tell us that he does not know what we shall be like

---

28. As far as the future of the body is concerned, note also Phil. 3:21: "Who . . . will transform our lowly bodies [lit., the body of our humiliation] so that they will be like his glorious body [lit., the body of his glory]."

in the future. But of one thing he is sure: "*we know* that when he appears we shall be like him, for we shall see him as he is." In other words, at the time of Christ's return, those who are in him will share his glory.[29]

When John says that we shall be *like him*, he is referring to Christ. There are two ways of understanding the last part of verse 2. One could understand John as saying that we shall be like Christ *because* we shall see him as he is. The thought then would be that our seeing Christ as he is results in our becoming perfectly like him.[30] Another possible interpretation, however, is that John is saying: "We shall be like Christ and *therefore* we shall see him as he is."[31] The latter interpretation seems to deserve the preference. So, then, the blessing promised to us at Christ's return is perfect and total likeness to him, a likeness that will enable us to do what we cannot do as long as we remain in our present, unglorified state: namely, to see him in his dazzling glory, face to face. Since Christ is God's perfect image, likeness to Christ will also mean likeness to God. This perfect likeness to Christ and to God is the ultimate goal of our sanctification. Whereas the image of God is now being progressively restored in those who are children of God, in the life to come that image will be totally and finally restored. We shall then be perfectly like God.

Summarizing, now, what we have learned from the Bible about the image of God, we note that from the Old Testament passages cited and from James 3:9 it is clear that there is a very important sense in which man today, fallen man, is still a bearer of the image of God, and must therefore still be so viewed. From the other New Testament passages consulted, however, we have learned that there is a sense in which fallen man needs more and more to be restored to the image of God—a restoration that is now in progress but will some day be completed. In other words, there is also a sense in which human beings no longer properly bear the image of God, and therefore need to be renewed in that image. We could say that in this latter sense the image of God in man has been marred and corrupted by sin. We must still see fallen man as an image-bearer of God, but as one who by nature, apart from the regenerating and sanctifying work of the Holy Spirit, images God in a distorted way. In the process of redemption that

29. Note Paul's testimony to this happy future expectation in Col. 3:4: "When Christ, who is your life, appears, then you also will appear with him in glory."
30. Cf. I. Howard Marshall, *The Epistles of John* (Grand Rapids: Eerdmans, 1978), *ad loc.*; John R. W. Stott, *The Epistles of John* (Grand Rapids: Eerdmans, 1964), *ad loc.*
31. Calvin, *I John*, trans. T. H. L. Parker (Grand Rapids: Eerdmans, 1979), *ad loc.*; S. Greijdanus, *I, II, and III Johannes* (Kampen: Kok, 1952), *ad loc.*

distortion is progressively taken away until, in the life to come, we shall again perfectly image God.

So, to be faithful to the biblical evidence, our understanding of the image of God must include these two senses: (1) The image of God as such is an unlosable aspect of man, a part of his essence and existence, something that man cannot lose without ceasing to be man. (2) The image of God, however, must also be understood as that likeness to God which was perverted when man fell into sin, and is being restored and renewed in the process of sanctification.

# CHAPTER 4

# The Image of God:
# Historical Survey

Clearly, according to the Scriptures man was created in the image of God. It is also clear that, in distinction from other creatures, only man has been made in God's image. What is not so clear, however, is the answer to the question "In what does the image of God consist?" This question involves three other questions: (1) What effect did man's fall into sin have on the image of God? (2) How does the moral and spiritual renewal of man in the process of redemption affect the image of God? (3) What is the final destiny of the image of God in the life to come?

Throughout the history of the church there have been various answers to these questions. In this chapter we shall look at some representative answers given by Christian theologians from the second century A.D. to the present time. By reflecting upon and evaluating these answers, we should arrive at a better understanding of what the image of God in man means.

## IRENAEUS

Irenaeus (*c.* 130-*c.* 200) was born in Asia Minor and in 177 became Bishop of Lyons in what is now southern France. In 185 he wrote his chief work, *Against Heresies,* in which he gave a strong refutation of the doctrinal errors of Gnosticism. In the beginning, Irenaeus taught, God created man in his image and after his likeness. Man's likeness to God, however, was lost in the Fall, whereas the image of God still remained. However, the lost likeness to God is being restored in believers in the process of redemption.[1]

Let us listen to Irenaeus's own words:

---

1. David Cairns, *The Image of God in Man,* rev. ed. (London: Collins, 1973), p. 80. I am indebted to Cairns for the main lines of the sketch of Irenaeus that follows.

> But if the Spirit be wanting to the soul, he who is such is indeed of an animal nature, and being left carnal, shall be an imperfect being, possessing indeed the image in his formation, but not receiving the similitude through the Spirit, and thus is this being imperfect.[2]

This description is of man as he is after the Fall (note the words "animal nature" and "carnal"). Fallen man, according to this statement, still possesses the image of God but needs the work of the Spirit in order to have restored to him the similitude or likeness to God that he lost in the Fall.

Irenaeus develops this point further:

> And then, again, this Word was manifested when the Word of God was made man, assimilating himself to man and man to himself, that by means of his resemblance to the Son, man might become precious to the Father. For in times long past, it was *said* that man was created after the image of God, but it was not yet *shown*; for the Word was as yet invisible, after whose image man was created. Wherefore also he did easily lose the similitude. When, however, the Word of God became flesh, he confirmed both these: for he both showed forth the image truly, since he became himself what was his image; and he re-established the similitude after a sure manner, by assimilating man to the invisible Father through means of the visible Word.[3]

Again we find Irenaeus saying that though man was created in the image of God, he lost the similitude or likeness to God in the Fall. Christ, however, showed us in his own person what the image of God truly was. Furthermore, Christ also restores the likeness of God in those who belong to him by making them one with God the Father.

For Irenaeus, the image of God meant man's "nature as a rational and free being, a nature which was not lost at the fall."[4] That Irenaeus thought of the image as consisting primarily of rationality is not surprising, since the classical Greek philosophers (Plato, Aristotle, the Stoics) taught that man's reason was his highest and most distinctive characteristic. But he also included as an aspect of the image of God man's freedom, his ability to make decisions, and his responsibility for those decisions.[5] Both man's rationality and his freedom, according to Irenaeus, are retained after the Fall.

The likeness of God, however, meant the "robe of sanctity" that the Holy Spirit had bestowed on Adam.[6] Interestingly, according to

2. *Against Heresies*, V.6.1, in *Ante-Nicene Fathers*, vol. 1, ed. Alexander Roberts and James Donaldson (Grand Rapids: Eerdmans, 1953), p. 532.
3. Ibid., V.16.2.
4. Emil Brunner, *Man in Revolt*, trans. Olive Wyon (New York: Scribner, 1939), p. 93.
5. See *Against Heresies*, IV.4.3, as cited by Cairns, *Image*, pp. 81-82.
6. *Against Heresies*, III.23.5.

Irenaeus believers have three components in their being: the body, the soul, and the spirit. Unbelievers, however, have only souls and bodies. The Holy Spirit creates man's spirit as an organ whereby the believer receives divine influence and knows divine truth.[7] It would appear, therefore, that the spirit within the human being is the bearer of the likeness to God. This likeness-bearing spirit was given to Adam before the Fall, was lost through the Fall, and is restored in the process of redemption.

We appreciate the fact that Irenaeus makes a distinction between an aspect of the image of God that was retained after the Fall and an aspect that was lost through the Fall and is regained through Christ. As we have seen in the previous chapter, this is an important biblical distinction.

Irenaeus was wrong, however, in associating these two aspects of *image* and *likeness*. As our biblical study has shown, these two words are used virtually as synonyms. Thus, although his teaching gave rise to a tradition that continued into the Middle Ages, his basic distinction is untenable.

Irenaeus also erred in thinking of the retained aspect of the image of God as being primarily rationality. Though many theologians after Irenaeus were to say the same thing, rationality, as we have already seen, is by no means the heart of the image of God.

We must also object to Irenaeus's view that believers are "made up of" body, soul, and spirit, whereas unbelievers "consist" only of body and soul. As we shall see in Chapter 11, the words *soul* and *spirit* are virtual synonyms in the Bible, and therefore one is not justified in affirming a trichotomous view of man. Further, Irenaeus's assertion that fallen man lost his spirit suggests that what human beings lost in the Fall was only something additional to them, something extra, something apart from which they could still be complete persons—a teaching that was to be further elaborated by the Scholastic theologians of the Middle Ages into the view that at the Fall man lost only a gift of God that had been added to him (the so-called *donum superadditum*).[8] This teaching, however, minimizes the effect of the Fall on human nature. Man's fall into sin did not result merely in the loss of something additional to his existence, but involved the total corruption of his entire being.

---

7. Cairns, *Image*, p. 84. He refers in this connection to *Against Heresies*, II.33.5 [the text mistakenly has II.35.5].
8. See below, p. 38.

## THOMAS AQUINAS

Thomas Aquinas (1225-1274) is often called the greatest philosopher and theologian of the medieval church. His views on the image of God are drawn from his magnum opus, *Summa Theologica* ("Summary of Theology").

Thomas finds the image of God primarily in man's intellect or reason. Only intelligent creatures can, properly speaking, be said to be in God's image.[9] Even in rational creatures, the image of God is found only in the mind.[10] In fact, Thomas continues, the image of God is found more perfectly in angels than in men, because the natures of angels are "more perfectly intelligent" than those of men.[11] Since Thomas finds the image of God particularly in man's intellect, it is clear that for him the intellect is the most Godlike quality in man.

According to Thomas, the image of God exists in man at three stages:

> The first stage is man's natural aptitude for understanding and loving God, an aptitude which consists in the very nature of the mind, which is common to all men. The next stage is where a man is actually or dispositively [or habitually; Lat. *actu vel habitu*] knowing and loving God, but still imperfectly; and here we have the image by conformity of grace. The third stage is where a man is actually knowing and loving God perfectly; and this is the image by likeness of glory. . . . The first stage of the image then is found in all men, the second only in the just, and the third only in the blessed.[12]

Thomas, therefore, finds the image of God in some sense in all people, in a richer or higher sense only in believers ("the just"), and in the highest sense in those who have been glorified. What is of interest to us at this point is that Thomas does indeed find the image of God in all human beings living today, after the Fall, whether they are believers or not. In this respect he follows Irenaeus, though he does not tie in this teaching, as Irenaeus did, with a distinction between image and likeness. Aquinas did not share the view that many medieval theologians, including Irenaeus, taught—that through the Fall man lost the likeness to God but retained the image of God. While granting that image and likeness may have somewhat different meanings,[13] he concedes that "there is nothing wrong in something being called 'image' in one context and 'likeness' in another."[14]

9. Thomas Aquinas, *Summa Theologica*, I.93.2.
10. Ibid., I.93.6.
11. Ibid., I.93.3.
12. Ibid., I.93.4. The translation is from the Latin-English edition published by Black-friars in conjunction with McGraw-Hill (New York, 1964), 13:61.
13. Ibid., I.93.9.
14. Ibid., *ad* 3.

The form in which the image of God is found in all people is "man's natural aptitude for understanding and loving God . . . which is common to all men." Note that Thomas described this first stage of the image as an aptitude for rather than, as in the case of the other two stages, an actual understanding and loving of God. The image of God, in other words, is described here in part in terms of a certain capacity or endowment found in all human persons, rather than in terms of the type of activity that flows from that endowment. This is an important distinction, to which we shall return later.

At this point we are inclined to ask Thomas: But is there also a sense in which all human beings not only have the aptitude for understanding and knowing God but actually do know God, apart from God's special grace? Thomas answers that, although man apart from God's special grace cannot know God as he is in himself, he can by the natural light of reason know that God is the first and preeminent cause of all things.[15] Thomas further teaches that man, without the help of grace, can know truth by himself—the truth about such intelligible things as we can learn through the senses. But man's intellect "cannot know intelligible things of a higher order unless it is perfected by a stronger light, such as the light of faith or prophecy, which is called 'the light of glory' since it is added to nature."[16]

Can natural man apart from grace love God? Again Thomas answers in the affirmative:

> There is, however, such a thing as natural knowledge and love of God. . . . And it is also natural to the mind that it has the power of using reason to understand God, and it was in terms of such a power that we said God's image remains always in the mind.[17]

According to Thomas, therefore, there is a sense in which every person bears the image of God, since everyone has not only a natural aptitude for understanding and loving God but also a natural knowledge and love of God. Thomas admits, however, that the image of God in man is not always equally bright. Thomas says that God's image remains always in the mind "*whether this image of God is so faint—so shadowy, we might say—that it is practically nonexistent,* as in those who lack the use of reason; *or whether it is dim and disfigured,* as in sinners; *or whether it is bright and beautiful,* as in the just."[18] He

15. Ibid., I.12.12.
16. Ibid., I-II.109.1, trans. A. M. Fairweather, in *Nature and Grace*, vol. 11 of the Library of Christian Classics (Philadelphia: Westminster, 1954), p. 139. Note here the typical two-level structure of scholastic theology.
17. Ibid., I.93.8, *ad* 3 (Blackfriars trans.).
18. Ibid.

would grant, therefore, that the image of God in those who are not believers is either dim, disfigured, or practically nonexistent.

What, then, did Thomas teach about the original state of man before the Fall? Two things must be said: First, there was in man as he was originally created a struggle between reason and the "lower passions" or "lower powers" (*inferiores vires*).[19] Second, man as he was originally created needed a gift of supernatural grace to enable him to control his "lower powers" by his reason. Thomas develops these thoughts in the *Summa*, where he addresses the question of "whether man was created in grace." He answers in the affirmative, for the following reason: When the human person was created, his reason was submissive to God, his lower powers were submissive to his reason, and his body was submissive to his soul. But, he goes on to say, this submission of body to soul and of lower powers to reason was not by nature—otherwise it would have persisted after man's fall into sin. "From this it is plain that that primary submissiveness in which the reason put itself under God was not something merely natural either, but was by a gift of supernatural grace (*supernaturalis donum gratiae*)."[20] In other words, when he was first created man was not able in his own strength to keep his "lower powers" under control; he needed a "gift of supernatural grace"[21] to enable him to do so.

There is another reason why man when he was first created needed divine grace: in order to merit eternal life. Thomas said that even before sin human beings needed grace to achieve eternal life; this is, in fact, the chief necessity for grace.[22] In other words:

> A man cannot, by his natural power, produce meritorious works commensurate with eternal life. A higher power is needed for this, namely, the power of grace. Hence a man cannot merit eternal life without grace.[23]

What, now, was the effect of the Fall on the image of God? Because of the Fall man lost the supernatural grace that God had bestowed upon him in the beginning: "Our first parents by their sin were deprived of the divine benefit which maintained in them the integrity of human nature."[24] Because man lost this supernatural grace,

---

19. Ibid., I.95.1. By "lower powers" Aquinas means such things as emotions (like anger) and appetites (hunger, sexual drive, etc.).

20. Ibid.

21. Other medieval theologians, beginning with Alexander of Hales (*Summa Theologica*, II.91.1, art. 3), called this grace a *donum superadditum naturae*, a "gift superadded to nature." Aquinas called this grace *gratia gratum faciens*, "a grace which makes one pleasing [to God]" (*Summa*, I.100.1, *ad* 2).

22. *Summa*, I.95.4, *ad* 1.

23. Ibid., I-II.109.6 (Fairweather trans.).

24. Ibid., II-II.164.2 (Blackfriars trans.). Cf. I.95.1.

he now no longer has the ability to control his "lower powers" by means of his reason:

> In his original state man was divinely endowed with the grace and privilege that, so long as his mind was subject to God, the lower powers of the soul would be subject to his rational mind, and his body to his soul. Man's mind by sin abandoned subordination to God, with the consequence that now his lower powers were no longer wholly responsive to his reason; and such was the rebellion of the flesh against reason that the body as well was no more wholly responsive to soul.[25]

Since this is so, fallen man needs to have this supernatural grace restored to him, for two reasons:

> Thus in the state of pure nature man needs a power added to his natural power by grace, for one reason, namely, in order to do and to will supernatural good. But in the state of corrupt nature he needs this for two reasons, in order to be healed, and in order to achieve the meritorious good of supernatural virtue.[26]

We appreciate the distinction Thomas makes between the image of God as still retained by man after the Fall and the image as it is spoiled by sin and restored in those who are the recipients of divine grace. We may also appreciate Thomas's insistence that apart from the grace of God humans today cannot properly image God—can neither know, love, nor serve God as they ought. We must, however, object to Aquinas's understanding of the image of God on five counts.

First, Aquinas finds the image of God solely in man's *intellectual* nature. This view has its roots in Greek thought rather than in Scripture. Both Plato and Aristotle called man's intellect divine; it was the spark of divinity within man.[27] When Thomas asserts that the image of God must be seen particularly in the intellect, since the intellect is the most Godlike aspect of man, he is echoing a typically Greek idea. We may admit that there is in human intellectual ability a reflection of God who is the supreme Knower, but to say that the image of God is found exclusively or even primarily in man's intellect is to render a judgment that is more Greek than Christian. The Bible says that God is love; nowhere does it say that God is intellect.

We may note further that to find the image of God primarily in the human intellect or reason tends to downplay if not remove altogether what we have found to be essential in the biblical view of the image: namely, man's relatedness to God and to others, that is, his

25. Ibid., II-II.164.1.
26. Ibid., I-II.109.2 (Fairweather trans.).
27. Plato, *The Timaeus*, 90 C; Aristotle, *De Anima*, Bk. 1, 408b; also *Nic. Ethics*, Bk. 10, 1177b.

capacity for loving God and loving his neighbor. Thomas's understanding of the image of God is an abstract, static conception, far removed from the dynamics of biblical language about man.

A second point of criticism is this: Thomas's view detracts from the goodness of man's original nature, by positing a struggle between the "lower" and "higher" aspects of human nature from the very moment of creation. The "lower aspects" of man could be kept under control by the "higher aspects" only by means of an added gift of supernatural grace. At the very beginning of man's existence, therefore, even before the Fall, he was somehow defective; he needed a *donum superadditum* (an added gift) of grace in order to enable him to be what he ought to be. How does this view comport with the biblical statement, "God saw all that he had made [including man], and it was very good" (Gen. 1:31)?

Third, Thomas's view of the image of God detracts from the seriousness of the Fall. That is, according to Thomas, man was essentially the same after the Fall as he was before it, merely without the gift of supernatural grace, or the *donum superadditum*. This gift, which man received before the Fall, was something *additional* to his nature, not something *essential* to his nature. Thus we can describe the effect of the Fall on human beings only in negative terms, in terms of the loss of an added gift. One could say that, according to this view, fallen man is not so much *depraved* as *deprived*. Thomas's view, in other words, fails to do justice to the devastating effects the Fall had on human nature.

A fourth point of criticism is that the opposition between reason and the "lower powers" taught by Aquinas suggests a kind of devaluation of the body as the seat of man's "lower nature." In Aquinas virtue is generally defined as the subjection of the passions to reason. "Now all that the virtues are is a set of perfections by which reason is directed towards God and the lower powers are managed according to the standard of reason."[28] One implication of this statement is that human reason is always right and never wrong—a conception that has more in common with Greek thought than with the biblical view of man.[29] Further, to speak of certain aspects of human nature as man's "lower powers" suggests an unscriptural dichotomy between what is "noble" in us (the intellect) and what is "ignoble" in us (the passions

---

28. *Summa*, I.95.3 (Blackfriars trans.).
29. Though Aquinas usually says that virtue means the subjection of the passions to reason, implying that reason is always right, he does admit, in I-II.74 of the *Summa*, that there may be sin in the reason and that reason may be in error (see particularly Art. 5). At this point, therefore, Aquinas seems to be following Scripture rather than Greek philosophy.

and emotions). According to Scripture, however, we do not find in man lower and higher powers; the human being as a totality has been created by God, and no aspect of his or her being is "lower" or "less noble" than other aspects.

A further implication of the view that virtue consists in the suppression of bodily appetites is that the body (where the "lower powers" are found) is the chief source of sin. A number of implications follow this. One can see, for example, how the monasticism common in the medieval church fits into this picture: monks and nuns who subjected themselves to severe bodily austerities, and who remained unmarried, were thought to attain a higher moral and spiritual level than those who gratified their appetites by living ordinary lives. One can also see how the requirement for clerical celibacy follows: a man who remains unmarried and denies himself the satisfaction of his sexual drives is thought to be on a higher level of holiness than someone who is married. The insistence of scholastic theologians like Aquinas[30] on the perpetual virginity of the Virgin Mary also has its roots in the view of human nature just described.

The idea that the chief moral struggle of man is that between his reason and his appetites has its roots not in the Scriptures but in Greek thought. Plato, for example, distinguishes between a rational (*nous* or *logistikon*) part of man and an irrational (*alogistikon*) part of man, declaring that it belongs to the rational part to rule over the irrational part (that is, over the passions and the appetites).[31] According to the Bible, however, the chief struggle of man is that between disobedience to God with the whole person (mind and appetites) and obedience to God with the whole person. According to Scripture the body is not a "lower nature" that must be suppressed but an aspect of God's good creation that must be used in his service.

A fifth and final point of criticism has to do with Thomas's teaching that man today, after his fall into sin, is still able (with the help of cooperating grace) to merit everlasting life.[32] "To merit" means to earn something by one's own efforts. But it is clear from Scripture that salvation is never earned, but is always a gift of grace—and grace is by definition God's undeserved favor: "For it is by grace you have been saved, through faith—and this not from yourselves, it is the gift of God" (Eph. 2:8); "For the wages of sin is death, but the gift of God is eternal life in Christ Jesus our Lord" (Rom. 6:23). When Thomas

30. Ibid., III.28.3.
31. *Republic*, 443 A.
32. *Summa*, I.95.4, *ad* 1; I-II.109.6; I-II.114.2.

also says that one can merit an increase of grace,[33] he would seem to be stating a contradiction in terms. For how can one merit what is not deserved?

## JOHN CALVIN

The Protestant Reformation brought about a return to a more biblical view of man as a reaction to the scholastic anthropology of the Middle Ages. It will therefore be extremely important for us to look next at the understanding of the image of God found in John Calvin, the great Reformer, who lived from 1509 to 1564.

The first question we ask about Calvin's view is this: *Where is the image of God in man to be found?* According to Calvin, the image of God is found primarily in man's soul: "For although God's glory shines forth in the outer man, yet there is no doubt that the proper seat of his [God's] image is in the soul."[34] However, Calvin is willing to grant that "although the primary seat of the divine image was in the mind and heart, or in the soul and its powers, yet there was no part of man, not even the body itself, in which some sparks did not glow."[35] Looking forward to the future, Calvin grants that when the image of God is restored to its fullness in the life to come, it will be restored in the body as well as in the soul.[36]

The next question we ask is this: *In what did the image of God originally consist?* In Book I of the *Institutes* Calvin answers the question this way:

> The integrity with which Adam was endowed is expressed by this word [image or likeness of God], when he had full possession of right understanding, when he had his affections kept within the bounds of reason, all his senses tempered in right order, and he truly referred his excellence to exceptional gifts bestowed upon him by his Maker.[37]

Calvin goes on to say that in the beginning God's image was visible "in the light of the mind, in the uprightness of the heart, and in the soundness of all the parts."[38] Elsewhere he adds the thought that at that time man truly excelled in everything good.[39]

---

33. Ibid., I-II.114.8.
34. *Institutes of the Christian Religion,* ed. John T. McNeill, trans. Ford Lewis Battles (Philadelphia: Westminster, 1960), I.15.3.
35. Ibid.
36. *Comm. on I Cor.* 15:49. It may be noted that, according to Calvin, even the angels were created according to the likeness of God (*Inst.,* I.15.3).
37. *Inst.,* I.15.3.
38. Ibid., I.15.4.
39. *Comm. on Genesis* 1:26.

On the basis of Colossians 3:10 and Ephesians 4:24 Calvin concludes that the image of God in man originally included true knowledge, righteousness, and holiness.[40] Among the "supernatural gifts" that human beings had at the beginning—gifts that have been lost through the Fall—were faith, love of God, charity toward one's neighbor, and zeal for holiness and righteousness.[41] In his original state man was capable of communicating with and responding to both God and other human beings.[42]

Calvin opposes those who find God's likeness in the dominion over the earth that has been given to man.[43] Yet he is willing to grant that man's having dominion over the earth comprises some portion, though small, of the image of God.[44]

Before the Fall, therefore, according to Calvin, man possessed the image of God in its perfection. The Fall, however, had a devastating effect upon that image. Before we go on to explore that effect, we must first ask Calvin this further question: *Is there a sense in which fallen man is still in the image of God?* Sometimes it seems as if Calvin's answer to this question would be a resounding No. For at times he speaks of the image of God as having been *destroyed* by sin,[45] *obliterated* by the Fall,[46] *wiped out* or *lost* by sin,[47] *cancelled* by sin,[48] "as it were, *blotted out . . . by Adam's sin,"*[49] or *utterly defaced* by sin.[50]

A closer look, however, reveals that there is a real sense in which, according to Calvin, fallen man is still in the image of God. The image of God, Calvin says, is not totally annihilated by the Fall but is frightfully deformed.[51] Elsewhere he says that in the diversity of fallen human nature we see "some remaining traces [*notas*] of the image of God, which distinguish the entire human race from the other creatures."[52] In other places Calvin calls these traces *lineaments*[53] or a *remnant*[54] of the image of God. Reason and will still remain in fallen

---

40. *Inst.*, I.15.4. Cf. *Comm. on Colossians* 3:10 and *Comm. on Ephesians* 4:24.
41. *Inst.*, II.2.12.
42. T. F. Torrance, *Calvin's Doctrine of Man* (London: Lutterworth, 1949), p. 45.
43. *Inst.*, I.15.4.
44. *Comm. on Genesis* 1:26.
45. Ibid.
46. *Comm. on Genesis* 3:1.
47. *Comm. on Ephesians* 4:24.
48. *Comm. on II Corinthians* 3:18.
49. *Sermon on Job* 14:16-17, quoted by Torrance, *Calvin's Doctrine*, p. 77.
50. *Sermon on Job* 32:4-5, paraphrased by Torrance, ibid., p. 78.
51. *Inst.*, I.15.4.
52. *Inst.*, II.2.17.
53. *Comm. on Genesis* 1:26; *Comm. on James* 3:9.
54. *Comm. on Genesis* 9:6.

man; these Calvin calls "natural gifts," which, though not lost, have been partly weakened and partly corrupted by sin.[55] In an important passage in his Commentary on Psalm 8 Calvin indicates what are some of these traces of the image of God that are still found in fallen man. Commenting on the words "Thou hast made him little lower than God," Calvin says that the Psalmist must have in mind

> the distinguished endowments which clearly manifest that men were formed after the image of God. . . . the reason with which they are endued and by which they can distinguish between good and evil; the principle of religion which is planted in them; their intercourse with each other, which is preserved from being broken up by certain sacred bonds; the regard to what is becoming, and the sense of shame which guilt awakens in them, as well as their continuing to be governed by laws; all these things are clear indications of pre-eminent and celestial wisdom.[56]

Calvin, therefore, would have us see remnants and traces of the image of God in fallen man. He expresses himself even more strongly, however, in a remarkable passage where he tells us that our recognition of the image of God in all men must motivate us to treat them with kindness and love:

> We are not to consider that men merit of themselves but to look upon the image of God in all men, to which we owe all honor and love. . . . Therefore, whatever man you meet who needs your aid, you have no reason to refuse to help him. . . . Say, "he is contemptible and worthless"; but the Lord shows him to be one to whom he has deigned to give the beauty of his image. . . . Say that he does not deserve even your least effort for his sake; but the image of God, which recommends him to you, is worthy of your giving yourself and all your possessions.[57]

Calvin urges his readers to love even those who hate them, for we should "remember not to consider men's evil intention but to look upon the image of God in them, which cancels and effaces their transgressions, and with its beauty and dignity allures us to love and embrace them."[58]

In answer to our question, therefore, Calvin does indeed affirm that, though sin has deformed and distorted the image of God, there is an important sense in which fallen man must still be seen as an image-bearer of God. In fact, he insists that our recognition of the

---

55. *Inst.*, II.2.12.
56. *Comm. on Psalm* 8:5.
57. *Inst.*, III.7.6.
58. Ibid. On the point that Calvin sees fallen man as still being an image-bearer of God, see Ronald S. Wallace, *Calvin's Doctrine of the Christian Life* (Grand Rapids: Eerdmans, 1961), pp. 148-52.

image of God in all people today should move us to honor them and to love them, even in a sacrificial way.

As is well known, however, Calvin had strong convictions about the disruptive effect of sin on the image of God. The next question we address to him, therefore, is this: *What, then, has man's fall into sin done to the image of God?*

Calvin answers as follows: "Therefore, even though we grant that God's image was not totally annihilated and destroyed in him [man], yet it was so corrupted [by sin] that whatever remains is frightful deformity."[59] Again, from the same section of the *Institutes*, "Now God's image is the perfect excellence of human nature which shone in Adam before his defection, but was subsequently so vitiated and almost blotted out that nothing remains after the ruin except what is confused, mutilated, and disease-ridden."

Similarly, in his Commentary on Genesis he says:

> But now, although some obscure lineaments of that image [the image of God] are found remaining in us, yet are they so vitiated and maimed, that they may truly be said to be destroyed. For besides the deformity which everywhere appears unsightly, this evil also is added, that no part is free from the infection of sin.[60]

And in one of the Sermons on Job he makes the following statement: "True it is that when we come into this world, we bring some remnant of God's image wherein Adam was created: howbeit that same image is so disfigured that we are full of unrighteousness and there is nothing but blindness and ignorance in our minds."[61] This distortion of the image means that man has become alienated from God, from himself, and from his fellows.[62]

In distinction from many medieval theologians and from Irenaeus as well, Calvin held that what happened in the Fall was not just a matter of losing the *likeness* of God and retaining the *image* of God, since Calvin saw no basic difference between these two.[63] What did happen, however, was that whatever gifts or abilities man retained, such as reason and will, were perverted and distorted by the Fall. "Now, all man's faculties are, on account of the depravity of nature, so vitiated and corrupted that in all his actions persistent disorder and

59. *Inst.*, I.15.4.
60. *Comm. on Genesis* 1:26 (King trans. [Grand Rapids: Eerdmans, 1948]).
61. *Sermon on Job* 14:13-14, quoted in Torrance, *Calvin's Doctrine*, p. 76.
62. Torrance, *Calvin's Doctrine*, p. 46. Reference is made to the *Comm. on Genesis* 3:1-2 and 9:6-7.
63. *Inst.*, I.15.3.

intemperance threaten."[64] Similarly, we read the following words from the Commentary on the Gospel of John:

> For since no part or faculty of the soul is not corrupted and turned aside from what is right, the fact that men live and breathe and are endowed with sense, understanding and will tends to their destruction. Thus it is that death reigns everywhere. For the death of the soul is alienation from God.[65]

According to Aquinas and most of the scholastic theologians, as we have seen, the Fall simply meant the loss of something additional to man's nature, the added gift of grace (*donum superadditum*), leaving man pretty much as he was beforehand.[66] Calvin rejects this view, insisting that sin has distorted and perverted all of man's nature and all of his gifts—so that man has now become spiritually dead. According to Calvin fallen man is not just *deprived* but *depraved*.

The next question we ask of Calvin is this: *How is the image of God in man renewed?* Looking at this question from God's side, we may say that the image is renewed by the Holy Spirit, who uses the Word of God as his instrument. "Man's answer [to the grace of God] is the work of the Holy Spirit who through the Word forms the image anew in man, and forms his lips to acknowledge that he is a child of the Father."[67] Calvin insists that we receive the renewed image of God not by our own achievement but by grace, particularly by the working of the Spirit through the Word.

> *Imago dei* [the image of God] is essentially a reflection in and by the soul of the Word of God which is itself the lively or quickening image of God. Therefore man has been made such that it is his "special duty to give ear to the Word of God"; while, on the other hand, it is the work of the Holy Spirit who "with a wondrous and special energy forms the ear to hear, and the mind to understand."[68]

Looking at the question from man's side, the renewal of the image of God is accomplished by faith. "Faith is the motion of man's response to the Word by which he becomes conformable to God, that is, has *imago Dei*."[69] That is, faith is our response to the Word of God—a response that we can make only through the working of the Holy Spirit in our hearts.

There is a dynamic aspect to this restoration of the image of God.

64. *Inst.*, III.3.12.
65. *Comm. on John* 11:25 (Parker trans. [Grand Rapids: Eerdmans, 1979]).
66. See above, p. 40.
67. Torrance, *Calvin's Doctrine*, p. 80.
68. Ibid., p. 56. Quotes are from *Inst.*, I.6.2 and II.2.20.
69. Ibid., p. 81.

The image is not restored in us all at once, but progressively. According to Calvin,

> The manner of the Spirit's working in the elect is that he creates faith in our hearts, so "that the image of God, which had been effaced by sin, may be stamped anew upon us, and that the advancement of this restoration may be continually going forward in us during our whole life, because God makes his glory shine forth in us by little and little" (*Comm. on II Cor.* 3:18).[70]

This renewal of the image is the goal of regeneration; it therefore involves our knowledge, righteousness, and holiness.[71] This renewed image of God means conformity to Christ: "Now we see how Christ is the most perfect image of God; if we are conformed to it, we are so restored that with true piety, righteousness, purity, and intelligence we bear God's image."[72]

The goal of this renewal of the image of God is that man will be enabled once again to reflect the glory of God:

> The *imago dei* in Calvin's exposition has always to do with the glory of God, i.e., with his grace. Only when a man seeks the glory of God, by acknowledging His Word and by responding to His grace thankfully and with the adoring love of a child for his father, does he reflect that Glory.[73]

It should be noted, therefore, that for Calvin the renewal of the image of God is both the work of God's grace and the responsibility of man. The Holy Spirit must renew us through the Word, but we, enabled by the Spirit, must respond to that Word by faith. "The *imago dei* is God's action on man in the imprint of His Truth by the Word, and man's action only in response to the communication of that Word."[74] Thus, in Calvin's thought "there are two important factors constitutive of the *imago dei*. One is the act of God's pure grace, and the other is the response of man to that act—and both are brought together in one in the doctrine of the *imago dei*."[75]

It is clear from the above that Calvin's conception of the renewal of the image of God in man is not static but dynamic. This renewal, as previously noted, is gradual and progressive, which leads us to ask Calvin a final question: *When will the renewal of the image of God be completed?* Calvin replies: Not until the life to come.

---

70. David Cairns, *Image*, p. 150.
71. *Inst.*, I.15.4.
72. Ibid.
73. Torrance, *Calvin's Doctrine*, p. 79; cf. *Inst.*, II.3.4.
74. Calvin's comments on John 17:17 in his *Comm. on John*, quoted in ibid., p. 57.
75. Ibid., p. 68.

For we now begin to bear the image of Christ, and we are daily being transformed into it more and more; but that image depends upon spiritual regeneration. But then [at the time of the resurrection] it will be restored to fulness, in our body as well as our soul; what has now begun will be brought to completion, and we will obtain in reality what as yet we are only hoping for.[76]

Elsewhere he says, "Observe that the purpose of the gospel is the restoration in us of the image of God which had been cancelled by sin, and that this restoration is progressive and goes on during our whole life. . . . Thus the apostle speaks of progress which will be perfection only when Christ appears."[77] And again: "The image of God was only shadowed forth in him [man] till he should arrive at perfection."[78] "Therefore in some part it [the image of God] now is manifest in the elect, in so far as they have been reborn in the spirit; but it will attain its full splendor in heaven."[79]

In our evaluation of Calvin's thought, we must express great appreciation for his view of the image of God as a sober and responsible attempt to reproduce biblical teaching on this subject. Calvin's teachings on the following points are particularly appreciated: (1) The integrity of the original image of God—there was no deficiency in man at the beginning that had to be kept in check by a superadded gift of grace. Human beings as they were first created were able to serve and glorify God as they ought. (2) The devastating results of the Fall on the image of God in man—for Calvin fallen man is not just *deprived* but *depraved*. (3) Fallen man is, however, still an image-bearer of God. This concept we found to be important both for Calvin's theology and for his ethics. (4) The rejection of the distinction between image and likeness. (5) The renewal of the image of God is both God's work in man and man's response to God—a product of both divine sovereignty and human responsibility. (6) The renewal of the image of God is progressive and dynamic, and will not be completed until the life to come.

By way of criticism, a few minor points may be mentioned: (1) Calvin is inconsistent when he speaks about the image of God in fallen man: sometimes he says that the image has been destroyed, obliterated, or blotted out by sin, whereas at other times he states that the image has not been totally destroyed but that we must still see the image of God in all people, conducting ourselves toward them in the

76. *Comm. on I Corinthians* 15:49 (Fraser trans. [Grand Rapids: Eerdmans, 1979]).
77. *Comm. on II Corinthians* 3:18 (Smail trans. [Grand Rapids: Eerdmans, 1979], p. 50).
78. *Comm. on Genesis* 1:26.
79. *Inst.*, I.15.4.

light of this understanding. (2) Calvin holds that man's dominion over the earth is not part of the image of God. Yet, as we have seen, this dominion is presented as an aspect of the image in Genesis 1:26. (3) Calvin does not do full justice to man's having been created male and female as an essential aspect of the image of God, and to the implications of this aspect for our understanding of the image.

## KARL BARTH

We turn now to the views of a more recent theologian, Karl Barth, often called the father of neo-orthodoxy, who lived from 1886 to 1968. Again, we need to ask the question that we have also addressed to Aquinas and Calvin: *Where is the image of God to be found?* For Barth the image of God in man is not to be found in his intellect or reason. Barth totally rejects the statement of Polanus, a sixteenth-century theologian, that man is "a being gifted with reason" (*animal ratione praeditum*)—a definition derived from Aristotle.[80] As we saw, it was precisely this aspect of man that Aquinas had characterized as the essence of the image of God. Further, Barth refuses to find the image of God in man in any kind of anthropological "description of the being of man, its structure, disposition, capacities, etc."[81] Though previous theologians spent a great deal of time trying to locate the exact structures and qualities in man in which the image of God consists, Barth concludes, they were all mistaken in looking there.

Previous theologians, Barth continues, all made the mistake of failing to look clearly and carefully at the Bible text that describes man's creation in the image of God: "So God created man in his own image, in the image of God he created him; male and female he created them" (Gen. 1:27, RSV).

> Could anything be more obvious than to conclude from this clear indication that the image and likeness of the being created by God signifies existence in confrontation, i.e., in this confrontation, in the juxtaposition and conjunction of man and man which is that of male and female. . . ?[82]

The fact that we were created male and female means for Barth that the human being was endowed by God with the possibility of confrontation between man and woman. Man can be an "I" to woman and woman can be an "I" to man. Man can also be a "thou" to woman, and woman can be a "thou" to man. This I-thou confrontation, how-

---

80. Karl Barth, *Church Dogmatics*, III/2 (Edinburgh: T. & T. Clark, 1960), pp. 76-77.
81. *Church Dogmatics*, III/1, p. 195.
82. Ibid., p. 195.

ever, concerns not only the relation between man and woman, but also the relation between man and man.

Barth calls this confrontational relationship the image of God because this same confrontational relationship exists between God and man. God is a being who confronts us and enters into an I-thou relationship with us. Man's having been created with the capacity for a similar relationship with his fellowman means therefore that he has been created in the image and likeness of God.

> Man is created by God in correspondence with this relationship and differentiation [between the I and the Thou] in God Himself: created as a Thou that can be addressed by God but also an I responsible to God; in the relationship of man and woman in which man is a Thou to his fellow and therefore himself an I in responsibility to this claim.[83]

> Thus the *tertium comparationis,* the analogy between God and man, is simply the existence of the I and the Thou in confrontation. This is first constitutive for God, and then for man created by God. To remove it is tantamount to removing the divine from God as well as the human from man.[84]

Between God and man there is therefore for Barth not an analogy of being (*analogia entis*) but an analogy of relation (*analogia relationis*). God created man for covenantal fellowship with himself and for fellowship with others; therefore he made him in this way. Barth summarizes all this as follows:

> That real man is determined by God for life with God has its inviolable correspondence in the fact that his creaturely being is a being in encounter—between I and Thou, man and woman. It is human in this encounter, and in this humanity it is a likeness of the being of its Creator.[85]

To the question we asked Irenaeus, Aquinas, and Calvin, *Has the image of God been lost in the Fall?,* Barth replies in the negative. To begin with, Barth does not recognize in the history of man a historical Fall from a condition of rectitude to a state of corruption.[86] There could therefore be no loss of the image of God after "the Fall." Further, Barth holds that the capacity for I-thou fellowship between God and man and between man and man is an essential and unlosable aspect of human existence.

Barth, in fact, goes so far as to say that the history of God's fellowship with man, far from being abrogated by the Fall, really begins

---

83. Ibid., p. 198.
84. Ibid., p. 185.
85. *Church Dogmatics*, III/2, p. 203.
86. *Church Dogmatics*, III/1, p. 200.

with the Fall.[87] It is hard to know what Barth means here by "the Fall," but it is clear that he would not allow for any fellowship between God and man in a state of integrity.

In Calvin we found an emphasis on the *renewal of the image of God* by the Holy Spirit in the lives of believers. Is there anything of this emphasis in Karl Barth? On this point Barth does not give us a clear answer. Sometimes he seems to say that the image of God in man is susceptible of renewal. For example, in commenting on Colossians 3:10, he says that the passage "is important because it shows that for Paul 'our' participation in the divine likeness of Christ does not rest on our decision and action but on a transformation which has happened to us."[88] The reference to a "transformation" would seem to suggest that the image of God here means more than a merely formal capacity for encounter. Barth has similar things to say about sanctification elsewhere in the *Church Dogmatics*:

> The sanctification of man, his conversion to God, is, like his justification, a transformation, a new determination, which has taken place *de jure* for the world and therefore for all men. *De facto*, however, it is not known by all men, just as justification has not *de facto* been grasped and acknowledged and known and confessed by all men, but only by those who are awakened to faith.[89]

Here Barth is saying that certain people grasp and acknowledge their sanctification by faith, and hence are subjectively changed and transformed. So, on the basis of statements of this sort, it would seem that there is a possibility that those created in the image of God can be progressively transformed and thus become more like God and more like Christ.

Yet in terms of Barth's definition of the image of God we must conclude that the image of God is not really capable of renewal. For the image is defined in purely formal terms: the ability to exist in confrontation with God and others; the capacity of hearing God as a thou and responding to him as an I, and the capacity of doing the same with fellow human beings. But if this capacity is an ineradicable aspect of man, and if it is understood as a mere capacity or ability as such, regardless of how it is used, one fails to see how it can be subject to improvement, renewal, or transformation.

We may grant that Barth's understanding of the image of God is a wholesome corrective to an overemphasis on the structure of man, particularly on his rationality, as the essential aspect of the image of

87. Ibid.
88. Ibid., p. 204.
89. *Church Dogmatics*, IV/2, p. 511.

God. As we saw in a previous chapter, we should not think of the image of God only as a noun but also as a verb: we are to *image* God by the way we live, and the heart of the image of God is love for God and for others. Barth's dynamic understanding of the image ties in with this important emphasis.

We must, however, criticize Barth's view of the image of God as being an inadequate reproduction of the biblical data. In Barth's view the image is purely relational, and therefore purely formal: the capacity for confrontation and encounter. But the image of God is surely more than a mere capacity. Are not Satan and the demons also beings in encounter with each other and with God? What is significant is not just the capacity for encounter but the way in which we encounter God and others. While we may grant that the possibility of an I-thou relationship with God and others is an aspect of our likeness to God, that likeness must surely show itself in concrete actions and attitudes, and not just in a formal similarity of capacity.

Further, Barth's denial of the historical Fall and his understanding of the image of God as purely relational make it impossible for him fully to recognize both the devastating effects of the Fall on the image of God and the need for the renewal of the image of God in the redemptive process. In these respects Barth's conception of the image of God falls far short of the biblical doctrine of man.

## EMIL BRUNNER

It will be profitable to look next at the conception of the image of God found in a contemporary of Barth's, also representing the so-called Dialectical Theology, Emil Brunner (1889-1966). We should note that, like Barth, Brunner rejects the historicity of Adam and of the fall of man into sin.[90] This does not mean, however, that Brunner denies the present sinfulness of man:

> If, on the one hand, we maintain that we cannot think in Copernican terms without giving up the *story* of Adam, then, on the other hand we must also say: that we cannot believe, in Christian and Biblical terms, without holding firmly to the distinction between Creation and Sin, and therefore the idea of a Fall. To give this up means to abandon the Biblical faith as a whole.[91]

In other words, while denying the historicity of the Fall, Brunner wants to maintain that man today is not in the same state or condition

---

90. Emil Brunner, *The Christian Doctrine of Creation and Redemption*, trans. Olive Wyon (Philadelphia: Westminster, 1953), pp. 48-49.
91. Ibid., p. 51.

in which God created him, but now exists in a sinful state. In fact, Brunner sometimes speaks about man's fall into sin, putting the phrase into quotation marks ("this split between formal and material image from God's point of view should not be; it is the result of the 'fall into sin ...' ").[92] This language is puzzling indeed. Brunner apparently wants to speak about man as if he had fallen into sin while at the same time insisting that one ought not to think about him as having experienced an actual historical fall into sin. He wants to hold that there has been a Fall, and even occasionally to speak of "the event"[93] of the Fall, while denying that there has ever been such an event.

If we should ask Brunner where the image of God in man is to be found, we should find him rejecting strongly, as does Barth, the conception that the image is found primarily in man's reason. Brunner disavows this understanding as a relic of medieval scholasticism. For him the image of God is to be found first of all in the area of man's relation to God, his responsibility to God, and the possibility of fellowship with God. Reason is therefore not the highest thing in man but only the means whereby man is able to fulfill his true function: that of having loving fellowship with God.

> Man may be described as an hierarchical system. In him there is an "above" and a "below." ... Idealism posits it [the "above"] as the Divine Reason in which man participates; the Christian faith posits it as the Word of God, that self-bestowing, challenging Word, in Whom man as man has his ground. ... Reason is, so to speak, only the organ of man's relation to God.[94]

In order to understand how Brunner conceives of the image of God, we must first note what he says about God's purpose in creating man: "God, who wills to glorify Himself and to impart Himself, wills man to be a creature who responds to His call of love with a grateful, responsive love."[95] Love, therefore, is at the heart of Brunner's understanding of man and of the purpose for his existence: God loves us and desires us to love him. God does not wish from man the response of an automaton or of an animal; he desires the response of a free person, since only such a person can truly love him.

> Hence the heart of the creaturely existence of man is freedom, selfhood, to be an "I," a person. Only an "I" can answer a "Thou," only a Self which is self-determining can freely answer God.[96]

92. "Reply to Interpretation and Criticism," in Charles W. Kegley, ed., *The Theology of Emil Brunner* (New York: Macmillan, 1962), p. 333.
93. "Frieden auf Erden," *Grundriss* 6, no. 5 (1944).
94. *Man in Revolt*, trans. Olive Wyon (New York: Scribner, 1939), p. 102.
95. *Doctrine of Creation*, p. 55.
96. Ibid., p. 56.

Man as originally created had this freedom. This was not freedom to do anything he pleased, but a restricted or limited freedom. Man was given this limited freedom in order that he might respond to God with love, so that through this response God might be praised and glorified.[97]

It is of the essence of this responsible freedom, Brunner goes on to say, that its purpose may or may not be fulfilled. And it is at this point that he introduces the distinction between the image of God in the *formal* and *material* sense:

> Thus it is part of the divinely created nature of man that it should have both a formal and a material aspect. The fact that man must respond, that he is responsible, is fixed; no amount of human freedom, nor of the sinful misuse of freedom, can alter this fact. Man is, and remains, responsible, whatever his personal attitude to his Creator may be. He may deny his responsibility, and he may misuse his freedom, but he cannot get rid of his responsibility. Responsibility is part of the unchangeable structure of man's being.[98]

By the *formal* aspect of the image of God, therefore, Brunner means man's responsibility, his capacity to respond to God's love, his need to give an answer to God. We ought to answer God's love with our own love, but even where we do not do so, we are still giving answers to God. This formal aspect of the image of God applies not only, however, to man's relation to God; it also concerns his relation to his neighbor: he has a responsibility to love and care for his fellowman.

Though the term *formal image* suggests an abstract concept, Brunner insists that the formal image has content. For example, he says that such things as freedom, reason, conscience, and language belong to the image in this sense.[99]

Further, the image of God in this formal sense cannot be lost; it is not abolished by man's sin. One cannot lose the formal image without ceasing to be a human being.

> Whatever kind of response man may make to the call of the Creator—in any case he does respond even if his reply is: "I do not know any Creator, and I will not obey any God." Even this answer *is* an answer, and it comes under the inherent law of responsibility. This formal essential structure cannot be lost. It is identical with human existence as such, and indeed with the quality of being which all human beings possess equally; it only ceases where true human living ceases—on the borderline of imbecility or madness.[100]

97. Ibid.
98. Ibid., pp. 56-57.
99. *Man in Revolt*, p. 510.
100. *Doctrine of Creation*, p. 57.

The image of God in this formal sense is what Brunner calls the Old Testament conception of the image: "In the thought of the Old Testament the fact that man has been 'made in the Image of God' means something which man can never lose; even when he sins he cannot lose it."[101] Brunner grants, however, that this aspect of the image of God is also taught in the New Testament in two passages: 1 Corinthians 11:7 and James 3:9.[102]

The New Testament simply assumes and presupposes the fact that man has been created in the image of God. What matters most, however, to the New Testament writers, particularly to the apostles, is that man should give the kind of answer the Creator intends, the kind of response that honors and glorifies God, the response of reverent and grateful love—a response that is to be given not just in words but by one's entire life. This proper response, which consists of love for God and love for the neighbor, is what Brunner calls the *material* aspect of the image of God.[103]

The New Testament reveals that man has not been giving this right answer to God; he has been giving the wrong answer, seeking himself instead of seeking God, glorifying himself and other creatures instead of giving glory to God.[104] Man now "lives in contradiction not only to the will of God, but also to his own creaturely nature, in contradiction with himself."[105] In this sense (the *material* aspect) man has lost the image of God—wholly, and not partially.[106]

The chief message of the New Testament is how this lost image of God in man is being restored in and through Jesus Christ. This restoration of the image is identical with the gift of God in Jesus Christ received by faith.[107] The restoration of the image is, in fact, the heart of the doctrine of reconciliation: "The whole work of Jesus Christ in reconciliation and redemption may be summed up in this central conception of the renewal and consummation of the Divine Image in man."[108]

Since Christ is the true image of God, the restoration of the image means existence in Christ, the Word made flesh.

Jesus Christ is the true *Imago Dei*, which man regains when through

---

101. Ibid., p. 57.
102. *Man in Revolt*, p. 500 (although Brunner does not use the expression *formal image* here).
103. *Doctrine of Creation*, pp. 57-58.
104. Ibid., p. 58.
105. "Reply to Criticism," in Kegley, p. 332.
106. *Doctrine of Creation*, p. 58.
107. Ibid.
108. *Man in Revolt*, p. 501.

faith he is "in Jesus Christ." Faith in Jesus is therefore the *restauratio imaginis* [restoration of the image], because he restores to us that existence in the Word of God which we had lost through sin. When man enters into the love of God revealed in Christ he becomes truly human. True human existence is existence in the love of God.[109]

Brunner insists that it is important for us to maintain the distinction between these two aspects of the image:

> It is evident that our thought will become terribly muddled if the two ideas of the *Imago Dei*—the "formal" and "structural" one of the Old Testament, and the "material" one of the New Testament—are either confused with one another or treated as identical. The result will be: either that we must deny that the sinner possesses the quality of humanity at all; or, that which makes him a human being must be severed from the *Imago Dei*; or, the loss of the *Imago* in the material sense must be regarded merely as an obscuring or a partial corruption of the *Imago,* which lessens the heinousness of sin. All these three false solutions disappear, once the distinction is rightly made.[110]

How, then, are these two aspects of the image related? As we have seen, the image in the material sense has been lost because of man's sinfulness, and must be restored in man through the redemptive process. The formal image, however, has not been lost. Man continues to be a responsible being who ought to give the right answer to God and who ought to give the right answer to his fellowman. "As man was made for love to God, so he is made for love to men. This is the true meaning and goal of his existence."[111] When man rebels against God, therefore, he still stands before God—only in the wrong way.

Brunner puts it this way: "The loss of the *Imago,* in the material sense, presupposes the *Imago* in the formal sense."[112] So the two aspects of the image of God must always be recognized, must always be held in tension. In one sense the image of God has been lost, but in another sense it has been retained. Brunner also puts it this way:

> Man's relation with God, which determines his whole being, has not been destroyed by sin, but it has been perverted. Man does not cease to be the being who is responsible to God, but his responsibility has been altered from a state of being-in-love to a state of being-under-the-law, a life under the wrath of God.[113]

Brunner goes on to make a rather puzzling statement: "From the

---

109. *Doctrine of Creation,* p. 58.
110. Ibid., p. 59.
111. David Cairns, *Image,* p. 157 (reproducing Brunner's thought).
112. *Doctrine of Creation,* p. 60.
113. *Man in Revolt,* p. 105.

side of God, therefore, this distinction between the 'formal' and the 'material' does not exist; it is not legally valid. But it does exist— wrongly."[114] I would have preferred to say that this distinction *ought not* to exist (rather than *does not* exist). What Brunner means, I presume, is that God did not intend that the image should be split into these two aspects. God intended the image to remain unitary, but sin has split it into these two aspects. When the image has been totally renewed, it will be unitary once again.

We may appreciate much about Brunner's exposition of the image of God: (1) his dynamic understanding of the image, which for him must be seen in the light of the encounter between God and man, which is basic to human existence; (2) his finding love to be central in the image of God, rather than reason or intellect; (3) his emphasis on the devastating effects of sin on the image of God; (4) his retention of the twofold aspect of the image; and (5) his insistence that fallen man is still in a very real sense in the image of God.

In other respects, however, I have some real problems with Brunner's view. First, Brunner's denial of the historical Fall repudiates Pauline teaching about the first Adam, and raises serious doubts about the historicity of the second Adam, namely, Jesus Christ. This point is extremely important. In Romans 5:12-21 Paul contrasts the condemnation we have received through the fall of the first Adam with the righteousness we receive through the obedience of the second Adam. If, however, the first Adam was merely figurative or symbolic, how can we be certain that the second Adam, to whom Paul refers in the same passage, is not also figurative or symbolic? In this passage Paul is obviously speaking of two heads—one through whom we fell into sin, and another through whom we are saved. If one should say that the first head never existed, what becomes of Paul's argument?

Paul Jewett's comments on this matter are very much to the point:

Paul's doctrine is: At a given time and in a given place the first man committed a sinful act of transgression against the will of God. If we remove the time-space form in which this proposition is cast, what is there left to talk about? Brunner may continue to speak of the fall as an "event" in quotes, he may call it primal history, or he may affirm, as he did in one place, that he does not know what the fall is, nor why and how it happened. But the prosaic mind can hardly escape the suspicion that an event which did not happen in time and space did not happen at all.

Furthermore, the idea that the historical form in which Paul cast his doctrine of the fall is immaterial to that doctrine, is only its "alphabet," so to speak, is preposterous. The whole thrust of Paul in Romans 5:12-21 is to illustrate how men can be justified on the basis of another's right-

114. *Doctrine of Creation*, p. 61.

eousness, not their own; namely, the righteousness of Christ, by an appeal to the way in which they are condemned on the basis of another man's sin, not their own; namely, Adam's. . . . To abandon the existence of the first Adam does not alter the *form* of such an argument, for the simple reason [that] there is no argument left to have a form. . . .

Brunner, by abandoning this Biblical parallelism, enervates the force of his argument for the absolute necessity of the Jesus event. It is obvious enough *why* he insists on this point. . . . What is not evident is *how* Brunner justifies his insistence upon this point. He has never anywhere indicated how it is possible to existentialize the first Adam and insist on the historicity of the second.[115]

A second point of criticism is this: Brunner's denial of the historical Fall also calls into question the distinction he wants to maintain between creation and sin. If there was no point in time in which man first rebelled against God and thus became sinful, how did man become sinful? Was it possibly because of some defect in the way he had been created?

Third, Brunner insists that the image of God in the formal sense has been retained despite man's sinfulness: man still remains a being who is answerable to God, even when he gives God the wrong answer. Yet, as we have seen, the formal image in Brunner has content: freedom, reason, conscience, and language are included in it. Is it then correct to say that this formal image has been completely retained? Has it been retained in its full integrity? Has not sin also affected this formal image, in the sense that man's reason, conscience, and freedom have been corrupted and perverted by sin (as Calvin so strongly affirmed)?

## G. C. BERKOUWER

We conclude this historical study by examining the conception of the image of God taught by a contemporary Dutch theologian, Gerrit C. Berkouwer. Born in 1903, he was Professor of Dogmatics at the Free University of Amsterdam from 1945 until his retirement in 1973. The volume in which he sets forth his views on man is *Man: The Image of God*.[116]

Like Barth and Brunner, Berkouwer rejects the thought that the image of God in man is to be found primarily in man's intellect or reason. He deems contrary to the Bible those definitions that find the

115. Paul K. Jewett, *Emil Brunner's Concept of Revelation* (London: James Clarke, 1954), pp. 148-49.
116. Trans. Dirk W. Jellema (Grand Rapids: Eerdmans, 1962). The original Dutch edition was published in 1957.

essence of man to be his reason, since they do not emphasize what the Scriptures present as the unique characteristic of man: namely, his inescapable relatedness to God.[117] For Berkouwer man must always be seen as he stands before the face of the Almighty, bound to God religiously in the totality of his existence. This relatedness to God, moreover, is not something added to man but is constitutive of his being. Whoever tries to see the human person apart from this relatedness to God will always fail to see him as he really is.

In this connection Berkouwer makes a comment that sounds a note of caution to all psychologists, sociologists, psychiatrists, physicians, and so on: "The sciences which deal with certain aspects of man can make no more than a partial contribution towards our understanding of man, and cannot unveil the secret of the whole man."[118]

The first major problem about the image of God that Berkouwer tackles is the question of whether we may properly speak about the image in both a broader and a narrower sense. Reformed theologians have traditionally made this kind of distinction when speaking about the image of God. For example, Louis Berkhof, in his *Manual of Christian Doctrine,* following the Dutch theologian Herman Bavinck, distinguishes between the image of God in a restricted and in a more comprehensive sense. The restricted or narrower image, Berkhof says, consists in "the spiritual qualities with which man was created, namely, true knowledge, righteousness and holiness." The image in the more comprehensive or broader sense means that man is "a spiritual being, rational, moral, and immortal; in the body, not as a material substance, but as the organ of the soul; and in man's dominion over the lower creation."[119] It is then usually also said that, whereas the image in its narrower sense has been completely lost through man's fall into sin, the image in the broader sense has not been lost but has been corrupted and perverted by sin.

Berkouwer suggests that Reformed theologians made this distinction for two reasons: they recognized that (1) man, though fallen, still remains man; and (2) man, through his fall into sin, has lost that conformity to God's will which marked his life before the Fall. Reformed scholars therefore began to concern themselves with the question of what in man was not lost through sin. This type of discussion led to the assertion that there is an aspect of the image of God that was not lost through sin.

117. *Man,* p. 34.
118. Ibid., p. 29. For a fuller treatment of what will follow, see my review, "Berkouwer on the Image of God," *Reformed Journal* 8, nos. 5 and 6 (May and June 1958).
119. Grand Rapids: Eerdmans, 1953, pp. 129-30.

Berkouwer questions the validity of this distinction between the broader and narrower aspects of the image of God.[120] In the second chapter of his book he sets forth five difficulties that he has with the so-called twofold-image concept:

1. The attempt to describe the image of God in the broader sense tends to make us think of the image primarily in terms of man's ontological and psychological structure. When we try to define the image of God by means of such concepts as reason, morality, and freedom, Berkouwer insists, we are soon involved in speculations that find no support in Scripture.[121]

2. If we begin our description of the image of God by trying to describe the "essence" or "being" of man, we then have to add man's relatedness to God as a kind of appendix. But this would be quite out of harmony with Scripture, which always puts man's relatedness to God at the center.[122]

3. If we try to speak of a narrower aspect of the image that has been lost and of a broader aspect that has been retained, are we not operating with two divergent and perhaps even contradictory conceptions of the image? By the narrower image we mean active conformity to God's will in a life of obedience, and by the broader image we mean an analogy of being to God's being, which consists of the possession of reason, will, and other qualities. But these two conceptions of the image are so diverse that it is impossible to unite them into a meaningful synthesis.[123]

4. The distinction between the broader and narrower image involves the danger of losing sight of man's radical corruption because of sin, by suggesting the possibility that the broader aspect of the image points to something in man that has not been affected by sin. Proponents of the double-image concept, continues Berkouwer, speak of an aspect of the image of God that is retained after the Fall. When they do so, are they not implying that there is something in man that sin has not perverted? To combat this possible implication, Berkouwer quotes Herman Bavinck to the effect that the image in the broader sense has been "corrupted and devastated" (*bedorven en verwoest*) by sin.[124] But then the question arises for Berkouwer whether the expression "image of God in the wider sense" still has any valid meaning. Has this image still been retained if it has been "corrupted and devastated"? Can one really say that man in revolt against God still bears

120. *Man*, p. 119.
121. Ibid., pp. 59-60.
122. Ibid., pp. 61-62.
123. Ibid., pp. 57, 61-62.
124. Ibid., p. 41 (the reference in Bavinck is to *Dogmatiek*, 2:595).

the image of God? Or should we not rather say that man in revolt is in many ways precisely the opposite of the image of God?

5. The distinction between the broader and narrower image involves a certain arbitrariness in the determination of what does and what does not belong to the image of God in the broader sense.[125] Various theologians come up with different attributes or qualities in man that allegedly belong to the broader image. These different descriptions of the broader image, however, neither agree with each other nor are specifically drawn from Scripture.

In Chapter 3 I argued that Genesis 9:6 and James 3:9 teach that there is a sense in which fallen man is still in the image of God.[126] How does Berkouwer interpret these passages? He reproduces with appreciation and obvious approval the views of Klaas Schilder, F. K. Schumann, and E. Schlink on the meaning of these texts. According to these scholars, Genesis 9:6 and James 3:9 do not intend to teach us that fallen man is still in the image of God, but only that God did make man in his image at the time of creation, and that, at some time in the future, he may again, through the instrumentality of God's grace, bear the image of God. In other words, these passages tell us what man was in the past and what he may be in the future, but say nothing about what fallen man apart from the redemptive work of God is at the present time. This is apparently Berkouwer's view of the meaning of these passages,[127] though it is regrettable that he nowhere himself gives us detailed exegeses of these important texts.

It may be noted in passing that Berkouwer does not see in man's having been given dominion over the rest of creation a description of the content of the image of God.[128]

While he grants that the Scriptures nowhere give us a systematic doctrine of what the image of God includes, Berkouwer follows Calvin and Herman Bavinck in calling attention to two ways in which the New Testament sheds light on the meaning of the image of God: (1) by what it says about the restoration of the image in the regenerate, and (2) by what it says about Christ, who is in a unique way the image of God.[129] Berkouwer therefore proceeds to discuss the *new self* (or "new man") as pictured in the New Testament, in contrast with the *old self* (or "old man"), as a way of showing what the Bible says about the meaning of the image.

The image of God becomes visible in the life of this *new self*, who

125. *Man*, p. 60.
126. Above, pp. 16-18, 19-20.
127. *Man*, pp. 58-59.
128. Ibid., pp. 70-72.
129. Ibid., pp. 87-89.

has put off the *old self*, has learned to know Christ, and has been taught in him. In this tremendous change that Christ brings about, man arrives at his true humanity.

> Thus when we consider the image of God in man as it is restored in Christ, we are not concerned with some "analogy" of ego or personality or self-consciousness, but rather with the fulness of the new life which can be described as a new relationship with God, and in *this* relationship as the reality of salvation.[130]

This new self is recognizable in the new direction of man's life. The new life is a new birth, a living in love, a walking in the truth, a passing out of death into life. It is a new inner disposition of heart that reveals itself in a new outward walk. This life is in conformity with the will of God. In it man, like the Prodigal Son, truly comes to himself. Therefore in this new life, described variously as newness, fellowship, peace, or joy, man is re-created after the image of God.[131]

In this connection Berkouwer discusses the dynamics of the imitation of God. He cites such biblical passages as Ephesians 5:1-2, "Be imitators of God, therefore, as dearly loved children and live a life of love, just as Christ loved us and gave himself up for us." The image of God is therefore not just a static entity; it is a dynamic challenge to consecrated living! The Christian must constantly strive in God's strength to be *like God* in his daily life. We must forgive as our Heavenly Father forgives; we must love as God loves; we must try to be perfect as our Father in heaven is perfect. This imitation of God must assume the form of an imitation of Christ. We must try to be like Christ, particularly by living in love.[132]

However, we must never think of this imitation of God apart from our fellowship with others. The renewal of the image of God must never be conceived of in an individualistic way, but always in connection with our relatedness to others. It is in this *analogy of love*, not in the scholastic *analogy of being*, that Berkouwer sees the image of God in man.

This renewal of man's life in the image of God is a product of God's redemptive work. However, this renewal also involves man's active participation. The passage in Ephesians 5 particularly stresses this aspect: we are to "be imitators of God. . . ."

The renewal of the image of God also has an eschatological dimension. It will not be completed during this present life; we shall

130. Ibid., p. 99.
131. Ibid., pp. 98-100.
132. Ibid., pp. 100-104.

not totally reflect the image of God until the life to come.[133] The apostle John puts it this way: "Beloved, we are God's children now; it does not yet appear what we shall be, but we know that when he appears we shall be like him" (1 John 3:2, RSV).

Berkouwer further observes that we can learn about the meaning of the image by looking at Jesus Christ, who is the perfect image of God (see 2 Cor. 4:4; Col. 1:15). This implies first of all that the most central thing in the image of God is not "reason" or "will" but love, since what comes most fully into focus as we look at Christ is his amazing love. This also implies that to be renewed in the image of God means to become more and more like Christ (Rom. 8:29; 2 Cor. 3:18).[134] Through regeneration and faith believers become one with Christ and become members of Christ, who is himself the unique image of God.[135]

Berkouwer also comments on the relation of the word *representation* to the image of God. To be in the image of God means that man represents God here on earth. This implies that man must make his likeness to God visible—not in the sense of "theatrical holiness" but in the sense of Matthew 5:16, "Let your light so shine before men, that they may see your good works and give glory to your Father who is in heaven" (RSV).[136]

We may sum up Berkouwer's conception of the meaning of the image of God by saying that it is dynamic, not static. For him the image does not consist in certain structural qualities that resemble similar qualities in God, but in concretely visible sanctification—that is, in the newness of life to which we are restored in Christ. This renewal of the image is both a gift from God and the task of man. The image of God and its renewal is therefore not a static entity but an ever-beckoning ideal, a challenge to consecrated living.

While rejecting the idea that fallen man has retained the image in the broader sense, Berkouwer does not mean to deny that fallen man is still man. What traditional Reformed theologians called the "retained broader image" Berkouwer calls man's "continuing humanity."[137] Scripture, however, emphasizes not only this retained humanity as such, but its corruption by sin. Man in his apostasy from God abuses his reason, perverts his will, and loves himself instead of God and others.[138] However, God's common grace restrains the

133. Ibid., pp. 104-6.
134. Ibid., pp. 107-12.
135. Ibid., p. 112.
136. Ibid., pp. 114-15.
137. Ibid., pp. 54, 56-57.
138. Ibid., chap. 4.

outward manifestation of this corruption in such a way that civilization, culture, and a certain measure of external conformity to the will of God (apart from the inner renewal of the heart) is still possible in this present world.[139]

Berkouwer has given us a challenging and stimulating study of the biblical concept of the image of God. We appreciate his insistence that we cannot understand man apart from his inescapable relatedness to God and to his fellowmen. Further, we also appreciate his balanced view of the present state of fallen man: apart from the redemptive work of God, man today is pervasively depraved, but yet there is a restraint of sin even in the unregenerate through God's common grace. We are especially grateful for what is probably his outstanding contribution: his dynamic view of the image of God as meaning our renewal by the Holy Spirit into an active and growing likeness to God.

On the other hand, however, I have some serious difficulties with Berkouwer's view—difficulties that center in his denial of the so-called twofold image. As we saw in Chapter 3, the Bible does lead us to see the image in a twofold sense, and to see fallen man as still in an important sense an image-bearer of God. Therefore, I have several objections to Berkouwer's position.

First, two passages of Scripture, Genesis 9:6 ("Whoever sheds the blood of man, by man shall his blood be shed; for in the image of God has God made man") and James 3:9 ("With the tongue we praise our Lord and Father, and with it we curse men, who have been made in God's likeness"), speak of fallen man as still being in the image of God. To be sure, passages like Colossians 3:10 and Ephesians 4:24 describe man's need to be renewed according to God's image. But these texts do not negate or nullify the clear biblical statements about the retention of the image. If we put these two types of passages together, we conclude that there must be a sense in which fallen man still bears the image of God, but that there must also be a sense in which he no longer bears that image. Hence the distinction between the broader and narrower aspects of the image is necessary.

Furthermore, Genesis 1:26 ("Then God said, 'Let us make man in our image, after our likeness . . .', " RSV) does not refer only to a certain way in which man should live, but to man himself in the totality of his existence. As was said above, I appreciate Berkouwer's emphasis on the image as meaning man's proper functioning in obedience to God, in conformity to God's will. This is indeed a biblical emphasis. According to the scriptural data, however, the image of God consists of more than mere functioning; it concerns not only what

139. Ibid., chap. 5.

man does but also what he is. For Berkouwer the image of God is *only a verb*: man ought to *image* God; since fallen man no longer *images* God, he is no longer an image-bearer of God. But the Genesis passage indicates that the image of God *is also a noun*, that that *image* refers to the uniqueness of man's existence, and that the image is inseparable from man's being man.

Finally, Berkouwer's distinction between man's continuing humanity (which persists after the Fall) and the image of God (which, according to him, was wholly lost in the Fall) implies that the image of God is somehow separable from man's essence. The image of God, in Berkouwer's thinking, is therefore something like an accessory on an automobile—something that may be desirable but is not really necessary. New automobiles today come equipped either with or without air-conditioning; if you, to save money, decide to order your next car without air-conditioning, you may not be as comfortable in the summer as your neighbor who has an air-conditioned car, but you will still be driving an automobile. Comparably, in Berkouwer's view, the image of God is so nonessential to human existence that man can still be man without it. But does not the Bible indicate that what is unique about man, in distinction from all other creatures, is that he was created to be an image-bearer of God, and that such image bearing is essential and not accidental to his existence?

Herman Bavinck has put it well:

> Man does not simply *bear* or *have* the image of God; he *is* the image of God.
>
> From the doctrine that man has been created in the image of God flows the clear implication that that image extends to man in his entirety. Nothing in man is excluded from the image of God. All creatures reveal traces of God, but only man is the image of God. And he is that image totally, in soul and body, in all faculties and powers, in all conditions and relationships. Man is the image of God because and insofar as he is true man, and he is man, true and real man, because and insofar as he is the image of God.[140]

---

140. *Dogmatiek*, 2:595-96 [trans. mine].

# CHAPTER 5

# The Image of God:
# A Theological Summary

**T**he purpose of this chapter will be to give a summarizing theological description of the meaning and significance of the doctrine of the image of God. As we have seen, it is said only about man—not about any other creature—that he or she has been created in the image of God. To be in the image of God, therefore, must be an indication of what is unique about humankind. The concept of the image of God is the heart of Christian anthropology.

When the Bible says that God created man in his own image, it certainly intends to say that man at the time of his creation was obedient to God and loved God with all his heart (note, e.g., Gen. 1:31, "And God saw everything that he had made, and behold, it was very good," RSV). But the statement "God created man in his own image" (v. 27) obviously intends to do more than just describe man's spiritual and moral integrity. That is, it sets man apart from the rest of God's creation, by indicating that he was formed in a unique way. The statement does not merely tell us in what direction man was living his life in the beginning (namely, in obedience to God); it describes him in the totality of his existence. Man, these words tell us, is a being whose entire constitution images and reflects God.

In our earlier discussion of Berkouwer's view of the image of God, I quoted Herman Bavinck, who said that according to the Bible man does not just *bear* or *have* the image of God but *is* the image of God, and that the image of God extends to man in his entirety.[1] All this implies that the image of God is not something accidental to man, which he can lose without ceasing to be man, but is essential to his existence.

The basic thought underlying the word *image* (*tselem* and *demūth*

---

1. See above, p. 65. Cf. Karl Barth, *Church Dogmatics*, III/1 (Edinburgh: T. & T. Clark, 1958), p. 184: "He [man] would not be man if he were not the image of God. He is the image of God in the fact that he is man."

in Hebrew) is that of likeness; these words tell us that man as he was created was *like God*. Genesis 1:26-28, which describes man's creation in the image of God, does not tell us precisely in what this likeness to God consists. More will be said later on this matter. But we should note at the outset that the concept of man as the *image* or *likeness* of God tells us that man as he was created was to *mirror* God and to *represent* God.

First, he was to *mirror* God. As a mirror reflects, so man should reflect God. When one looks at a human being, one ought to see in him or her a certain reflection of God. Another way of putting this is to say that in man God is to become visible on earth. To be sure, other creatures, and even the heavens, declare the glory of God, but only in man does God become visible. Reformed theologians speak of God's general revelation, in which he reveals his presence, power, and divinity through the works of his hands. But in the creation of man God revealed himself in a unique way, by making someone who was a kind of mirror image of himself. No higher honor could have been given to man than the privilege of being an image of the God who made him.

This fact is tied in with the prohibition of image making found in the second commandment of the Decalogue: "You shall not make for yourself a graven image" (Ex. 20:4, RSV). God does not want his creatures to make images of him, since he has already created an image of himself: a living, walking, talking image.[2] If you wish to see what I am like, God is saying, look at my most distinguished creature: man. This means that when man is what he ought to be, others should be able to look at him and see something of God in him: something of God's love, God's kindness, and God's goodness.

Second, man also *represents* God. Man was created in such a way that he was able to do this. If it is true that when one looks at man he should see something of God in him, it follows that man represents God on earth. Ancient rulers often set up images of themselves in distant parts of their realms; an image of this sort then represented the ruler, stood for his authority, and reminded his subjects that he was indeed their king. In Daniel 3, for example, we read that King Nebuchadnezzar set up an image on the plain of Dura, commanding his subjects to fall down in worship before it. Though the biblical text does not specifically say so, we may presume that the image was a likeness of Nebuchadnezzar himself, and thus represented the king.

Man, then, was created in God's image so that he or she might represent God, like an ambassador from a foreign country. As an am-

2. On this point, see Berkouwer, *Man*, pp. 81-82.

bassador represents his country's authority, so man (both male and female) must represent the authority of God. As an ambassador is concerned to advance the best interests of his country, so man must seek to advance God's program for this world. As God's representatives, we should support and defend what God stands for, and should promote what God promotes. As God's representatives, we must not do what we like, but what God desires. Through us God works out his purposes on this earth. In us people should be able to encounter God, to hear his word, and to experience his love. Man is God's representative.[3]

If it is true that the whole person is the image of God, we must also include the body as part of the image. Unfortunately, theologians have often denied this. J. Gresham Machen, for example, put it this way: "The 'image of God' cannot well refer to man's body, because God is a spirit; it must therefore refer to man's soul."[4] Calvin, as we have seen, was not quite so one-sided; though he found the primary seat of the image of God to be in the soul, he admitted that "there was no part of man, not even the body itself, in which some sparks [of the image] did not glow."[5] Herman Bavinck, however, clearly affirmed that man's body is included in the image:

> Man's body also belongs to the image of God. . . . The body is not a tomb but a wondrous masterpiece of God, constituting the essence of man as fully as the soul . . . it belongs so essentially to man that, though through sin it is violently torn away from the soul [in death], it is nevertheless again united with the soul in the resurrection.[6]

When we think of man in connection with the various relationships in which he functions, we are confirmed in the conclusion that the image of God in man does not concern only a part of him (the "soul" or the "spiritual" aspect) but the entire person.

## STRUCTURAL AND FUNCTIONAL ASPECTS

In our discussion of Berkouwer's views, I raised the question of the distinction between the broader and narrower aspects of the image of God. In this connection, I cited Louis Berkhof as a proponent of the view that the image of God has these two aspects, and we dis-

---

3. The above sketch of man as one who mirrors and represents God describes human beings as they were originally created, before they fell into sin. One could say that what has been pictured here describes God's intention for man.
4. *The Christian View of Man* (New York: Macmillan, 1937), p. 169.
5. *Inst.*, I.15.3.
6. *Dogmatiek*, 2:601 [trans. mine]. Cf. Berkouwer, *Man*, pp. 75-77, 229-32.

cussed his understanding of what is included in each of these aspects. According to this view, the image of God in the narrower sense was totally lost through man's fall into sin; the image in the broader sense, however, was not lost but was corrupted and perverted.

This distinction concerns the question of the relation between what could be called the structural and the functional aspects of man. The problem is this: Must we think of the image of God in man as involving only what man is and not what he does, or only what he does and not what he is, or both what he is and what he does? Is "image of God" only a description of the way in which the human being functions, or is it also a description of the kind of being he or she is? Some theologians lay most of their emphasis here on the structural aspect (what kind of being man is), whereas other theologians lay most of their emphasis on the functional aspect (what man does).

It is my conviction that we need to maintain both aspects. Since the image of God includes the whole person, it must include both man's structure and man's functioning. One cannot function without a certain structure. An eagle, for example, propels itself through the air by flying—this is one of its functions. The eagle would be unable to fly, however, unless it had wings—one of its structures. Similarly, human beings were created to function in certain ways: to worship God, to love the neighbor, to rule over nature, and so on. But they cannot function in these ways unless they have been endowed by God with the structural capacities that enable them to do so. So structure and function are both involved when we think of man as the image of God.

On this question a certain shift has taken place in Christian theology. Earlier theologians said that the image of God in man was to be found primarily in his structural capacities (his possession of reason, morality, and the like),[7] whereas his functioning was thought of as a kind of appendix to his structure. More recent theologians, however, have affirmed that the functioning of man (his worshiping, serving, loving, ruling, etc.) constitute the essence of the image of God.[8] The danger involved in the latter view is the temptation to think of the image *only* in terms of function—a conception just as one-sided as that which sees image only in terms of structure.[9]

The image of God involves both structure and function. Various terms have been used to describe these two aspects: broader and nar-

---

7. See Chap. 4 above, noting particularly the views of Irenaeus and Aquinas.
8. Note here the views of Barth and Berkouwer.
9. For the reasons given above (pp. 64-65) I believe that Berkouwer's view of the image tends in the direction of this one-sidedness.

rower image (H. Bavinck,[10] L. Berkhof), formal and material image (Brunner), substance and relationships (Hendrikus Berkhof),[11] endowment and creativity (David Cairns).[12] But both are essential facets of the image of God. Herman Bavinck put it this way:

> By means of their distinction between the image of God in the broader and narrower sense Reformed theologians have most clearly maintained the connection between substance and quality, nature and grace, creation and redemption.[13]

But, one may ask, what belongs to the image of God in the broader, formal, or structural aspect? Theologians have given various answers to this question. Early in the history of Christian theology, as we have seen, man's intellectual and rational powers were singled out as one of the most important, if not *the* most important, features of the image of God in this broader sense. Certainly included in the image here is man's moral sensitivity (his ability to distinguish between right and wrong) and his conscience. Included also is the capacity for religious worship (what Calvin called the *sensus divinitatis* or "awareness of divinity"). An important human quality frequently mentioned by recent theologians is that of responsibility: man's ability to respond to God and to his fellowmen, and his being held responsible for the way in which he makes these responses.

We could mention a great many other capacities or qualities, such as, for example, man's volitional powers, or his ability to make decisions.[14] Another quality is man's aesthetic sense, whereby human beings not only can appreciate the beauty that God has lavished on his creation, but also can create artistic beauty of their own—in painting, sculpture, poetry, and music. In fact, the gifts of speech and of song are also qualities of man that belong to this aspect. Indeed, we could make this list much longer. In sum, then, we may say that by the image of God in the broader or structural sense we mean the entire

10. *Dogmatiek*, 2:590-94.
11. *De Mens Onderweg* (The Hague: Boekencentrum, 1962), pp. 46-47.
12. *The Image of God in Man*, rev. ed. (London: Collins, 1973), p. 199.
13. *Dogmatiek*, 2:594 [trans. mine]. Though Brunner by his distinction between the formal and material image of God does not mean exactly the same thing as is intended by the traditional Reformed distinction between the broader and the narrower image, his discussion of the image of God (see pp. 52-57 above) confirms the point that both aspects of the image are essential.
14. Leonard Verduin puts it this way: "In the Christian view man is a creature of options, one who is constantly confronted with alternatives between which he chooses, saying yes to the one and no to the other" (*Somewhat less than God* [Grand Rapids: Eerdmans, 1970], p. 84). For a fuller development of this thought, see the entire chapter (pp. 84-108).

endowment of gifts and capacities that enable man to function as he should in his various relationships and callings.

The question may be asked, Why should the gifts and capacities just mentioned be thought of as belonging to the image of God? The answer is that in all of these capacities man is like God, and therefore images him. Man's rational powers, for example, reflect God's reason, and enable man now, in a sense, to think God's thoughts after him. Man's moral sensitivity reflects something of the moral nature of God, who is the supreme determiner of right and wrong. Our capacity for fellowshiping with God in worship reflects the fellowship that Father, Son, and Holy Spirit have with each other. Our ability to respond to God and to fellow human beings imitates God's ability and willingness to respond to us when we pray to him. Our ability to make decisions reflects in a small way the supreme directing power of him "who works out everything in conformity with the purpose of his will" (Eph. 1:11). Our sense of beauty is a feeble reflection of the God who scatters beauty profusely over snow-crowned peaks, lake-jeweled valleys, and awe-inspiring sunsets. Our gift of speech is an imitation of him who constantly speaks to us, both in his world and in his word. And our gift of song echoes the God who rejoices over us with singing (Zeph. 3:17).

What, now, do we mean by the image of God in the narrower, material, or functional sense? Traditionally, Reformed theologians have described the image of God in this sense as consisting in true knowledge, righteousness, and holiness.[15] They derived this description in part from two Scripture passages: Colossians 3:10 ("... and have put on the new self, which is being renewed in knowledge in the image of its Creator") and Ephesians 4:24 ("... and to put on the new self, created to be like God in true righteousness and holiness"). Various theologians have described this aspect of the image in several ways: as man's giving the right answer to God (Brunner);[16] as man's living in love toward God and toward his neighbor (Otto Weber);[17] as man's living in the right relationship to God, the neighbor, and creation (Hendrikus Berkhof);[18] or as "concretely visible sanctification"

---

15. See H. Bavinck, *Dogmatiek*, 2:599; J. G. Machen, *The Christian View of Man*, pp. 174-77; and L. Berkhof, *Systematic Theology*, rev. & enl. ed. (Grand Rapids: Eerdmans, 1941), p. 207. Cf. also Heidelberg Catechism, Q. 6; Westminster Confession, IV.2; Westminster Shorter Catechism, Q. 10.

16. *The Christian Doctrine of Creation and Redemption*, trans. Olive Wyon (Philadelphia: Westminster Press, 1953), p. 58.

17. *Foundations of Dogmatics*, vol. 1, trans. Darrell L. Guder (Grand Rapids: Eerdmans, 1981), p. 574.

18. *De Mens Onderweg*, pp. 31-41.

(G. C. Berkouwer).[19] Thus, the image of God in the narrower sense means man's proper functioning in harmony with God's will for him.

These two aspects of the image of God (broader and narrower, structural and functional, or formal and material) can never be separated. Whenever we look at the human person, both aspects must always be taken into account. Man's fall into sin, however, has done damage to the way he images God. Whereas before the Fall we imaged God in the proper way, after the Fall we are no longer able to do so in our own strength, since we are now living in a state of rebellion against God.

This being so, one might conceivably think that man after the Fall is no longer an image-bearer of God (and, as we have seen, some theologians have indeed taught this). From the scriptural data we examined earlier, however, it is clear that we ought not to say this. According to the biblical evidence (as we noted in Chap. 3), fallen man is still considered to be an image-bearer of God, although other evidence shows that he no longer images God properly, and therefore must again be restored to the image of God. Thus, there is a sense in which fallen man is still an image-bearer of God but also a sense in which he must be renewed in that image. We ought not therefore to say that the image of God has been totally lost through man's fall into sin; we ought rather to say that the image has been perverted or distorted by the Fall. Yet the image is still there. What makes sin so serious is precisely the fact that man is now using God-given and God-imaging powers and gifts to do things that are an affront to his Maker.

The distinction between the structural and the functional aspects of the image of God helps us to verbalize man's pre-Fall and post-Fall condition. When man was created, he possessed the image of God in the structural or broader sense, and at the same time imaged God properly in the functional or narrower sense, since he lived in perfect obedience to God. After man had fallen into sin, however, he retained the image of God in the structural or broader sense but lost it in the functional or narrower sense. That is to say, fallen human beings still possess the gifts and capacities with which God has endowed them, but they now use these gifts in sinful and disobedient ways.[20] In the process of redemption God by his Spirit renews the image in fallen human beings—that is, enables them once again to use their God-reflecting gifts in such a way as to image God properly—at least in

---

19. *Man*, p. 112.
20. Brunner puts it this way: "The loss of the *Imago* in the material sense presupposes the *Imago* in the formal sense" (*Doctrine of Creation*, p. 60).

principle. After the resurrection of the body, on the new earth, re-deemed humanity will once again be able to image God perfectly.

The image of God in man must therefore be seen as involving both the structure of man (his gifts, capacities, and endowments) and the functioning of man (his actions, his relationships to God and to others, and the way he uses his gifts). To stress either of these at the expense of the other is to be one-sided. We must see both, but we need to see the structure of man as secondary and his functioning as primary. God has created us in his image so that we may carry out a task, fulfill a mission, pursue a calling. To enable us to perform that task, God has endowed us with many gifts—gifts that reflect something of his greatness and glory. To see man as the image of God is to see both the task and the gifts. But the task is primary; the gifts are secondary. The gifts are the means for fulfilling the task.

## Christ as the True Image of God

As we continue to ask what we must understand by the image of God, we are reminded of the fact that in the New Testament Christ is called the image of God par excellence; he is the "image of the invisible God" (Col. 1:15). If, therefore, we wish to know what the image of God in man is really like, we must first look at Christ. This means, among other things, that what is central in the image of God is not such matters as reason or intelligence but rather love, since what stands out more than anything else in the life of Christ is his amazing love. In Christ, in other words, we see clearly what is hidden in Genesis 1: namely, what man as the perfect image of God should be like.

When we look at Jesus Christ, we realize that there is a twofold strangeness about him. There is, first, the strangeness of his deity. He is the God-man, the one who is bold enough to say that he and the Father are one—a statement that made the Jews accuse him of blasphemy (John 10:31-33). He is the one who forgives sins—something only God is supposed to do. He is the one who even dares to say, "Before Abraham was born, I am!" (John 8:58).

But there is also the strangeness of his humanity. Though genuinely human, he is unique in his humanity. He is totally sinless. His obedience to the Father is perfect, his prayer life is unexcelled, his love for people is fathomless. And then we realize that this strangeness makes us ashamed, because it tells us what we all should be like. The strangeness of the human Jesus holds a mirror before us; it is an exemplary strangeness, for it tells us what God's intentions are for each of us.

When we look more closely at the life of Christ we see that he was, first of all, *wholly directed toward God*. At the beginning of his ministry, though sorely tempted by the devil, Jesus resisted temptation, in obedience to the Father. He often spent whole nights in prayer to the Father. He once said, "My food is to do the will of him who sent me, and to finish his work" (John 4:34). At the end of his earthly life, when he was facing the terrible suffering he would have to undergo as the Savior of his people, he prayed, "My Father, if it is possible, may this cup be taken from me. Yet not as I will, but as you will" (Matt. 26:39).

Second, we note that Christ is *wholly directed toward the neighbor*. When people came to him in need, whether that need was for healing, food, or forgiveness, he was always ready to help them. When, tired out from a walking tour, Jesus was resting at a well, he was willing to forget his own fatigue in order to minister to a Samaritan woman. To Zacchaeus he said, "The Son of Man came to seek and to save what was lost" (Luke 19:10). At another time Jesus said to his disciples, "For the Son of Man did not come to be served, but to serve, and to give his life as a ransom for many" (Mark 10:45). Once Jesus indicated what is the greatest love one can show to another: "Greater love has no one than this, that he lay down his life for his friends" (John 15:13). This is the kind of love Jesus himself revealed: he laid down *his* life for his friends.

Third, Christ *rules over nature*. With a word of command Jesus stilled the tempest that threatened the lives of his disciples on the Lake of Galilee. Later he walked on the water to show his mastery over nature. He was able to bring about a miraculous catch of fish. He multiplied the loaves and changed water into wine. He healed many diseases, drove out many demons, made the deaf hear, the blind see, the lame walk, and even raised the dead.

Were these miraculous deeds evidence of Christ's deity or revelations of what Christ could do in his humanity in dependence upon his Father in heaven? We cannot separate Christ's human and divine natures; as the Council of Chalcedon put it, these two natures are always together without mixture, change, division, or separation. Yet certain biblical statements suggest that Jesus performed these miracles in his perfect humanity, in dependence on divine power: "But if I drive out demons by the Spirit of God, then the kingdom of God has come upon you" (Matt. 12:28); " 'Men of Israel, listen to this: Jesus of Nazareth was a man accredited by God to you by miracles, wonders and signs, which God did among you through him, as you yourselves know' " (from Peter's Pentecost sermon, Acts 2:22).

One cannot be dogmatic about this, however. Jesus was the God-man, and therefore whatever he did, he did as one who was both divine and human. Obviously we cannot perform miracles as Jesus did; we cannot still the storm or raise the dead. But we do learn from Christ's life that rulership over nature is an essential aspect of the functioning of the image of God—one that we must now find our own ways of implementing.

In sum, from looking at Jesus Christ, the perfect image of God, we learn that the proper functioning of the image includes being directed toward God, being directed toward the neighbor, and ruling over nature.[21]

## MAN IN HIS THREEFOLD RELATIONSHIP

Just as Christ, the true image of God, functioned in three relationships, so also must man. Genesis 1:26-28, describing man's creation in God's image, says,

> (26) Then God said, "Let us make man in our image, after our likeness; and let them have dominion over the fish of the sea, and over the birds of the air, and over the cattle, and over all the earth, and over every creeping thing that creeps upon the earth." (27) So God created man in his own image, in the image of God he created him; male and female he created them. (28) And God blessed them, and God said to them, "Be fruitful and multiply, and fill the earth and subdue it; and have dominion over the fish of the sea and over the birds of the air and over every living thing that moves upon the earth." (RSV)

God has placed man into a threefold relationship: between man and God, between man and his fellowmen, and between man and nature. The references to God's creation of man, to God's blessing of man, and to the mandate given him by God indicate the primary relationship in which man stands: his relationship to God. Man's relationship to his fellowmen is indicated in the words "male and female he created them." Our relationship to nature is alluded to in God's giving us dominion over the earth.

Let us now look at each of these relationships in greater detail. As we do so, we shall discover what is God's purpose with us, how God intends us to live.

*To be a human being is to be directed toward God.* Man is a creature who owes his existence to God, is completely dependent on God, and is primarily responsible to God. This is his or her first and most important relationship. All of man's other relationships are to be seen as dominated and regulated by this one.

21. For this discussion of the image of God as seen in the life and work of Christ, I am indebted to Hendrikus Berkhof, *De Mens Onderweg*, pp. 19-26.

To be a human being in the truest sense, therefore, means to love God above all, to trust him and obey him, to pray to him and to thank him. Since man's relatedness to God is his primary relationship, all of his life is to be lived *coram Deo*—as before the face of God. Man is bound to God as a fish is bound to water. When a fish seeks to be free from the water, it loses both its freedom and its life. When we seek to be "free" from God, we become slaves of sin.

This vertical relationship of man to God is basic to a Christian anthropology, and all anthropologies that deny this relationship must be considered not only un-Christian but anti-Christian. All views of man that do not take their starting-point in the doctrine of creation and that therefore look upon him as an autonomous being who can arrive at what is true and right wholly apart from God or from God's revelation in Scripture are to be rejected as false.

Many years ago Augustine put it this way: "Thou [God] hast made us for thyself, and our hearts are restless until they find their rest in thee."[22] Calvin expressed a similar thought when he wrote, "All men are born to live to the end that they may know God."[23] G. C. Berkouwer has similarly emphasized man's inescapable relatedness to God: "Scripture is concerned with man in his relation to God, in which he can never be seen as man-in-himself."[24]

This means, further, that we are completely responsible to God in all that we do. Man has been created as a self, as a person, capable of self-consciousness and self-determination,[25] capable therefore of responding to God, of answering God, of fellowshiping with God, and of loving God. This has implications not only for our worship but for our entire life. God's intention with man is that he might do whatever he does in obedience to God and for the glory of God, so that he uses all his powers, gifts, and capacities in God's service.

*To be a human being is to be directed toward one's fellowmen.* Again we go back to Genesis 1. Note the close juxtaposition, in verse 27, of "in the image of God he created him" and "male and female he created them." More than sexual differentiation is involved here, since this is found also in animals, and the Bible does not say that animals have been created in the image of God. What is being said in this verse is that the human person is not an isolated being who is complete in himself or herself, but that he or she is a being who needs the fellowship of others, who is not complete apart from others.

22. *Confessions*, I.1.
23. *Inst.*, I.3.3.
24. *Man*, pp. 59-60.
25. By self-determination I mean the ability to choose one's acts without external compulsion. I am not implying that fallen man is able in his own strength to change his basic preference for sin to love for God.

This point is made even more vividly in Genesis 2, which describes the creation of Eve: "The LORD God said, 'It is not good for the man to be alone. I will make a helper suitable for him' " (v. 18). The Hebrew expression rendered "a helper suitable for him" is *'ēzer kᵉnegdō*. *Neged* (the word translated as "suitable for him") means "corresponding to" or "answering to." Literally, therefore, the expression means "a help answering to him." The words imply that woman complements man, supplements him, completes him, is strong where he may be weak, supplies his deficiencies and fills his needs. Man is therefore incomplete without woman. This holds for the woman as well as for the man. Woman, too, is incomplete without the man; man supplements woman, complements her, fills her needs, is strong where she is weak.

What has just been said, however, must not be interpreted as implying that only a married person can experience what it means to be truly and fully human. Marriage, to be sure, reveals and illustrates more fully than any other human institution the polarity and interdependence of the man-woman relationship. But it does not do so in an exclusive sense. For Jesus himself, the ideal man, was never married. And in the life to come, when humanity will be totally perfected, there will be no marriage (Matt. 22:30).

The man-woman relationship, therefore, implies the need for fellowship between human beings. But what is said in Genesis 1 and 2 about this relationship has implications also for our relationship to our fellowmen in general. Not only is man incomplete without woman and woman incomplete without man; man is also incomplete without other men and woman is also incomplete without other women. Men and women cannot attain to true humanity in isolation; they need the fellowship and stimulation of others. We are social beings. The very fact that man is told to love his neighbor as himself implies that man needs his neighbor.

Man cannot be truly human apart from others. This is true even in a psychological and social sense. Near the end of the eighteenth century, in the region near the French town of Aveyron, a small boy was apparently abandoned by his parents and left to fend for himself in the forest of Lacaune. Years later the boy was found. He resembled an animal more than a human being. He ate nuts, acorns, and wild fruits. His speech consisted of grunts; he never did learn to talk coherently.[26] It would appear that apart from contact and fellowship with other human beings a person cannot develop into normal manhood or womanhood.

---

26. For the story of this boy and his later history, see Harlan Lane, *The Wild Boy of Aveyron* (Cambridge: Harvard Univ. Press, 1976).

The fact that we can only be complete human beings through encounters with fellow human beings is true in other ways as well. It is only through contacts with others that we come to know who we are and what our strengths and weaknesses are. It is only in fellowship with others that we grow and mature. It is only in partnership with others that we can fully develop our potentialities. This holds for all the human relationships in which we find ourselves: family, school, church, vocation or profession, recreational organizations, and the like.

We enrich each other. This holds true even in a collective sense. We are enriched by people of different races, different backgrounds, different levels and types of education, different callings and professions than our own. It is not good for a person to have social fellowship only with others "of his own kind."

Man's relatedness to others means that every human being should not view his or her gifts and talents as an avenue for personal aggrandizement, but as a means whereby he or she can enrich the lives of others. It means that we should be eager to help others, heal their hurts, supply their needs, bear their burdens, and share their joys. It means that we should love others as ourselves. It means that every human being has a right to be accepted by others, to belong to others, and to be loved by others. It means that man's acceptance of and love for others is an essential aspect of his humanness.[27]

*To be a human being is to rule over nature.* Genesis 1:26-28 also describes man as one who rules over or has dominion over nature. Man is given dominion over the earth and all that is in the earth. Theologians, however, have differed over the significance of this ruling. Some have thought of this dominion as only a side effect of man's having been created in the image of God, not as an essential aspect of the image.[28] Most interpreters, however, have believed—and rightly so—that man's having been given dominion over the earth is an essential aspect of the image of God.[29] As God is revealed in Gen-

---

27. One could add that acceptance of others requires a proper acceptance of oneself. There is a wrong love of self, as Augustine said long ago, but there is also a right or healthy love of self, which is both a result of and a support for our service to God and others. More will be said about the question of man's self-image in Chap. 6.

28. E.g., J. Skinner, *Critical and Exegetical Commentary on Genesis* (New York: Scribner, 1910), p. 32; H. Gunkel, *Genesis* (Göttingen: Vandenhoeck and Ruprecht, 1902), p. 99; Berkouwer, *Man*, pp. 70-72. Calvin's cautious opinion on this point has been quoted above: "Man's having dominion over the earth comprises some portion, though small, of the image of God" (above, p. 43).

29. Luther, *Lectures on Genesis* (St. Louis: Concordia, 1958), p. 64; John Laidlaw, *The Bible Doctrine of Man* (Edinburgh: T. & T. Clark, 1905), p. 163; Bavinck, *Dogmatiek*, 2:569-70, 603; L. Vander Zanden, *De Mens als Beeld Gods* (Kampen: Kok, 1939),

esis 1 as ruling over the whole creation, so man is pictured here as God's vicegerent, who rules over nature as God's representative. Having dominion over the earth, therefore, is essential to man's existence. He is not to be thought of apart from this dominion, any more than he should be thought of apart from his relationship to God or to his fellow human beings.

Two words are used in Genesis 1:28 to describe this relationship of man to nature: *subdue* and *have dominion*. The verb rendered *subdue* is a form of the Hebrew verb *kābash*, which means "to subdue" or "bring into bondage." This verb tells us that man is to explore the resources of the earth, to cultivate its land, to mine its buried treasures. Yet we must not think simply about land, plants, and animals; we must also think about human existence itself insofar as it is an aspect of God's good creation. Man is called by God to develop all the potentialities found in nature and in humankind as a whole. He must seek to develop not only agriculture, horticulture, and animal husbandry, but also science, technology, and art. In other words, we have here what is often called the *cultural mandate*: the command to develop a God-glorifying culture. Though these words occur as part of God's blessing upon man, the blessing implies a mandate.

The other word used in Genesis 1:28 to describe this relationship is translated as "have dominion," a form of the Hebrew verb *rādāh*, meaning "to rule" or "to dominate." It is specifically said that humankind shall have dominion over the animals. Note in this connection also Genesis 9:2, in which God says to Noah, as the representative of postflood humanity, "The fear and dread of you will fall upon all the beasts of the earth . . . they are given into your hands." Psalm 8 not only echoes this thought but expands upon it:

> Thou [God] hast made him [man] little less than God,
> and dost crown him with glory and honor.
> Thou hast given him dominion over the works of thy hands;
> thou hast put all things under his feet. (vv. 5-6, RSV)

It is important, however, to note that the proper relationship of man to nature is not simply that of ruling over it. When we go from Genesis 1 to Genesis 2, we find that Adam was given a specific task to perform: to work (*'ābad*) and to take care of (*shāmar*) the Garden of Eden in which he had been placed (v. 15). The Hebrew word *'ābad* literally means "to serve." The word *shāmar* means "to guard, watch

---

pp. 51-54; L. Berkhof, *Systematic Theology*, p. 205; H. Berkhof, *De Mens Onderweg*, pp. 37-41; L. Verduin, *Less than God*, pp. 27-48; and Cairns, *The Image of God in Man*, p. 28.

over, preserve, or care for." Adam, in other words, was not only told to rule over nature; he was also told to cultivate and care for that portion of the earth in which he had been placed. If human beings had been commanded only to *rule* over the earth, this command might easily have been misconstrued as an open invitation to irresponsible exploitation of the earth's resources. But the injunction to *work* and *take care of* the Garden of Eden implies that we are to serve and preserve the earth as well as to rule over it.[30]

This third relationship into which man has been placed by God means that man, while standing below God, stands above nature as its ruler, as the one who is summoned to admire its beauties, discover its secrets, and explore its resources. But man—that is, *we* — must rule over nature in such a way as to be its servant as well. We must be concerned to conserve natural resources and to make the best possible use of them. We must be concerned to prevent the erosion of the soil, the wanton destruction of forests, the irresponsible use of energy, the pollution of rivers and lakes, and the pollution of the air we breathe. We must be concerned to be stewards of the earth and of all that is in it, and to promote whatever will preserve its usefulness and beauty to the glory of God.

How are these three relationships (to God, to each other, and to nature) related to each other? Do they stand loosely next to each other without any connection, or is there a close connection between them? Is one of these more prominent than the other two? These are significant questions. For centuries the Christian church has maintained that only the first of these three is really important, and that the other two relationships are important only as means for fulfilling the first one. Perhaps we could call this first one the *vertical* relationship. In recent years, however, there has arisen a kind of *horizontalizing* version of Christianity. Many have taught that the most important relationship is the second one, and that the relationship to God can only find expression in man's relationship with his neighbor. To this must be added the fact that in our technological age the third relationship seems to be eclipsing the other two. In the industrial nations at least it seems that most of our energy is being devoted to this third relationship—to the maintenance and improvement of technology. Some now feel that this third relationship is so dominating our lives that modern man is fast becoming a slave of the machine and of the computer.

30. For a further elaboration of this point, see chaps. 13-15 (esp. pp. 208-11) of *Earthkeeping*, ed. Loren Wilkinson (Grand Rapids: Eerdmans, 1980).

In point of fact, however, God has placed man into all three of these relationships. Each one is as important and as indispensable as are the other two; we can neither exist nor function properly without any one of them. Further, they are interrelated. Man is inescapably related to God; this is indeed the prior and most important relationship. But this relationship does not exist without the other two, and is not realized apart from the other two. Our relationship to the neighbor is a form in which our relationship to God realizes itself; as the Bible often teaches, we show our love for God by means of our love for the neighbor. A person who does not love his neighbor is a liar if he says that he loves God (1 John 4:20). Our love for God and for the neighbor, further, should also reveal itself in our rule over and care for God's creation. When we love the neighbor and when we work responsibly with God's creation, we are at the same time serving God.[31]

We ought now to observe that no other creature lives in precisely the same threefold relationship. When we say that human beings are responsible to God and that their lives must be consciously directed toward him, we ascribe to man a relationship to God found in no other creatures except the angels. When we say that human beings are capable of conscious fellowship with their fellowmen and that their lives are to be directed toward their neighbors, we ascribe to man a relationship found in no other creatures, probably not even the angels, who are not bound to each other in the same way that human beings are. And when we say that human beings have been appointed by God to rule over and to care for the earth, we ascribe to man a relationship found in no other creatures, not even the angels.

Each of these three relationships, further, is a reflection of God's own being. Man's responsibility to God and conscious fellowship with God is a reflection of God's fellowship with and love for man. Man's fellowship with his fellowmen is a reflection of the inter-Trinitarian fellowship within the Godhead (cf. John 17:24, "Because you [Father] loved me [the Son] before the creation of the world"). And man's dominion over the earth reflects the supreme dominion of God the Creator over all that he has made—so much so that the author of Psalm 8 can say, in connection with man's rule over the works of God's hands, "Thou hast made him [man] little less than God" (v. 5, RSV).

Since this threefold relationship is unique to man, and since he images God in each of these relationships, we may conclude, as we did when we looked at Christ as the true image of God, that the proper functioning of the image of God is to be channeled through these

---

31. For these insights into man's three relationships and their interconnections, I am again indebted to Hendrikus Berkhof, *De Mens Onderweg*, pp. 41-44.

three relationships: to God, to the neighbor, and to nature. Man has been endowed by God with the qualities and gifts whereby he is able to function in these relationships. The image of God is to be seen, however, not just in these capacities, important though they are, but primarily in the way man functions in these relationships.

## THE ORIGINAL IMAGE

This leads us to a fuller consideration of something mentioned earlier: namely, that to understand the image of God in its full biblical content, we must see it in the light of creation, fall, and redemption. What we see at the beginning, before man fell into sin, was *the original image*. Though we do not know exactly how the image of God revealed itself at that stage of man's history,[32] we may assume that the original human pair imaged God sinlessly and obediently. Man was then, to quote Augustine, "able not to sin."[33] We may therefore also assume that at this stage Adam and Eve functioned sinlessly and obediently in all three of the relationships we have just discussed: in worshiping and serving God, in loving and serving each other, and in ruling over and caring for that area of creation where God had placed them.

A further comment needs to be made, however. Though the first human pair were sinless, living in what earlier theologians used to call "the state of integrity," they were not yet at the end of the road. They were not yet fully developed image-bearers of God; they should have advanced to a higher stage where their sinlessness would have been unlosable. At the stage where they existed, there was still the possibility of sin. Bavinck puts it this way:

> Adam thus stood not at the end but at the beginning of the road; his condition was a provisional and temporary one, which could not remain this way, and which had to pass over either into a state of higher glory or into a fall into sin and death.[34]

Bavinck goes on to suggest that the fact that Adam and Eve still had to live with the possibility of sinning was, so to speak, the *boundary* of the image of God:

> Adam . . . had the *posse non peccare* [able not to sin] but not yet the *non posse peccare* [not able to sin]. He still lived in the possibility of sin . . . ; he did not yet have the perfect, unchangeable love which excludes all

---

32. As is evident from this statement, the position taken in this book is that the Fall recorded in Genesis 3 was a historical event. This point will be taken up in greater detail in Chap. 7.
33. *On Correction and Grace*, 33. In the original Latin, *"posse non peccare."*
34. *Dogmatiek*, 2:606 [trans. mine].

fear. Reformed theologians therefore correctly affirmed that this possibility, this changeableness, this still being able to sin ... was not an aspect of or the content of the image of God, but rather the boundary, limitation, or edge of the image of God.[35]

This much is clear: the integrity in which Adam and Eve existed before the Fall was not a state of consummate and unchangeable perfection. Man, to be sure, was created in the image of God at the beginning, but he was not yet a "finished product." He still needed to grow and to be tested. God wished to determine whether man would be obedient to him freely and voluntarily, in the face of an actual possibility of disobedience. For this reason God gave Adam a "probationary command": "You are free to eat from any tree in the garden; but you must not eat from the tree of the knowledge of good and evil, for when you eat of it you will surely die" (Gen. 2:16-17). If Adam and Eve had kept that command, who knows what the further history of the human race would have been like. But, sad to say, they disobeyed the command, and thereby plunged themselves, and the human race that was to follow them, into a sinful state.

## THE PERVERTED IMAGE

After man's fall into sin, the image of God was not annihilated but perverted. The image in its structural sense was still there—man's gifts, endowments, and capacities were not destroyed by the Fall—but man now began to use these gifts in ways that were contrary to God's will. What changed, in other words, was not the structure of man but the way in which he functioned, the direction in which he was going. Again Bavinck has put it well:

> Man through the fall ... has not become a devil who, incapable of redemption, can no longer reveal the features of the image of God. But while he has remained really and substantially man and has still preserved all his human faculties, capacities, and powers, the form, nature, disposition, and direction of all these powers have been so changed that now instead of doing the will of God they fulfill the law of the flesh.[36]

Because of the Fall, therefore, the image of God in man, though not destroyed, has been seriously corrupted. Calvin, it will be recalled, described this image as deformed, vitiated, mutilated, maimed, disease-ridden, and disfigured.[37] Herman Bavinck at one time even

---

35. Ibid., p. 617 [trans. mine]. Cf. also Wm. Shedd, *Dogmatic Theology*, vol. 2 (1888; Grand Rapids: Zondervan, n.d.), pp. 150-52.
36. *Dogmatiek*, 3:137 [trans. mine].
37. See above, pp. 43-45.

used the word *devastated* (*verwoestte*) to depict what sin has done to the image of God in man[38] (though he would not deny that fallen man still retains the image of God in a sense).

How has this perversion of the image affected man's functioning in the three relationships into which God has placed him? Man was created, as we have seen, in order to be properly directed toward God; he is inescapably related to God. But fallen man, instead of worshiping the true God, worships idols. In the first chapter of Romans Paul indicates the inexcusableness of this perversion of the God-man relationship:

> So they [men who by their wickedness suppress the truth] are without excuse; for although they knew God they did not honor him as God or give thanks to him, but they became futile in their thinking and their senseless minds were darkened. Claiming to be wise, they became fools, and exchanged the glory of the immortal God for images resembling mortal man or birds or animals or reptiles. (vv. 20-23, RSV)

Whereas primitive man made idols out of wood and stone, modern man, seeking something to worship, makes idols of a more subtle type: himself, human society, the state, money, fame, possessions, or pleasure. All such idolatries are perversions of man's capacity for worshiping God.

We could go on to say that instead of using his reason as a means for praising God, fallen man now uses it as a means for praising himself or human accomplishments. The moral sense with which man has been endowed he or she now uses in a perverted way, calling wrong right and right wrong. The gift of speech is used for cursing God instead of praising him. Instead of living in obedience to God, man is now "man in revolt," living in defiance of God and of God's laws.

The perversion of the image has also affected the second of man's three relationships. Instead of using his capacity for fellowship to enrich the lives of others, fallen man now uses this gift to manipulate others as tools for his selfish purposes. He uses the gift of speech to tell lies instead of the truth, to hurt his neighbor instead of helping him. Artistic abilities are often prostituted in the service of lust, and God-given sexual powers are used for perverse and debasing goals. Pornography and drugs have become big businesses; their purpose is not to help others but to exploit them. The motto of many in today's world seems to be, "Every man for himself, and the devil take the hindmost." Man is still inescapably related to others, but instead of loving others he is inclined to hate them.

38. *Dogmatiek*, 2:595.

In contemporary society this tendency to hate others often takes the form of indifference or alienation. Indifference toward others is a common phenomenon in our growing urban civilization, where many people hardly know their next-door neighbors and, what is worse, do not care to know them. Alienation in its extreme form is well expressed in Jean-Paul Sartre's famous dictum, "Hell is other people."[39] One sees this alienation at its worst in the criminal who so totally hates his neighbor that he will steal, brutalize, or murder in order to obtain what he wants.

Perversion has also occurred in the third relationship, that between man and nature. Instead of ruling the earth in obedience to God, man now uses the earth and its resources for his own selfish purposes. Having forgotten that he was given dominion over the earth in order to glorify God and to benefit his fellowmen, man now exercises this dominion in sinful ways. He exploits natural resources without regard for the future: stripping forests without reforestation, growing crops without crop rotation, failing to take measures to prevent soil erosion. His factories pollute rivers and lakes, and his chimneys pollute the air—and nobody seems to care. His discovery of the secret of nuclear fission, instead of being a boon to humankind, has become a bone-chilling threat that hangs over our heads like a sword of Damocles. And in his cultural achievements—his literature, his art, his science, his technology—man's goal is to magnify himself instead of praising his God.

In all these ways, therefore, the image of God in man has been perverted after the Fall. The image is now malfunctioning—and yet it is still there. The loss of the image of God in the functional sense presupposes the retention of the image in the structural sense. To be a sinner one must be an image-bearer of God—one must be able to reason, to will, to make decisions; a dog, which does not possess the image of God, cannot sin. Man sins with God-imaging gifts.

In fact, the very greatness of man's sin consists in the fact that he is still an image-bearer of God. What makes sin so heinous is that man is prostituting such splendid gifts. *Corruptio optimi pessima*: the corruption of the best is the worst.

## THE RENEWED IMAGE

Since the image of God has been perverted through man's fall into sin, it needs to be renewed. This renewal or restoration of the image is what takes place in the redemptive process. Does this restoration

39. *No Exit*, in *No Exit and Three Other Plays* (New York: Vintage Books, 1949), p. 47.

mean that an image that was utterly and totally lost is now given back? No; it is better to say that the image of God that has become perverted, though not totally lost, is being rectified, is being set straight again. What happens in the redemptive process is that man who was using his God-imaging powers in wrong ways is now again enabled to use these powers in right ways.

In Chapter 3 we noted the New Testament teaching about the restoration of the image of God in the process of redemption.[40] This restoration begins in regeneration, sometimes called "being born again"—an event that could be defined as "that act of the Holy Spirit, not to be separated from the preaching and teaching of the Word, whereby he initially brings a person into living union with Christ and changes his or her heart so that he or she who was spiritually dead becomes spiritually alive, now ready and willing to believe the gospel and to serve the Lord." The renewal of the image is continued in what the Bible calls the work of sanctification—which can be defined as "that gracious and continuing operation of the Holy Spirit, involving man's responsible participation, by which the Spirit progressively delivers the regenerated person from the pollution of sin, and enables him or her to live to the praise of God."

We should therefore note that the renewal of the image of God in man is primarily the work of the Holy Spirit. Since man, because of his fall into sin, is now spiritually dead, the Spirit must first give him new spiritual life in regeneration.[41] Since fallen man now uses his God-imaging gifts in perverse ways, the Spirit must enable him to use these gifts in a God-glorifying way; this is what happens in the process of sanctification. Sanctification, therefore, ought to be understood as the progressive renewal of man in the image of God. This renewal, further, does not take place apart from the influence, through preaching, teaching, or study, of the word of God found in the Bible; by means of this word the Spirit instructs God's people on how they are to live in a new obedience, and enables them to live in this way.

In this renewal of the image we are once again enabled to live in love, in three directions: toward God, toward the neighbor, and toward nature. In other words, the renewal or restoration of the image of God means that man is once again empowered to function properly in his threefold relationship.

The renewal of the image, therefore, means first of all that man is now enabled to be properly directed toward God. This includes

40. See above, pp. 22-28.
41. Cf. Eph. 2:4-5, "But because of his great love for us, God ... made us alive with Christ even when we were dead in transgressions."

worshiping God in the right way, praying to God for all his needs, and thanking God for all his blessings. It includes loving God with all his heart, with all his soul, with all his mind, and with all his strength (Mark 12:30). Since our most basic relationship is to God, the renewal of the image means that we are given strength to do whatever we do in obedience to God and for the glory of God. This includes using our rational powers in God-glorifying ways: to think God's thoughts after him, to discern behind the orderliness of nature the planning of an all-wise God, and to admire the wisdom with which the Creator has fashioned the universe. It includes using our volitional powers to will what God wants us to will, and to will nothing contrary to God's will. It includes using our aesthetic sense to appreciate the beauty God has lavished on his creation, and to praise the author of that beauty. It includes using our gift of speech in a God-glorifying way. It includes the ability to function in our relationship to our neighbors and in our relationship to nature in obedience and praise to God.

The renewal of the image means, in the second place, that man is now enabled to be properly directed toward the neighbor. This includes loving our neighbors as ourselves. It includes a readiness to forgive others when they sin against us. It includes praying for the neighbor, and being deeply concerned for his or her welfare. It means being concerned for social justice, for human rights, and for meeting the needs of the poor and destitute. It even includes loving our enemies, since, as Jesus said, this is an activity in which we are uniquely imaging God (Matt. 5:44-45). It implies loving the neighbor not because we find him so lovable, but because God loved him first.

The restoration of the image in this second relationship means that man is enabled to live for others rather than for himself or herself. It includes using all his gifts in the service of his fellowmen. This means using his rational and volitional powers to help him do what is for the neighbor's best interest. This means giving herself to her neighbor: sharing her joys and sorrows, helping her in time of need. It includes using the gift of speech not to run down the neighbor or ruin his reputation, but to maintain the neighbor's good name and to encourage him. It means resisting the temptation to look down upon a person because of the color of his or her skin, and being ready and eager to accept and respect people of different races and nationalities as fellow image-bearers of God. It includes using his or her creative and artistic abilities to create beauty in various artistic media, so that the lives of others might be enriched. As God so loved the world that he gave his only Son, we must so love our neighbors that we give ourselves to them.

The renewal of the image means, in the third place, that man is now enabled properly to rule over and care for God's creation. That is to say, he is now empowered to exercise dominion over the earth and over nature in a responsible, obedient, and unselfish way. This means that man is now enabled to look upon himself as a steward of the earth and all that is in it, rather than an overlord with absolute and completely arbitrary power. This includes holding property, tilling the soil, growing fruit trees, mining coal, and drilling for oil not for personal aggrandizement but in a responsible way, for the benefit and welfare of one's fellowmen. In our present world this also includes concern for the conservation of natural resources, and opposition to all wasteful or thoughtless exploitation of those resources. It includes concern for the preservation of the environment and for the prevention of whatever hurts that environment: erosion, wanton destruction of animal species, pollution of air and water. It includes concern for adequate distribution of food, the prevention of famine, and the improvement of sanitation. It also embraces the advancement of scientific investigation, research, and experimentation, including the continuing conquest of space, in such a way as to honor God's commands and to give him the praise.

This further includes concern for the development of a Christian culture, as the proper fulfillment of the so-called cultural mandate. In other words, we should attempt to do philosophical, scientific, historical, and literary work in a uniquely Christian way. This also includes concern for the development of a Christian world-and-life view, which will influence all that man thinks, says, and does.

The renewal of the image of God, therefore, involves a broad, comprehensive vision of the Christian view of man. The process of sanctification affects every aspect of life: man's relationship to God, to others, and to the entire creation. The restoration of the image does not concern only religious piety in the narrow sense, or witnessing to people about Christ, or "soul-saving" activities; in its fullest sense it involves the redirection of all of life.

The renewal of the image of God is described in the New Testament in various ways. One of these we have already looked at: the "taking off" of the old self and the "putting on" of the new self.[42] Other figures, however, are also used. This new life means holding fast the word in an honest and good heart, bringing forth fruit with patience (cf. Luke 8:15, RSV). The new life means being transformed by the renewing of the mind (Rom. 12:2). It means living by the Spirit and producing the fruit of the Spirit (Gal. 5:16, 22). It means

42. See above, pp. 24-28.

living a life of love (Eph. 5:2), walking in the truth (2 John 4), living not for self but for Christ (2 Cor. 5:15).

Being renewed in the image of God means, further, that we become more and more like God, that God becomes more and more visible in our words and deeds. Since God is love (1 John 4:16), our living in love is an imitation of God.

Because Christ is the perfect image of God, becoming more like God also means becoming more like Christ. This means following Christ's example, trying to live as he lived. But there is more to say about this. Galatians 3:27 calls the putting on of the new self or the new person putting on or clothing ourselves with Christ (cf. Rom. 13:14). To put on Christ means new existence as a member of Christ's body (1 Cor. 12:12-13); the believer therefore images God as one who belongs to the body of that Christ who is uniquely God's image.[43]

This suggests that the renewal of the image has an ecclesiastical aspect. It does not concern individuals in isolation; it has to do with believers as members of Christ, and therefore with the church that Christ is sanctifying (Eph. 5:26). This means that the image of God today is seen in its richest form in Christ together with his church, or in the church as the body of Christ.[44] But this also implies that the restoration of the image of God in man takes place in the church, through the fellowship of Christians with each other. Believers learn what Christ-likeness is by observing it in fellow Christians. We see the love of Christ reflected in the lives of our fellow believers; we are enriched by Christ through our contact with them; we hear Christ speaking to us through them. Believers are inspired by the examples of their fellow Christians, sustained by their prayers, corrected by their loving admonitions, and encouraged by their support.

So far we have been speaking about the renewal of the image of God as the result of God's enablement, as a fruit of the Holy Spirit's work in the hearts and lives of believers. It is important to remember, however, that the renewal of the image involves both the Spirit's gracious working within and the responsibility of man. In other words, this renewal is both God's gift and our task.

We have touched on this point already. In Chapter 2 I pointed out that because man is a creature, God in his sovereign grace must restore the divine image in him, but because man is also a person he has a responsibility in this restoration. In Chapter 3 we examined

43. Herman Ridderbos, *Paul: An Outline of His Theology*, trans. John R. De Witt (Grand Rapids: Eerdmans, 1975), p. 225. Cf. F. W. Eltester, *Eikon im Neuen Testament* (Berlin: Töpelmann, 1958), p. 159.
44. Weber, *Foundations of Dogmatics*, 1:578.

scriptural evidence which showed that our being transformed into the image of God in the process of sanctification is both the work of the Holy Spirit and something that involves our own efforts.[45]

Without repeating what was said before, we may note some other ways in which the Bible emphasizes both facets of this truth. In 1 Thessalonians 5:23 Paul expresses the following wish for his believing readers: "May God himself, the God of peace, sanctify you through and through." But in another letter, written to the Corinthians, he writes, "Since we have these promises, dear friends, let us purify ourselves from everything that contaminates body and spirit, perfecting holiness out of reverence for God" (2 Cor. 7:1). The interesting thing about this passage is that the last clause literally reads "bringing holiness to its goal" (*epitelountes,* from the word *telos,* meaning "goal"). Although usually we think of God as the one who will bring our holiness to its goal, here believers are enjoined to do exactly that. Whereas in Romans 6:6 Paul says, "We know that our old self was crucified with him [Christ]," in Colossians 3:9 he says, "Do not lie to each other, since you have taken off your old self with its practices." The first passage states that the crucifixion or putting to death of our old self is something that was done for us when Christ died on the cross, but the second passage tells us that the putting off of our old self is something we have done. Further, while Paul assures his readers that "neither death nor life, neither angels nor demons, neither the present nor the future, nor any powers, neither height nor depth, nor anything else in all creation, will be able to separate us from the love of God" (Rom. 8:38-39), the writer of the Epistle of Jude enjoins his believing readers to "keep yourselves in God's love" (v. 21).

Perfecting holiness, taking off the old self, and keeping ourselves in the love of God are all ways in which the renewal of the image of God takes place. Other New Testament injunctions to live the new life similarly underscore the believer's responsibility in this renewal: "Let your light . . . shine before men" (Matt. 5:16); "Live a life worthy of the calling you have received" (Eph. 4:1); "So whether you eat or drink or whatever you do, do it all for the glory of God" (1 Cor. 10:31). The passage that sums it all up has already been quoted: "Be imitators of God, therefore, as dearly loved children" (Eph. 5:1).

From passages of this sort emerges a view of the image of God that is not static but dynamic. The image of God in the New Testament is not like a museum piece that is there simply to be admired; rather, it is more like a living example that we are urged to follow— the example of Christ. New Testament teachings about the image are

45. See above, pp. 8-10, 28-30.

not so much like a professor's lecture that we are trying to copy into a notebook; they are more like the words of a coach who is trying to help us play a better game. The image of God and its renewal challenge us to a new way of thinking, talking, and living. At the heart of this renewal is a summons to love as God loves.

The renewal of the image of God, therefore, is not an experience in which we remain passive, but one in which we must take an active part. But—and this deserves emphasis—this renewal is still *primarily* the work of the Holy Spirit. We are not able to renew ourselves in our own strength. The image of God can be restored in us only as we remain in union with Christ. Christ himself put this very clearly: "If a man remains in me and I in him, he will bear much fruit [another figure for the renewal of the image]; apart from me you can do nothing" (John 15:5).

This renewal of the image, as we observed before,[46] is not completed during a person's lifetime. It is a process that continues as long as one lives. We must never forget that while they are in this present life believers are *genuinely* new but not yet *totally* new. They are incomplete new persons.

This implies that we do not yet see the image of God in its fullest sense on this side of the final resurrection. To be sure, we see that image fully in Jesus Christ as he is revealed to us on the pages of Holy Writ. But Christ no longer walks the earth. And on this earth, even in those who are being renewed, we see the image of God only as "through a glass, darkly." What we see now are only hints and intimations of what the renewed image of God will be like. Only in the life to come will the full richness of the image finally come into view; only then shall we see God imaged perfectly and scintillatingly by a glorified humankind. To that perfection of the image we now turn.

## THE PERFECTED IMAGE

It is not until the time of the final glorification of man that the renewal of the image of God will be brought to completion. This final perfection of the image will be the culmination of God's plan for his redeemed people. We are reminded again of Romans 8:29, "For those God foreknew he also predestined to be conformed to the likeness of his Son"—totally conformed, we may be sure. And the likeness of God's Son is nothing less than the perfected image of God.

In order to see the Christian view of man in its total brilliance, therefore, we must not just go back to man as he was originally cre-

46. See above, pp. 30-31.

ated; rather, we must go forward to man as he will some day be. We must see man in the light of his final destiny. For, as was mentioned earlier, Christ through his redemptive work brings us higher than Adam was before the Fall. Adam could still lose his sinlessness and blessedness, but the glorified saints will no longer be able to do so. Adam was "able not to sin and die" (*posse non peccare et mori*), but the saints in glory will "not be able to sin and die" (*non posse peccare et mori*). This unlosable perfection is what man is destined for—and nothing less!

One may ask, however, How do we know that the final state of redeemed man is one in which he will "not be able to sin and die"? Scripture clearly teaches that there will be no death in the life to come: "He [God] will swallow up death forever" (Isa. 25:8); "The body that is sown is perishable, it is raised imperishable" (1 Cor. 15:42); "When the perishable has been clothed with the imperishable, and the mortal with immortality, then the saying that is written will come true: 'Death has been swallowed up in victory' " (1 Cor. 15:54); "There will be no more death" (Rev. 21:4).

Further, a number of New Testament passages teach that glorified saints will be sinless in the life to come. In Ephesians 5:27 Paul affirms that Christ's ultimate purpose for the church is "to present her to himself as a radiant church, without stain or wrinkle or any other blemish, but holy and blameless." The author of Hebrews tells his readers, with an obvious reference to deceased believers who are now in heaven awaiting the resurrection, "You have come [as those who are members of 'the church of the firstborn'] to the spirits of righteous men made perfect" (Heb. 12:23). John sees the Holy City or the New Jerusalem coming down out of heaven from God, and describes it as being "prepared as a bride beautifully dressed for her husband"—a reference to the final perfection of the glorified church (Rev. 21:3). This perfected church, John says further, will be permitted to go through the gates into the city of God's glorified people on the new earth, whereas those who have not been perfected will have no part in it: "Outside are . . . the sexually immoral, the murderers, the idolaters, and everyone who loves and practices falsehood" (Rev. 22:14-15).

The perfection of the image of God in man is intimately connected with the glorification of Christ. Since Christ and his people are one, his people will also share in his glorification. The final perfection of the image, therefore, will not only be brought about by Christ; it will also be patterned after Christ. In the life to come we shall "bear the likeness of the man of heaven" (1 Cor. 15:49). In the resurrection our "lowly bodies" (lit., "the bodies of our humiliation") will be transformed so that they will be like "his glorious body" (lit., "the body of his glory"; Phil. 3:21). So we shall be totally like the glorified Christ, not only in our spirits but even in our bodies. The apostle John sums it all up: "Dear friends, now we are children of God, and what we will be has not yet been made known. But we know that when he [presumably Christ] appears, we shall be like him, for we shall see him as he is" (1 John 3:2).

As we continue to reflect on the future perfection of the image, we realize that it is impossible for us to visualize in an exact or precise way what that perfected image will be like. We may, to be sure, find analogies between our present life and our future existence. But they will be only analogies and no more. How can we know exactly what it will be like to be glorified—to have what Paul calls a "spiritual body" (1 Cor. 15:44)? We shall only be able to speak about that future existence in figurative language, as the Bible does, particularly in the Book of Revelation. But insofar as this figurative language can be translated into anthropological concepts, it gives us a picture of man in which his functioning in the previously mentioned threefold relationship is brought to its final perfection.

This perfection will concern, first and most importantly, our relation to God. Man will then be wholly directed toward God. We shall then worship, obey, and serve God faultlessly, without any imperfection. Praise and adoration of God will then be as natural and constant as breathing is now. The Book of Revelation suggests what some of those praises may sound like: "Great and marvelous are your deeds, Lord God Almighty" (15:3);[47] "Hallelujah! for our Lord God Almighty reigns. Let us rejoice and be glad and give him glory!" (19:6-7). The nations (here, presumably, the glorified saints) will walk by God's light (Rev. 21:24), and no longer by their own understanding. The servants of God will serve him (Rev. 22:3)—no longer fragmentarily, inadequately, and sinfully, but perfectly.

The perfection of the image will also concern our relation to our neighbors. Man will then love and serve his fellowmen perfectly; whatever hindrances to such loving now exist will then be gone. There will then be perfect fellowship in a perfect society. All the barriers that now separate people will be gone—national, racial, linguistic, cultural, or religious. There will then be only one church, of which Christ will be the head. There will then be only one "nation," of which Christ will be the king. All dwellers on the new earth will be members of the family of God, bound to each other with intimate and

---

47. When my wife and I were traveling in Switzerland some years ago, we were thrilled to find these words on a plaque erected at the spot from which one could see the majestic Matterhorn!

unbreakable ties. Yet in the midst of this oneness there will still be many differences. Glorified believers will not all be alike, as peas in a pod. They will retain their unique talents and gifts, purged of all imperfection—talents that will be used for the enrichment of all. As a symphony orchestra produces a unified sound from many different instruments, so the fellowship of the life to come will be marked by unity in the midst of great but harmonious diversity.

In the third place, the perfection of the image will concern our relationship to nature. In the beginning man was given the so-called cultural mandate—the command to rule over the earth and to develop a God-glorifying culture. Because of man's fall into sin, not even believers have carried out that cultural mandate in the way God intended it to be done. Only on the new earth will that mandate be perfectly and sinlessly fulfilled.

One of the promises given to believers is that they shall some day reign with Christ (2 Tim. 2:12). In Revelation 22:5 we are even told that glorified believers will reign forever. And in the song of redemption in the same book the point is specifically made that this reigning will take place on the earth (Rev. 5:10).

How are we to understand this? The Heidelberg Catechism, perhaps the best-known Reformation creed, gives us the clue: it will be a reigning by glorified believers *over all creation*.[48] In the life to come resurrected and glorified saints will not be flitting from cloud to cloud somewhere off in space, but will be living on a renewed earth.[49] Then for the first time man will rule over and care for nature in the way God intended him to do. Human beings will then be stewards, not exploiters, of the earth, exploring its resources and admiring its beauties in a way that will bring unending praise to God.[50] We shall then reign perfectly over all creation, with and under Christ.

Revelation 21:24-26 tells us that "the kings of the earth will bring their splendor into it [the holy city that will be found on the new earth]," and that "the glory and honor of the nations will be brought into it." These fascinating words suggest that the best contributions of each nation will enrich life on the new earth, and that whatever potentialities and gifts have been of value in this present life will somehow, in some way, be retained and enriched in the life to come. This implies that there will be continuity as well as discontinuity between the present life and the life to come, and that therefore our

48. Heidelberg Catechism, Answer 32: "and afterward to reign with Christ over all creation for all eternity" (1975 trans., Christian Reformed Church).
49. For a fuller statement of biblical teaching on the new earth, see my *The Bible and the Future*, rev. ed. (Grand Rapids: Eerdmans, 1982), chap. 20.
50. Cf. the so-called song of creation in Rev. 4:11.

cultural, scientific, educational, and political endeavors today help us to prepare for a fuller and richer life on the new earth.[51]

The possibilities that now rise before us boggle the mind. Will there be "better Beethoven in heaven," as one author has suggested?[52] Shall we see better Rembrandts, better Raphaels, better Constables? Shall we read better poetry, better drama, and better prose? Will scientists continue to advance in technological achievement, will geologists continue to explore the treasures of the earth, and will architects continue to build imposing and attractive structures? We do not know. But what we do know is that man's dominion over nature shall then be perfect. God will then be magnified by our culture in ways that will surpass our most fantastic dreams.

In the life to come, therefore, the threefold relationship for which man was created will be maintained, deepened, and infinitely enriched. We shall then love God above all, love our neighbors as ourselves, and rule over creation in a totally God-glorifying way. The image of God in man will then have been perfected.

It might be helpful at this point to summarize briefly in what the image of God consists, as a brief synopsis of this chapter. The image of God, we found, describes not just something that man *has,* but something man *is.* It means that human beings both mirror and represent God. Thus, there is a sense in which the image includes the physical body. The image of God, we found further, includes both a structural and a functional aspect (sometimes called the broader and narrower image), though we must remember that in the biblical view structure is secondary, while function is primary. The image must be seen in man's threefold relationship: toward God, toward others, and toward nature. When originally created, humans imaged God sinlessly in all three relationships. After the Fall the image of God was not annihilated but perverted, so that human beings now function wrongly in each of the three relationships. In the process of redemption, however, the image is being renewed, so that man is now enabled to be properly directed toward God, others, and nature. The renewal of the image of God is seen in its richest form in the church. The image is therefore not static but dynamic—a constant challenge to God-glorifying living. In the life to come the image of God will be perfected; glorified human beings will then live perfectly in all three relationships. After the resurrection, redeemed man will be in a higher state

51. Cf. Hendrikus Berkhof, *Christ the Meaning of History,* trans. L. Buurman (Grand Rapids: Baker, 1979), pp. 188-92. For a fuller treatment of this point, see Richard Mouw, *When the Kings Come Marching In* (Grand Rapids: Eerdmans, 1983).
52. Edwin H. Palmer, "Better Beethoven in Heaven?", *Christianity Today,* Feb. 16, 1979, p. 29.

than man before the Fall, since he will then no longer be able either to sin or to die.

## Concluding Observations

A few concluding observations about the image of God may still be made. First, *we must always see man in the light of his destiny.* This is an important point to remember. As we think about man we must see him not just as he is now but also as he may some day become. So far we have dealt with the future of the image of God only in terms of those who are believers. The Bible clearly teaches that the future of the person who is in Christ is everlasting life in a glorified resurrection body—the perfected image. But that same Bible also teaches that the future of the person who rejects Christ and continues to live in rebellion against God without repentance or faith is eternal perdition.[53] We must therefore live with ourselves and with each other in the light of that future destiny.

The possibility of future perdition for those who are not in Christ should constrain us to cut off the offending hand or to pluck out the offending eye, as Jesus counseled us to do, rather than to spend eternity in hell. The thought of such a future destiny for people whom our lives touch should be a strong incentive for us to witness to them about Christ and his salvation. At the same time the prospect of "the glory that will be revealed in us" should help us to bear "our present sufferings" with patience (Rom. 8:18), and encourage us to "press on toward the goal" (Phil. 3:14). And the thought that our brothers and sisters in Christ are likewise on their way to ultimate perfection should help us to think of them not just as poor, stumbling sinners who have many irksome faults but rather as those who shall some day shine as the sun.

C. S. Lewis expresses this thought vividly and concretely:

> It is a serious thing . . . to remember that the dullest and most uninteresting person you talk to may one day be a creature which, if you saw it now, you would be strongly tempted to worship, or else a horror and a corruption such as you now meet, if at all, only in a nightmare. All day long we are, in some degree, helping each other to one or the other of these destinations. It is in the light of these overwhelming possibilities, it is with the awe and the circumspection proper to them, that we should conduct all our dealings with one another, all friendships, all loves, all play, all politics. . . .

53. See, e.g., Matt. 5:22, 29-30; 10:28; 18:8-9; 25:46; Mark 9:43; John 3:36; 2 Thess. 1:7-9; Rom. 2:5, 8-9; Heb. 10:28-29, 31; 2 Pet. 2:17; Jude 7, 13; Rev. 14:10-11; 21:8. For a discussion of these passages, see *The Bible and the Future,* chap. 19.

It is immortals whom we joke with, work with, marry, snub, and exploit—immortal horrors or everlasting splendors.[54]

A second observation is this: *Man and woman together are the image of God.* We have already made the point, in Chapter 3, that man's having been created male and female is an essential aspect of the image of God. Karl Barth, as we saw, lays great stress on this point: man's existence as male and female is not something secondary to the image, but is at the very heart of the image of God. This is so not just because of the difference in sex between man and woman—since this distinction is found also among the animals—but because of far-reaching differences in personality between the two. Man's existence as male and female means that man as a masculine being has been created for partnership with another being who is essentially like him but yet mysteriously unlike him. It means that woman is the completion of man's own humanity, and that man is wholly himself only in his relationship with woman.[55]

This implies that man is not the image of God by himself, and that woman cannot be the image of God by herself. Man and woman can only image God through fellowship with each other—a fellowship that is an analogy of the fellowship God has within himself. The New Testament teaches that God exists as a Trinity of "Persons"—Father, Son, and Holy Spirit.[56] Human fellowship, as between man and woman, reflects or images the fellowship between God the Father, God the Son, and God the Holy Spirit. And yet there is a difference. For persons as we know them are separate beings or entities, whereas God is three "Persons" in one Divine Being. Human fellowship, therefore, is only a partial analogy of divine fellowship—yet it is an analogy.[57]

It is therefore unfortunate that the English language has no word like the German *Mensch* or the Dutch word *mens*, both of which mean "human being, whether male or female." The English word *man* has to serve a double purpose: it may mean either (1) "male or female human being" (the generic sense) or (2) "male human being." This double use of the word *man* seems to betray a typical masculine kind of arrogance, as if the male is the carrier of all that is involved in being human. But man can only be fully human in fellowship and partnership with woman; woman complements and completes man, as man complements and completes woman.[58] When we use the word *man* in

54. C. S. Lewis, *The Weight of Glory* (Grand Rapids: Eerdmans, 1966), pp. 14-15.
55. Cf. Paul Jewett, *Man as Male and Female* (Grand Rapids: Eerdmans, 1975), pp. 38-39.
56. Cf. Matt. 28:19; 2 Cor. 13:14.
57. Jewett, *Man as Male and Female*, p. 45.
58. H. Berkhof, *De Mens Onderweg*, pp. 34-35.

the generic sense, therefore (as is often done in this book), we must always keep this in mind.

The fact that man and woman together image God will still be true in the life to come. Jesus once said, "When the dead rise, they will neither marry nor be given in marriage; they will be like the angels in heaven" (Mark 12:25). The similarity to angels, however, means only that there will be no marriage at that time; it does not mean that the differences between men and women will no longer exist. In the final resurrection we shall not lose our individuality; that individuality will be not only retained but enriched, and our maleness or femaleness is of the essence of that individual existence.[59]

In the life to come, therefore, not only shall we continue to image God as men and women together, but we shall then be able to do this perfectly. We do not know how such fellowship and partnership between men and women will be carried out in a situation where there will be no marriage. But we do know this: Only then shall we see what the relationship between men and women can be like in its richest, fullest, and most beautiful sense.

Third, *the doctrine of the image of God has important implications for the evangelistic task of the church.* Though, as we have seen, the Bible teaches that man's fall into sin has seriously perverted the image of God in him, it also teaches that fallen man is still to be regarded as an image-bearer of God.[60] This fact implies that we must look upon every person, whoever he or she may be, of whatever nationality or race, of whatever social or economic status, whether Christian or non-Christian, as a person who is in the image of God. This is what is unique about human beings; this is what gives them dignity and worth. Even a person who is living a disreputable life, who has become an outcast from society, who has not a friend in the world—even such a person still bears God's image, and that image we must honor. Because everyone whom we meet is an image-bearer of God, we may not curse him or her (James 3:9), but we must love that person and do him or her good.

John Calvin, who was as deeply aware of the sinfulness and unworthiness of man as anyone has ever been, expressed this same thought in a striking way:

> We are not to consider that men merit of themselves but to look upon the image of God in all men, to which we owe all honor and love. . . . Therefore, whatever man you meet who needs your aid, you have no reason to refuse to help him. . . . Say, "he is contemptible and worthless";

59. Jewett, *Man as Male and Female*, pp. 40-43.
60. See above, pp. 15-20.

but the Lord shows him to be one to whom he has deigned to give the beauty of his image. ... Say that he does not deserve even your least effort for his sake; but the image of God, which recommends him to you, is worthy of your giving yourself and all your possessions.[61]

As the church does its evangelistic or missionary work, it must keep alive the conviction that every person on this earth is an image-bearer of God. Every person whom we encounter as we seek to bring the gospel is someone who bears God's image. He or she is therefore a person in whom we should respect and recognize that image. If this person is outside of Christ, he or she has been using God-imaging gifts in the service of sin. Though this person is now, because of his or her sinful life-style, unworthy in God's sight, he or she is not worthless. God can still use that person in his service. God can by his transforming power enable him to use his God-reflecting talents to the praise of his Creator. Because she has been created in the image of God, there are tremendous potentialities in this person. Therefore we now bring the gospel, urging him or her to be reconciled to God in the hope that these potentialities may yet bear fruit for God's kingdom. Our concern, then, in evangelizing people is not just to "save people's souls," but to restore the image of God to its proper functioning in all of life, to the greater glory of God.

In the life to come the fruits of the church's evangelistic and missionary work will be fully revealed. Then God will be honored in the final gathering together of those whom Christ has purchased by his blood out of every tribe and nation. Then the gifts and talents of all those blood-bought saints will be used everlastingly to God's praise. Our evangelistic and missionary work should be done with a view to that great future.

A fourth and final observation is this: *the image of God in its totality can only be seen in humankind as a whole.* Herman Bavinck has effectively stated this point:

Not the individual man, and not even man and woman together, but mankind as a whole is the fully developed image of God. ... The image of God is far too rich to be completely represented by a single human being, no matter how gifted he might be. That image can only be disclosed in its depth and riches in the whole of humanity with its millions of members. As the traces of God [*vestigia Dei*] are spread out over many works of God, both in space and time, so the image of God can only be seen in its totality in a humanity whose members exist both after and next to each other. ... To that humanity belong its development, its history, its expanding mastery of the earth, its advancement in knowledge and art, and its dominion over all other creatures. All of this is an un-

61. *Inst.*, III.7.6.

folding of the image and likeness of God according to which man was created. Just as God has not revealed himself only at the time of creation but continues and enlarges that revelation from day to day and from age to age, so it is also with the image of God: it is no unchangeable magnitude but one which unfolds and develops itself in the forms of space and time.[62]

To this may be added a recent comment by Richard Mouw:

One of the more fascinating proposals which has been made in theological discussions of the biblical notion of "the image of God" is that this image has a "corporate" dimension. That is, there is no one human individual or group who can fully bear or manifest all that is involved in the image of God, so that there is a sense in which that image is collectively possessed. The image of God is, as it were, parceled out among the peoples of the earth. By looking at different individuals and groups we get glimpses of different aspects of the full image of God.[63]

This implies that we can only see the full riches of the image of God as we take into account all of human history and all of man's diverse cultural contributions. Whatever great artists, scientists, philosophers, and the like have added to our store of knowledge, art, and technological achievements reflects the greatness of the God who has endowed humankind with all these gifts. We could even put it this way: whatever is in God—his virtues, his wisdom, his perfections—finds its analogy and likeness in man, though in a finite and limited form. Of all of God's creatures, the human person is the highest and most complete revelation of God.[64] "The proper study of mankind is man," said Alexander Pope; but when we study man we are also learning about the majesty of God.

This means that we must not look down upon the contributions of different groups of people from various nationalities and races; rather, we must welcome these contributions as adding to our enrichment. A proper appreciation of the doctrine of the image of God, therefore, should rule out all racism—all denigration of races other than our own, as if they were inferior to us. God made all human beings in his image, and all of them can enlighten and enrich us. "The idea of man as made in the image of God demands . . . today a deliberate transcending of national and class barriers."[65]

Even those who live in rebellion against God and who do their cultural work without consciously praising God reflect God through

---

62. *Dogmatiek*, 2:621-22 [trans. mine].
63. *When the Kings*, p. 47.
64. Bavinck, *Dogmatiek*, 2:603-4.
65. Jürgen Moltmann, *Man*, trans. John Sturdy (Philadelphia: Fortress Press, 1974), p. 111.

the gifts he has given them—gifts for which we may thank the Lord. But those in whom the image of God is being renewed reveal that image voluntarily and self-consciously. In this renewal of the lives of God's people we see the image of God far more fully than we do in the contributions of non-Christians. We see God's image in its greater richness and wider splendor only as we look at the Christian community throughout the ages and throughout the world—in other words, in the universal church.[66] When we look at great saints of the past and of the present—the apostle Paul, Francis of Assisi, Martin Luther, John Calvin, Dietrich Bonhoeffer, Mother Teresa, and Billy Graham, to mention just a few—we see what God is like. And when we taste the joys of Christian fellowship in a group of believers where there is "total acceptance, honest sharing, and genuine loving,"[67] we see a reflection of God's love for us.

In the life to come we shall see the image of God not only in its perfection but also in its completion. All of God's people, from every age and every place, resurrected and glorified, will then be present on the new earth, with all the God-reflecting gifts that have been given them. And all of these gifts, now completely purged of sin and imperfection, will be used by man for the first time in a perfect way. Then, throughout eternity, God will be glorified by the worship, service, and praise of his image-bearers in a scintillating and totally flawless reflection of his own marvelous virtues. And the purpose for which he created humankind will have been accomplished.

66. Note in this connection Calvin's comment on John 13:34, "A new commandment give I unto you, that ye love one another." Calvin says: "Love is, indeed, extended to those outside, for we are all of the same flesh and are all created in the image of God. But because the image of God shines more brightly in the regenerate, it is proper that the bond of love should be much closer among the disciples of Christ" (*Comm. on John*, Parker trans. [Grand Rapids: Eerdmans, 1979], *ad loc.*).
67. Marion Leach Jacobsen, *Saints and Snobs* (Wheaton: Tyndale, 1972), pp. 28-29.

# CHAPTER 6

# *The Question of the Self-Image*

In the discussion of the image of God, we looked at man in his three-fold relationship: to God, to others, and to nature. But is there not also a possible fourth relationship, namely, man's relationship to himself? We could say that this relationship is not specifically taught in the Bible. We could, however, go on to point out that a person's relationship to himself or herself might be an extremely unhealthy one. What about, for example, the man who hates himself, or the woman who thinks of herself as worthless? On the other hand, it is also possible for a person to have a sound or healthy relationship to himself or herself—a relationship of self-confidence. Such a healthy self-image is never an end in itself; it is rather the presupposition for, a help in, and a result of, one's proper functioning in the threefold relationship just described.[1]

We should not, therefore, think of man's relationship to himself as a fourth relationship alongside of the other three. It is, rather, a relationship that underlies all the others, and makes possible a person's proper performance in his or her relationships toward God, others, and nature. For example, a person who has an extremely negative self-image, who thinks of himself as totally worthless, will not be able effectively to love his neighbor as himself; he will not dare to give himself to his neighbor in fellowship, since he feels he has nothing worthwhile to give. On the other hand, a person with a positive self-image, who has at least a modicum of self-confidence, will be willing to give herself to another in fellowship, and thus fulfill the command to love the neighbor. So, though the relationship of human beings to themselves is not a fourth relationship in addition to the other three, it is nevertheless an extremely important one, and should be taken into account in our discussion of the Christian view of man.

1. Cf. Hendrikus Berkhof, *De Mens Onderweg* (The Hague: Boekencentrum, 1962), p. 27.

First, a word about terminology. Two terms commonly used in discussions about this subject will not be used in this chapter: *self-love* and *self-esteem*. The term *self-love* may imply that we are to love what we ourselves are by nature, apart from God's grace. Love of this kind is next door to pride; a Christian ought therefore not to indulge in it. I agree with Jay Adams that when Christ told us to love our neighbors as ourselves, he was not commanding us to love ourselves but simply assuming that self-love is natural and therefore does not need to be commanded.[2] I also basically agree with Paul Brownback that self-love may easily lead to self-worship:

> The greatest peril of self-love is that it is worship of self. It is idolatry with self as the idol, the antithesis of the legitimate blessedness that comes from being poor in spirit. It leads to pride toward God and selfishness.[3]

What I do not like about Brownback's statement, however, is its absoluteness. I believe that a proper self-love is possible for the Christian, when he loves the new person God by his grace is creating within him, thus praising God rather than himself. But because of the ambiguity of the term *self-love*, I prefer not to use it.

I also prefer not to use the term *self-esteem*, defined in *Webster's Ninth New Collegiate Dictionary* as "a confidence and satisfaction in oneself." For here again the emphasis seems to be on one's satisfaction with oneself as he or she is by nature, apart from the grace of God. Though one who is not a Christian may well be very much satisfied with himself apart from God's grace, this is not the kind of relationship to himself that a Christian should seek to have.

I prefer to use the term *self-image*, defined by Webster as "one's conception of oneself or of one's role." This is a neutral term—one's conception of himself or herself may be either positive (one sees oneself as a person of worth) or negative (one sees oneself as a person of no worth or of little worth). This term also lends itself well to a Christian understanding: seeing ourselves not just as we are by nature, but as we are by grace. In this chapter I will attempt to develop briefly what a Christian's self-image ought to be, as an important aspect of the Christian doctrine of man.

Before the Fall, when Adam and Eve were still in the state of integrity, they had, we may presume, very positive images of them-

---

2. Jay E. Adams, *The Christian Counselor's Manual* (Grand Rapids: Baker, 1973), pp. 142-43.
3. Paul Brownback, *The Danger of Self-Love* (Chicago: Moody Press, 1982), p. 130. Cf. Paul C. Vitz, *Psychology as Religion: The Cult of Self-Worship* (Grand Rapids: Eerdmans, 1977).

selves. They were not aware of any guilt, since they had not sinned against God. Neither would there have been any possibility of their feeling guilty because they had sinned against each other. Genesis 2:25, in fact, pictures a state of perfect harmony and of a total absence of shame: "The man and his wife were both naked, and they felt no shame."

## The Perversion of the Self-Image

At the time of the Fall there occurred a twofold perversion of the self-image. First, the Fall was preceded by an inordinate heightening of man's self-image. Adam and Eve wanted to be higher than God. Genesis 3 tells the story. Satan, speaking through the serpent, told Eve that if she were to eat the forbidden fruit her eyes would be opened, and she would be like God (v. 5). "When the woman saw that the fruit of the tree was good for food and pleasing to the eye, and also desirable for gaining wisdom, she took some and ate it. She also gave some to her husband, who was with her, and he ate it" (v. 6). In disobeying God's clear command not to eat of the tree of the knowledge of good and evil, our first parents virtually put themselves above God, taking it into their own hands to decide what was right and what was wrong. This act revealed their sinful pride: it meant that they were "thinking of themselves more highly" than they ought to have thought (Rom. 12:3). This pride, this conceit, this perversion of the self-image in an upward direction, was the cause of man's first sin.

After the sin had been committed, the second perversion of the self-image occurred, this time in a downward direction. Adam and Eve now felt ashamed of themselves; their self-image became negative. The Genesis narrative continues: "Then the eyes of both of them were opened, and they realized they were naked" (v. 7). Awareness of their nakedness meant that they now had a sense of shame. They both realized that they had done wrong, and their self-image began to plummet. Adam revealed his sense of shame when he responded to God's call by saying, " 'I heard you in the garden, and I was afraid because I was naked; so I hid' " (v. 10). Shame now revealed itself in fear— Adam was afraid of God. He also evaded the real issue: he should have said, "I was afraid because I sinned"; but instead he said, "I was afraid because I was naked." Here, then, was shame coupled with an attempt to cover up guilt.

We can observe this same twofold perversion of man's self-image after the Fall. Man's self-image is sometimes inordinately high (in the form of sinful pride) or excessively low (in the form of feelings of shame or worthlessness).

In the first place, ever since the Fall man has tended to have too high an opinion of himself. Augustine said it long ago: pride is the root sin of man. Apart from the grace of God, human beings tend to think of themselves as autonomous, or as a law to themselves. Refusing to bow before God and his commandments, they wish to live as they please. In man by nature there is no sense of dependence on God, but rather pride in his or her own achievements and an exaggerated sense of self-importance. Perhaps the most dramatic biblical example of this attitude is King Nebuchadnezzar who, while walking on the roof of his royal palace, said, "Is not this the great Babylon I have built as the royal residence, by my mighty power and for the glory of my majesty?" (Dan. 4:30). A more recent example of the same trait would be Adolf Hitler, a man so intoxicated with his own sense of greatness that he was willing to let millions of people be killed for the purpose of exalting his own ego.[4] This, again, is the first perversion of the self-image.

The second type of perversion is also commonly found in fallen man: that of an inordinately low self-image. Because a man realizes that he falls far short of what he should be, he often tends to look down on himself, despise himself, perhaps even hate himself. Sometimes, in fact, people may think of themselves as totally worthless. Criminologists tell us that most criminals have negative self-images; they hate themselves and hate society, expressing their hatred in acts of violence. But this phenomenon is not limited to criminals. Psychiatrists, psychologists, and pastoral counselors report that a great many of their counselees come to them with inferiority feelings and negative self-images. Carl Rogers, the well-known proponent of client-centered therapy, puts it this way: "The central core of difficulty in people as I have come to know them . . . is that in the great majority of cases they despise themselves, regard themselves as worthless and unlovable."[5]

Both of the deviations just sketched are perversions of the self-image God intended us to have. Pride and conceit are detestable in his sight, for "God opposes the proud but gives grace to the humble" (1 Pet. 5:5). The opposite perversion, that of an extremely negative self-image, might be thought of as more salutary than pride, since a low self-image is the necessary condition for true repentance. For example, in Jesus' parable, the self-castigating tax collector went home justified, not the self-congratulating Pharisee (Luke 18:9-14). One must indeed first realize the magnitude of his sins against God

4. See Alan Bullock, *Hitler: A Study in Tyranny* (New York: Harper and Row, 1971).
5. Carl R. Rogers, "Reinhold Niebuhr's *The Self and the Dramas of History*: A Criticism," *Pastoral Psychology* 9 (June 1958):17.

(and this will certainly bring with it a nonflattering self-image) before he will feel the need of repenting of his sin and turning to Christ in faith.[6] Paul makes this very point in 2 Corinthians 7:10, "Godly sorrow brings repentance that leads to salvation." All this is sound scriptural teaching, but it remains true that God does not intend to have his people kept perpetually in bondage to an extremely low self-image.

## THE RENEWAL OF THE SELF-IMAGE

In the redemptive process, as we saw, the image of God in man, which was perverted through the Fall, is being progressively renewed. This implies that in this process man's self-image, which because of the Fall has also been perverted, is similarly being renewed. This renewal of the self-image takes place in two directions.

First, when God by his Spirit renews us, he enables us to renounce sinful pride, the first perversion of the self-image. He helps us to cultivate true humility. This includes, among other things, *an honest awareness of both our strengths and weaknesses,* so as to give us a realistic image of ourselves. The biblical passage that comes to mind in this connection is Romans 12:3, "For by the grace given me I say to every one of you: Do not think of yourself more highly than you ought, but rather think of yourself with sober judgment." Humility includes, further, *a readiness to consider others better than ourselves* (Phil. 2:3)—that is, to be more eager to praise others than to have others praise us. This humility also involves *a recognition that all our gifts and talents come from God,* thus pulling out pride by the roots.

---

6. In connection with this point, I wish to take issue with the view of the Christian self-image developed in Robert H. Schuller's recent book, *Self-Esteem: The New Reformation* (Waco, TX: Word Books, 1982). While appreciating Schuller's emphasis on the importance of a positive self-image for the Christian, I am unhappy with what seems to me to be a shallow view of sin. On p. 65 Schuller says that to call sin "rebellion against God" is "shallow and insulting to the human being." I reply, however, that it is not just theologians but the Bible itself that calls sin rebellion against God (Isa. 1:2; Ezek. 2:3-5; Dan. 9:5). On p. 127 Schuller states that the gospel message is "potentially dangerous if it has to put a person down before it attempts to lift him up." But must not a person know his or her sin before feeling the need of turning to Christ for forgiveness and salvation? And does not Paul in Romans first show that "Jews and Gentiles alike are all under sin" (3:9) before he brings his uplifting message about justification by faith? The Bible teaches a very serious view of sin, whereas Schuller does not. And if one detracts from the seriousness of sin, does one not also detract from the greatness of God's grace? (Cf. Dennis Voskuil, *Mountains into Goldmines* [Grand Rapids: Eerdmans, 1983], pp. 146-51; also Kenneth S. Kantzer with Paul W. Fromer, "A Theologian Looks at Schuller," *Christianity Today* 28, no. 11 [Aug. 10, 1984]: 22-24.)

Paul puts it very vividly in 1 Corinthians 4:7, "What do you have that you did not receive? And if you did receive it, why do you boast as though you did not?" And in 2 Corinthians 3:5 he writes, "Not that we are competent to claim anything for ourselves, but our competence comes from God." Finally, humility means *a willingness to use our gifts in the service of God and in the service of others.* When we look at our gifts in this way, we shall always realize that we could have used them far more unselfishly than we actually did—and thus we shall be kept from a self-image that is inordinately high.

Does the redemptive process also help to correct the second type of perversion we have looked at: namely, that of an inordinately low self-image? The answer is Yes, when the Bible is understood in a balanced way. Unfortunately, many evangelical Christians seem to have a self-image that is much more negative than positive, since, when they look at themselves, what is in the center of their field of vision is their continued sinfulness and inadequacy rather than their newness in Christ. But to associate this kind of negative self-image with biblical Christianity is, I believe, a serious distortion. When the Christian faith is grasped in its totality, it will be found to contain tremendous resources for a positive self-image. Such a positive self-image is one of the salutary results of the redemptive process, and an aspect of the renewing of the image of God.

In exploring the biblical resources for a positive self-image, I should like briefly to discuss scriptural teachings on both justification and sanctification. Justification is that act of God by which he imputes to (that is, credits to the account of) the believer the perfect satisfaction and righteousness of Christ. What this means is that God totally forgives all the sins of those who are in Christ by faith. The Bible takes sin very seriously; it teaches us that when we do wrong we sin not just against other people but against God himself. The Bible also shows us, however, that God has provided a way whereby we can be delivered not just from the feelings of guilt but from guilt itself. Since Christ bore our guilt (1 Pet. 2:24) and suffered the punishment for our sins on the cross (Rom. 3:24-25; 2 Cor. 5:21), God now frees from guilt all those who are in Christ. This means that when God looks at us who are in Christ, he no longer sees our sin and guilt, but sees instead the perfect righteousness of Jesus Christ. This marvelous truth of divine forgiveness is the foundation for a positive Christian self-image.

Sanctification is that work of God by which the Holy Spirit progressively delivers the believer from the pollution of sin and makes him or her more and more like Christ. What is evident from this definition is that because of what happens in the process of sanctification the believer is no longer the same person he or she was before conversion, but is a changed person. This change is the second reason why the Christian should have an image of himself or herself which is primarily positive.

Three biblical concepts—*new self versus old self, life in the Spirit,* and *the new creature*— help to illustrate this changed life. We will first look at the question of *new self versus old self.* Many Christians think that the believer is both an "old self" (or "old man") and a "new self" (or "new man"). Before conversion the one who is now a believer was only an old self; at the time of conversion he or she became a new self—without, however, totally losing the old self. There is, then, a constant struggle between these two aspects or parts of the believer's being, since the "taking off" or "crucifixion" of the old self is considered to be a lifelong process.

As we saw earlier, however, in connection with an exposition of Colossians 3:9-10,[7] this understanding of the relation between the old self and the new self is not in harmony with biblical teaching.[8] The late Professor John Murray put it very graphically:

> The old man is the unregenerate man; the new man is the regenerate man created in Christ Jesus unto good works. It is no more feasible to call the believer a new man and an old man, than it is to call him a regenerate man and an unregenerate.[9]

The Christian, in other words, should look upon himself or herself as someone who in the strength of the Spirit has decisively taken off the old self and just as decisively put on the new self—which new self, however, is still being progressively renewed. On the basis of God's redemptive work, therefore, the believer's self-image ought to be positive, not negative.

A second way in which the Bible shows us the change that takes place in the believer as a result of the process of sanctification is its teaching on *life in the Spirit.* In his letter to the Christians in Rome, Paul contrasts the "mind of the flesh" with the "mind of the Spirit," and then says, "But you are not in the flesh, you are in the Spirit" (8:9, RSV). The question we now face is, What does Paul here mean by "flesh" and "Spirit"? By "Spirit" in this passage he probably means the Holy Spirit. By "flesh" here Paul does not mean the body, but

---

7. See above, pp. 25-26.

8. This is not to say that there is no struggle in the Christian life. But that struggle should not be understood as being between the old self (that is, the total person enslaved by sin) and the new self (the total person under the direction of the Holy Spirit), but rather as a struggle between the new self and the remnants of indwelling sin that still remain in us.

9. *Principles of Conduct* (Grand Rapids: Eerdmans, 1957), p. 218.

rather the tendency within fallen man to disobey God in every area of life—with the mind as well as with the body. "Flesh" in this sense is roughly equivalent to "indwelling sin."

To be sure, believers must still contend with "indwelling sin" or "the flesh" as long as they live on this side of the resurrection.[10] But Paul here takes pains to say that in spite of this fact believers are not *in the flesh* (that is, enslaved to the flesh) but *in the Spirit* (that is, under the liberating regime of the Holy Spirit). Instead of being totally dominated and controlled by the flesh, they are now being directed by the Spirit into a way of life that is pleasing to God and helpful to others. So here again a positive self-image emerges: Christians should look upon themselves not as being partly in the flesh and partly in the Spirit but as being in the Spirit and as having been delivered from the tyranny of enslavement to the flesh.

One might, however, still raise the question: But does not the Bible teach that there is a continuing struggle between the Spirit and the flesh in the life of the believer, and does not this continuing struggle imply the possibility of a negative self-image? Not necessarily. It is instructive to see how Paul talks about this struggle in Galatians 5:16, "But I say, walk by the Spirit, and you will not carry out the desire of the flesh" (NASB).

To be sure, Paul is here describing the Christian life as one involving perpetual struggle between the Holy Spirit and the flesh. But he is by no means implying that as they engage in this struggle believers will always lose, will always give way to the flesh. Rather, the atmosphere of this verse is one of encouragement: if you keep on walking or living by the Spirit, you will not keep on fulfilling the lusts or evil desires of the flesh. The verse contains a promise, not a threat. If you do the one, you will not be doing the other. So, Paul is saying, engage in the struggle against sin not expecting defeat but confident of victory. For in the strength of the Spirit you are able to say No to the flesh. Again we see that the Christian's self-image ought to be a positive one.

A third way in which the New Testament describes this change is by what it says about the believer as *a new creature*. The passage

10. "Flesh" in this sense must not be thought of as identical to "the old self" or "the old man." Note John Murray's perceptive comment:

> The term "old man" does not lend itself to the same kind of usage which we have in the case of "sin" and "the flesh." "Old man" is a designation of the person in his unity as dominated by the flesh and sin. Though Paul, indeed, identifies himself, his ego, with sin . . . and then also with righteousness, . . . yet he does not call the former his "old ego" and the latter his "new ego." In like manner he does not call the "sin" and "the flesh" in him "the old man." (*Principles of Conduct*, p. 218n.7)

that springs to mind in this connection is 2 Corinthians 5:17: "Therefore if any man is in Christ, he is a new creature; the old things passed away; behold, new things have come" (NASB). The word rendered here as "creature" (*ktisis* in Greek) basically means "creation," and is so rendered in a number of recent versions of the Bible. What the passage means is probably something like this: the person who is in Christ is to be seen as a member of God's new creation, as someone who belongs to the new era ushered in by Christ. The Christian, in other words, no longer belongs to the old era of enslavement to sin; he or she now belongs to the new era of salvation, joy, and peace inaugurated by Christ's resurrection. As one who belongs to that new creation, therefore, the believer is in a very real sense a new creature.

Commonly we think of this concept of "the new creation" as applying only to the life to come. To be sure, the full implications of this new creaturehood will not be revealed until we who are in Christ have been raised in glory and are living on the new earth. But the words of 2 Corinthians 5:17 are in the present tense. To those who are in Christ Paul says, You are new creatures *now*! Not *totally* new, to be sure, but *genuinely* new. And we who are believers should see ourselves in this way: no longer as depraved and helpless slaves of sin, but as those who have been created anew in Christ Jesus.

The Christian life involves not just believing something about Christ but also believing something about ourselves. We must believe that we are indeed part of Christ's new creation. Our faith in Christ must include believing that we are exactly what the Bible says we are.[11]

All this implies that the Christian believer may have—and should have—a self-image that is primarily positive. Such a positive self-image does not mean "feeling good about ourselves" on the basis of our own achievements or virtuous behavior.[12] This would be sinful pride. The Christian self-image means looking at ourselves in the

11. For a fuller discussion of the biblical resources for a positive Christian self-image, see my *The Christian Looks at Himself*, rev. ed. (Grand Rapids: Eerdmans, 1977), pp. 31-60.

In this connection I should like to express my disagreement with the main thesis of Paul Brownback's recent book, *The Danger of Self-Love*. Brownback is critical of *The Christian Looks at Himself* because he feels that the Bible does not teach us to think positively about ourselves but rather urges us to have no self-image at all (pp. 133, 137). But this solution is quite unrealistic. Further, Brownback fails to do justice to the real change brought about within the believer in the process of sanctification—that is, the change described above. It is significant that this author nowhere refers to the chapters in *The Christian Looks at Himself* (chaps. 3, 4, and 5) in which this change is set forth.

12. Brownback, *Danger*, p. 14.

light of God's gracious work of forgiveness and renewal. It involves giving God all the praise for what he by his grace has done and is still doing within us and through us. It includes confidence that God can use us, despite our shortcomings, to advance his kingdom and to bring joy to others.

This Christian self-image, when properly understood, is the opposite of spiritual pride. It goes hand in hand with a deep conviction of sin and a recognition that we are still far from what we ought to be. It means glorying not in self but in Christ.

The Christian self-image is never an end in itself. It is always a means to the end of living for God, for others, and for the preservation and development of God's creation. It leads us outside of ourselves. It delivers us from preoccupation with ourselves and releases us so that we may happily serve God and love others.

Our self-image as Christians, therefore, must not be static but dynamic. The believer may never be satisfied with himself or herself. He or she must always be pressing on, in the strength of Christ, toward the goal of Christian perfection. Christians should see themselves as new persons who are being progressively renewed by the Holy Spirit.[13]

It is said that sometimes an airplane pilot is not sure whether the plane he is piloting is flying upside down or right side up. At such times he needs to look at his instrument panel to find the answer to his question. By way of analogy, perhaps we could think of the Bible as our instrument panel. Keeping our eyes on the Bible will help us to remember who we really are.

---

13. It is sometimes said that John Calvin, by his strong emphasis on the sinfulness of man, taught his followers to have a self-image that is far more negative than positive (cf., e.g., W. M. Counts, "The Nature of Man and the Christian's Self-Esteem," in *The Journal of Psychology and Theology* 1, no. 1 [Jan. 1973]:28-44). For a competent and thorough refutation of this erroneous opinion, see Louis A. Vos, "Calvin and the Christian Self-Image," in *Exploring the Heritage of John Calvin*, ed. David E. Holwerda (Grand Rapids: Baker, 1976), pp. 76-109.

# CHAPTER 7

# *The Origin of Sin*

The origin of sin is obviously an important topic. Man was created in the image of God. But that image has now been perverted. Human beings are now sinners, inclined to all varieties of evil, sometimes sinking to unbelievable depths of iniquity. The question therefore naturally arises, Where did sin come from? Did God create man as a sinful being? Or, if this was not the case, did man become sinful some time after his creation? And if he became a sinner, how did this happen?

In the history of Christian thought the traditional answer to these questions has been this: God created man good, without any sinful thoughts or desires. But sin came into the world through the fall and disobedience of our first parents, Adam and Eve. Since the Fall human nature has become so corrupted that apart from the grace of God man is now unable to do any true good and inclined toward all kinds of evil.[1]

## WAS ADAM A HISTORICAL PERSON?

In recent years a number of theologians standing in what is generally called the Reformed tradition have advanced the view that Adam and Eve were not actual persons who once lived on this earth but symbols of man's divine origin and of his fall into sin. As these theologians see it, the narrative of the Fall in Genesis 3 does not describe something that actually happened in history. According to Karl Barth, for example, the narrative of Genesis 3:1-7 is not history but only "saga";[2] Adam was not a historical figure but *exemplarily* the representative of all who followed him;[3] furthermore, at no time was man not a trans-

---

1. Cf., e.g., the following Reformed creeds: Heidelberg Catechism, Qq. 6-8; Belgic Confession, Art. 14; Canons of Dort, I.1; III-IV.2; Westminster Confession, Chap. 6.
2. Karl Barth, *Church Dogmatics*, IV/1, trans. G. W. Bromiley (Edinburgh: T. & T. Clark, 1961), p. 508.
3. G. C. Berkouwer, *The Triumph of Grace in the Theology of Karl Barth*, trans. H. Boer (Grand Rapids: Eerdmans, 1956), p. 84.

**112**

gressor and therefore guiltless before God.⁴ Emil Brunner, as we saw earlier, rejects what he calls "the historicity of the story of Adam"; for modern man, he insists, the possibility of accepting such historicity no longer exists.⁵ More recently, H. M. Kuitert, a professor of theology at the Free University of Amsterdam, has stated that we must not understand Adam as a historical figure, but rather as a pedagogical example or a "teaching model"—an illustration of what happens to every man, which helps us to understand the significance and reality of Jesus Christ.⁶

It is my conviction that the denial that Adam and Eve were actual persons who once lived on this earth and the understanding of Adam and Eve as symbols or "teaching models" is based on an incorrect understanding of Scripture. The Genesis account is not the only biblical reference to the first man. The genealogy in the first chapter of 1 Chronicles begins with Adam (v. 1), obviously treating him as a historical person. Similarly, the genealogy of Jesus in Luke 3 ends with the following words: "the son of Enos, the son of Seth, the son of Adam, the son of God" (v. 38). This verse clearly places Adam at the beginning of a list of historical persons, and indicates that Adam came into existence not through natural generation but by the creative act of God.

Furthermore, when the Pharisees questioned Jesus about divorce (Matt. 19:4-6; Mark 10:6-8), he referred to statements found in Genesis 1:27 and 2:24. These passages state that God made man male and female, and that a man shall leave his father and mother and be joined to his wife. Jesus' appeal to the beginning of things as recorded in Genesis would have no relevance for the situation in his day if the man and woman described in these verses were mere symbols. Jesus' words assume the existence of an actual human pair.

Paul, too, accepted the historicity of our first parents. In 1 Timothy 2:13 he gives the following ground for his injunction that women should not teach or have authority over men: "For Adam was formed

---

4. Barth, *Church Dogmatics*, IV/1, p. 495.

5. Emil Brunner, *The Christian Doctrine of Creation and Redemption*, trans. Olive Wyon (Philadelphia: Westminster Press, 1952), p. 48.

6. H. M. Kuitert, *Do You Understand What You Read?*, trans. Lewis B. Smedes (Grand Rapids: Eerdmans, 1970), p. 40. We should further note, however, that the denial of the historicity of the Fall is not new, but goes back to the ancient period. The Jewish scholar Philo (c. 30 B.C.–c. A.D. 45) taught that the story of Adam and Eve was not an account of something that had happened in history but was simply a myth (J. N. D. Kelly, *Early Christian Doctrines* [London: Adam and Charles Black, 1958], p. 20). And Origen, an Alexandrian theologian (c. 185–c. 254), taught that the Genesis narrative of the Fall was a cosmic myth, mirroring the experience of every man and woman, since all human beings had fallen into sin during a state of preexistence (ibid., pp. 180-82).

first, then Eve." These words indicate that Paul accepted the temporal sequence of the creation of Eve after Adam as described in Genesis; temporal sequence implies historical succession. Paul adds, "And Adam was not deceived, but the woman was deceived and became a transgressor" (v. 14, RSV). The statement "the woman was deceived" reflects the words of Genesis 3:13, where Eve is quoted as saying, "The serpent deceived me, and I ate." Paul's words here indicate that he fully accepted the historicity of the biblical account of the Fall.

Paul again refers to Adam in his letter to the Corinthians: "For as by a man came death, by a man has come also the resurrection of the dead. For as in Adam all die, so also in Christ shall all be made alive" (1 Cor. 15:21-22, RSV). Note that Paul here contrasts two men: one through whom death came into the world, and another through whom the resurrection has come; verse 22 specifies that the first man was Adam and that the second man was Christ. Here Adam and Christ are placed side by side. Paul obviously believed that Christ was a historical figure—a person who lived on this earth during a certain period in history. Does not Paul's placing Adam next to Christ imply that he believed that Adam was also a historical person? If Adam was only a mythical or symbolical figure, as some recent theologians insist, we could paraphrase verse 22 somewhat as follows: "As in Pandora [a character from Greek mythology who is said to have opened the box out of which flew all the evils that have since plagued mankind] all die, so also in Christ shall all be made alive." But does this understanding not wreck the structure of Paul's thought? Is not Paul here clearly contrasting one head of the human race with another? And if the second head was a historical person, are we not compelled to conclude that the first head was also a historical person? Paul speaks here of two men; if the first was only a symbol, what ground have we for believing that the second (our Lord Jesus Christ) was not a symbol?

A little later in the same letter Paul again speaks of Adam as the first man in contrast to Christ as the second man: "So it is written: 'The first man Adam became a living being'; the last Adam, a life-giving spirit.... The first man was of the dust of the earth, the second man from heaven" (15:45-47). John Murray's comment on these passages is to the point:

> The parallelism and contrast [in these verses] demand for Adam as the first man a historical identity comparable to that of Christ himself. Otherwise the basis of comparison and contrast is lost. Adam and Christ sustain unique relations to the human race, but in order to sustain these

relations there must be to both such historical character as will make those relations possible and relevant.[7]

We find in Paul's letter to the Romans a passage of crucial and decisive significance for the topic under discussion. In 5:12-21 Paul contrasts the bad results that have come to us through Adam, our first head, with the blessings that have come to us through Christ, our second head, of whom Adam was a type (*typos*). Paul's point is not that death and condemnation have come upon us because all of us somehow, at some time or other, sin,[8] but that death and condemnation have come upon us because of the transgression *of one man*, whom Paul, following the biblical narrative, calls Adam.

Paul begins his discussion by saying, "Therefore as sin came into the world through one man and death through sin . . ." (v. 12, RSV). If Barth, Brunner, and Kuitert are right in their understanding of what the Bible means by "Adam," we really ought to interpret Paul here as saying, "Therefore as sin came into the world *through no one man*, and death through sin"—since Adam never existed as a person but is simply a symbol standing for all people. Paul, however, says nothing of the kind. Rather, he says "as sin came into the world *through one man.*"

Verse 14 reads: "Yet death reigned from Adam to Moses, even over those whose sins were not like the transgression of Adam, who was a type of the one who was to come" (RSV). Note that Paul is thinking of a specific period of time, running from the time of a specific person, Adam, to that of Moses. Obviously, Paul is referring to a person who lived at a certain time in history; it makes no sense to say, "from mankind in general to Moses." Further, Paul writes about people "whose sins were not like the transgression of Adam." If Adam's transgression was simply the transgression of every man, symbolically expressed in the form of a story or teaching model, what point would there be in talking about people *whose sins were not like the transgression of Adam*? Ask yourself what sense it would make if we understood verse 14 as follows: "Yet death reigned . . . even over those whose sins were not like the transgression of every man." Who is there whose sins are not like the transgression of every man?

In verse 15 Paul writes, "For if many died through one man's trespass, much more have the grace of God and the free gift in the grace of that one man Jesus Christ abounded for many" (RSV). The thrust of the passage rests on the contrast between the one and the many. If "one man" in the first clause simply stands for "many," as

7. John Murray, "Historicity of Adam," ISBE, 1:50.
8. This understanding would seem to be implied in the teaching of all those theologians who deny the historicity of Adam.

the position of Barth, Brunner, and Kuitert implies, Paul's entire point is lost. "The one and the many" are surely not the same as "the many and the many." Further, note again the parallel between Adam and Christ. None of us would care to assert that in this verse Christ simply stands for a totality of men. Paul, in fact, describes Christ here as "that one man Jesus Christ." Paul's point is: through what one man (Adam) did, many died; but through what another man (Christ) did, the grace of God abounded to many. The statement becomes meaningless if the relation between the one and the many in the first clause is allegorized away. If Paul thought of Jesus Christ here (and in v. 17) as a historical person, what right has anyone to suggest that he thought of Adam, whom he describes in each of these verses with an expression identical to the one used for Christ ("one man . . . one man"), as not a historical person?

The denial of the historical Adam has disastrous effects on the interpretation of verse 19: "For as by one man's disobedience many were made sinners, so by one man's obedience many will be made righteous" (RSV). All evangelical Christians would reject the thought that we are made righteous through our own obedience; we insist that we are made righteous only through the obedience of Christ on our behalf—and we quote the latter half of verse 19 to prove this. But if "one man's disobedience" in the first half of this verse really means "the disobedience of all men, exemplified in the symbolical story of Adam and Eve," then the parallelism of the verse would require that we interpret the second half in a similar way. But we would all recognize such an interpretation as going directly contrary to Paul's teaching.[9]

The denial of the historicity of Adam is not only contrary to Scripture; it also has devastating results for the doctrine of man. Professor Kuitert believes that the story of the Fall is not the narration of a historical event but a teaching model, that there was no time when man was not a sinner, and that there was no state of integrity previous to our present state of corruption. If this understanding of the Genesis narrative were correct, however, it would seem that the human person, as he comes from the hand of his Creator, is a being who invariably and inevitably falls into sin. Such a view would tie sin inseparably to

9. On the question of the historicity of Adam see also J. P. Versteeg, *Is Adam a "Teaching Model" in the New Testament?*, trans. Richard B. Gaffin, Jr. (Nutley, NJ: Presbyterian and Reformed, 1978)—a direct reply to Kuitert. Cf. further J. Murray, "Historicity of Adam"; Paul K. Jewett, *Emil Brunner's Concept of Revelation* (London: James Clarke, 1954), pp. 148-49; G. C. Berkouwer, *Sin*, trans. Philip C. Holtrop (1958, 1960; Grand Rapids: Eerdmans, 1971), p. 274; E. J. Young, *In The Beginning* (Edinburgh: Banner of Truth, 1976), pp. 86, 90-91; James Daane, "The Fall," ISBE, vol. 2 (1982):277-78.

man's finiteness, to man's creatureliness, to man's humanity. But if sin is inevitably locked in with man's humanity, is redemption from sin possible? Does the human person then have to become a completely different type of creature—say, an angel—before he or she can become sinless?

The narrative of the Fall, however, tells us that man was created in a state of integrity but fell into a state of corruption through an actual event that occurred in time. Though the narration of this event in Genesis 3 does not give us an *explanation* for the entrance of sin (this is a mystery that can never be explained), it does tell us that at a certain point in time sin entered the world of humankind. This means that sin is accidental, not essential to man. It means, further, that redemption from sin is possible: human beings can again become sinless without ceasing to be human. Since sinfulness is not essential to humanness, Jesus Christ, though sinless, was a genuine man. Through the first head, Adam, we became sinful; through the second head, Christ, we can become sinless.

One could rightly observe that Paul's main purpose in setting forth the parallel between Adam and Christ in Romans 5:12-21 is to set forth the blessings that come to us through Christ—blessings that far outweigh the deleterious results of our oneness with Adam. This is true. But we must not forget that the work Christ did for us is here put into a framework of redemptive history—a history that begins with our relation to Adam, our first head. Herman Ridderbos puts it this way: "The parallel between Christ and Adam is of far-reaching significance for the understanding of the salvation-history background of Paul's preaching of the gospel."[10] On this same point J. P. Versteeg has some incisive words to say:

> The redemptive-historical correlation between Adam and Christ determines the framework in which—particularly for Paul—the redemptive work of Christ has its place. That work of redemption can no longer be confessed according to the meaning of Scripture if it is divorced from the framework in which it stands there. Whoever divorces the work of redemption from the framework in which it stands in Scripture no longer allows the word to function as the norm that determines *everything*.[11]

## SHOULD WE SPEAK OF A COVENANT OF WORKS?

From the Scripture passages just quoted it is obvious that the origin of sin must be tied in with the fall of man, and particularly with Adam

10. *Aan de Romeinen* (Kampen: Kok, 1959), p. 112 [trans. mine].
11. *Teaching Model*, p. 66.

as our first head. This leads us to consider the question, What is the exact relationship between Adam and humankind?

The traditional Reformed conception of this relationship is that Adam was the head of the first covenant God made with man, commonly called the *covenant of works*. Herman Bavinck, who devotes many pages to this doctrine in his *Gereformeerde Dogmatiek*, represents this approach. Adam and Christ, he maintains, are both covenant heads. The covenanting parties in the covenant of works were God and Adam. Adam was not only the father of the human race, but also our head and representative. The promise of the covenant of works was eternal life in its fullest sense—an eternal life in which Adam and his descendants would have been raised above the possibility of sinning. The condition of the covenant of works was perfect obedience, not only to the moral law that Adam and Eve knew by nature, but particularly to the so-called probationary or test command: the command not to eat of the tree of the knowledge of good and evil. The penalty of the covenant of works was death in its fullest sense: physical, spiritual, and eternal. Since Adam and Eve broke this covenant, they were driven out of the garden, and guilt and corruption came upon all humankind. Because our first parents failed in this first covenant, God graciously made a second covenant with humankind, the *covenant of grace*. In this second covenant Christ, the new head, not only suffered the punishment for the sin of Adam and Eve and the sins of their descendants, but also rendered to God the perfect obedience that Adam and Eve failed to render, thus earning for all who belong to Christ eternal life. Bavinck considers the doctrine of the covenant of works so important that he states more than once that the covenant of works and the covenant of grace stand or fall together.[12]

Other Reformed theologians who have taught and defended the doctrine of the covenant of works include Charles Hodge,[13] Robert L. Dabney,[14] William G. T. Shedd,[15] Geerhardus Vos,[16] and Louis Berkhof.[17] More recently, the doctrine of the covenant of works has been

---

12. For Bavinck's teaching on the covenant of works, see *Dogmatiek*, 2:602-24; 3:90-96, 137, 176-77, 229, 236-40. An English summary of this material can be found in my *Herman Bavinck's Doctrine of the Covenant* (Th.D. diss., Princeton Seminary, 1953), pp. 70-102. A copy of this dissertation can be found in the Calvin Theological Library, Grand Rapids, Mich.

13. *Systematic Theology*, vol. 2 (1871; Grand Rapids: Eerdmans, 1940), pp. 117-22.

14. *Lectures in Systematic Theology* (1878; Grand Rapids: Zondervan, 1972), pp. 302-5.

15. *Dogmatic Theology*, vol. 2 (1888; Grand Rapids: Zondervan, n.d.), pp. 152ff.

16. *Dogmatiek*, I.2 (Grand Rapids, 1910; mimeographed), pp. 34-39, 95-96. See also his *Biblical Theology* (Grand Rapids: Eerdmans, 1948), pp. 32, 37-51.

17. *Systematic Theology*, rev. and enl. ed. (Grand Rapids: Eerdmans, 1941), pp. 211-18.

defended by two Old Testament theologians, Meredith Kline[18] and O. Palmer Robertson.[19] Both Kline and Robertson, however, prefer to call this covenant with Adam before the Fall "the covenant of creation."

In recent years, however, some Reformed theologians have objected to the concept of a covenant of works before the Fall. Already in 1958 G. C. Berkouwer wrote about his problems with the covenant-of-works doctrine.[20] In his *Reformed Dogmatics*, published in 1966, Herman Hoeksema rejects the doctrine of the covenant of works, developing five objections to it.[21] John Murray, in an essay on "The Adamic Administration," gives two reasons why the term "covenant of works" ought not to be used.[22]

Though not necessarily agreeing with all the objections mentioned by these three authors, I share their conviction that we ought not to call the arrangement God made with Adam and Eve before the Fall a "covenant of works."

First, the idea of calling this arrangement a covenant of works does not do justice to the elements of grace that entered into this "Adamic administration." For, though it is true that Adam and Eve were to receive the blessing of continued life in fellowship with God along the path of "works" (that is, by perfect obedience to God's commands), it by no means follows that they would by such obedience earn or merit this continued fellowship, understood by many to include everlasting life. God was indeed entitled to perfect obedience from his human creatures; he was not obligated, however, to give them a reward for such obedience. That he promised (by implication) to give man such a reward must be understood as a gift of God's grace.

Second, the Bible does not call this arrangement a covenant. The only possible exception is Hosea 6:7, which describes the transgressions against God of the people of Ephraim. It reads: "Like Adam, they have broken the covenant—they were unfaithful to me there." If this passage has been properly translated, it would seem that there was indeed a covenant that Adam transgressed in Paradise. However, the translation of *keʾādām* (the Hebrew original rendered "like Adam" in the NIV) is not at all certain. Even the NIV has a footnote here: "Or *As at Adam*; or *Like men*." Other translations have "like men" (KJV, ASVmg), or "as a man" (Septuagint). Still other transla-

---

18. *By Oath Consigned* (Grand Rapids: Eerdmans, 1968), pp. 27-29, 32, 37.
19. *The Christ of the Covenants* (Grand Rapids: Baker, 1980), pp. 55-57, 67-87.
20. *Sin*, pp. 207-8.
21. *Reformed Dogmatics* (Grand Rapids: Reformed Free Publishing Association, 1966), pp. 217-20.
22. "The Adamic Administration," *Collected Writings of John Murray*, vol. 2 (Edinburgh: Banner of Truth Trust, 1977), p. 49.

tions suggest that $k^e$ ("like") should be read as $b^e$ ("in" or "at"), and therefore render the words in question as "at Adam" (RSV, Jerusalem Bible). It would not seem wise, therefore, to base a doctrine on a single passage of this sort, the translation and meaning of which is not altogether certain.

A third objection to the concept of a covenant of works before the Fall is that there is no indication in these early chapters of Genesis of a covenant oath or a covenant ratification ceremony. When we read about the probationary or test command in Genesis 2:16-17, nothing is said about either a covenant oath or a ratification ceremony. Much light has been shed on the nature of covenants in ancient times, including those mentioned in the Bible, by recent research into ancient Near Eastern covenantal treaties. These researchers found that the covenants of the Old Testament—particularly those described in the later chapters of Genesis (beginning with chap. 15), Exodus, and Deuteronomy—were always ratified by an oath and commonly accompanied by a ceremony, which in some cases involved the cutting up and/or sacrificing of animals. If such confirmatory oaths were characteristic of covenants in those days, as the evidence now indicates, we do not seem to be warranted in concluding that the arrangement God made with Adam and Eve before the Fall was covenantal in nature.

This view of the nature of covenants in biblical times is supported by several scholars. M. Weinfeld puts it this way:

> *Berith* as a commitment has to be confirmed by an oath . . . : Gen. 21:22ff.; 26:26ff.; Dt. 29:9ff.; Josh. 9:15-20; II K. 11:4; Ezk. 16:8; 17:13ff.; which included most probably a conditional imprecation: "May thus and thus happen to me if I violate the obligation." The oath gives the obligation its binding validity, and therefore we find in the Bible as well as in the Mesopotamian and Greek sources the pair of expressions: *berith ve'alah*, "covenant and oath" (Gen. 26:28; Dt. 29:11, 13, 20 [12, 14, 21]; Ezk. 16:59; 17:18) in Hebrew.[23]

George E. Mendenhall, whose 1954 articles gave the initial impetus to recent research in ancient Near Eastern covenantal treaties, calls a covenant "essentially a promissory oath."[24] According to Meredith G. Kline, whose book *By Oath Consigned* indicates familiarity with Near Eastern treaty research,

---

23. "Berith," in the *Theological Dictionary of the Old Testament*, ed. G. J. Botterweck and H. Ringgren, trans. J. T. Willis, vol. 2, rev. ed. (Grand Rapids: Eerdmans, 1977), p. 256.

24. "Ancient Oriental and Biblical Law," *The Biblical Archaeologist* 17, no. 2 (May 1954): 28. See also his "Covenant Forms in Israelite Tradition," ibid., 17, no. 3 (Sept. 1954):56-57.

Every divine-human covenant in Scripture involves a sanction-sealed commitment to maintain a particular relationship or follow a stipulated course of action. In general, then, a covenant may be defined as a relationship under sanctions. The covenantal commitment is characteristically expressed by an oath sworn in the solemnities of covenant ratification.[25]

My fourth objection to the use of the expression "covenant of works" for God's dealings with Adam and Eve before the Fall is that the word *covenant* in Scripture is always used in a context of redemption.[26] God establishes his covenant with fallen man, in order to provide a way whereby fallen humankind can be redeemed from sin. It does not therefore seem proper to apply this word to an arrangement God made with his human creatures before the Fall.

Though we should not, therefore, read the opening chapters of Genesis as a description of a "covenant of works" between God and Adam before the Fall, we must indeed maintain the doctrinal truths that lie behind the concept of the covenant of works. We must, for example, insist that Adam was indeed the head and representative of the human race that was to descend from him; that he was given a "probationary command" to test his obedience; that his disobedience to that command brought sin, death, and condemnation into the world; and that he was therefore a type of Christ, our second head, called "the last Adam" in 1 Corinthians 15:45, through whom we are delivered from the sad results of the first Adam's sin.

## THE FALL OF THE ANGELS

And so we come back at this point to the question of the origin of sin. Before we focus on the Genesis narrative of the Fall, which describes the origin of sin in the life of the human race, however, we must

---

25. *By Oath Consigned*, p. 16. Cf. also Meredith G. Kline, *Treaty of the Great King* (Grand Rapids: Eerdmans, 1963); Dennis J. McCarthy, *Treaty and Covenant* (Rome: Pontifical Biblical Institute, 1963); and M. Weinfeld, "The Covenant of Grant in the Old Testament and in the Ancient Near East," *Journal of the American Oriental Society* 90 (1970):184-203.

To the argumentation given above one could counter, correctly, that there is no mention of a covenant oath or a covenant ratification ceremony in the case of the covenant with Noah, described in Gen. 6:18 (preflood) and in Gen. 9:11-13 and 15-17 (postflood). But since the Bible clearly calls this bestowal of divine grace a covenant, we must also acknowledge it to be such, even though there is no record of either a covenant oath or a covenant ratification. Nowhere in Scripture, however, except in the uncertain reference found in Hos. 6:7, is the arrangement God made with Adam and Eve before the Fall called a covenant.

26. With the possible exception of Hosea 6:7.

observe that sin originated previous to the fall of man in the fall of the angels. Adam and Eve were tempted in the Garden of Eden by a creature called "the serpent" (Gen. 3:1). From other scriptural statements, however, it becomes apparent that the serpent was an instrument of or "spokesman" for Satan, a supremely evil being who, though created by God, rebelled against God and became the leader of a host of fallen angels.[27] Since the serpent tempted our first parents to sin against God, and since the serpent was a tool of Satan, we conclude that sin was present in the angelic world before it began in the human world. Satan, who obviously belonged to the angelic order of beings, was created good, but must have fallen from his state of integrity into an evil state, apparently taking with him a host of angels.[28]

That the angels were created by God is clearly taught in Colossians 1:16,[29] and is implied in passages that speak of God's creation of all things (Ps. 33:6; Neh. 9:6; John 1:3; Rom. 11:36; Eph. 3:9). Though we cannot be certain about the time of the creation of the angels, we may be sure that they were created before the time when God is said to have rested from all his work—"God saw all that he had made, and it was very good" (Gen. 1:31).

Nothing is said in Scripture about the time or the nature of the fall of the angels. It must have occurred before the fall of man. The passage that comes closest to describing the nature of the angels' sin is Jude 6: "And the angels who did not keep their positions of authority [Gk.: *archēn*] but abandoned their own home [*apolipontas to idion oikētērion*]—these he has kept in darkness, bound with everlasting chains for judgment on the great Day." It would seem that these angels were not satisfied with the place where God had put them, but desired a position of higher authority. The root of their sin would therefore appear to be pride, which led to rebellion against God. That the root sin of Satan and the angels was pride is further alluded to in 1 Timothy 3:6, "He [a person who wishes to be an overseer in the church] must not be a recent convert, or he may become conceited and fall under the same judgment as the devil."

What is significant here is that sin did not originate in the world of human beings but in the world of spirits. These spirits were not tempted to sin by some force or power outside of themselves; they fell

---

27. Note, e.g., Rev. 12:9 and 20:2, where "the devil or Satan" is identified with "that ancient serpent."

28. Peter refers to angels that sinned (2 Pet. 2:4). By way of contrast, Paul speaks of "elect angels" in 1 Tim. 5:21.

29. "For by him [Christ] all things were created: things in heaven and on earth, visible and invisible, whether thrones or powers or rulers or authorities [a reference to various kinds of angelic beings]; all things were created by him and for him."

in and by themselves. Jesus, in fact, says that the devil was a murderer "from the beginning," and that when he lies, he speaks "according to his own nature" (John 8:44, RSV; Gk.: *ek tōn idiōn*). In other words, the devil as the leader of the fallen angels brought the lie out of himself.[30]

In the human world, however, the temptation to sin came from the outside. Adam and Eve were tempted by the devil, who appeared in the form of a serpent. The devil, through the serpent, appealed to what the New Testament calls "the lust of the flesh, the lust of the eyes, and the pride of life" (1 John 2:16, RSV). Though this fact by no means excuses man's sin, nor provides an explanation for it, it does indicate an important difference between the sin of man and the sin of the angels.[31]

## WAS THERE A SPEAKING SERPENT?

In our earlier discussion of the historicity of Adam and Eve and of the Fall we concluded that Adam and Eve were persons who lived at a certain time in history and that the Fall was a historical event. But this does not fully answer the question of the interpretation of the narrative of the Fall (Gen. 3). While we grant that the Fall occurred at some time in history, should we therefore interpret literally all aspects of this narrative? Or should we interpret some aspects in a non-literal or symbolic way?

The first thing we should note is that the literary genre of Genesis 1 to 3 is different from the types of literature found in other parts of the Bible, particularly in other historical sections. Ordinarily, Bible writers wrote history based on what they or their informers had witnessed or experienced; sometimes they even had access to certain written documents.[32] But there were no actual witnesses to some of the events described in Genesis 1–3, such as the creation of the universe and what happened on each of the creation days, the forming of the man from the dust of the earth, and the formation of the woman

---

30. On the fall of the angels see H. Bavinck, *Dogmatiek*, 3:11, 52-53, 60. See also L. Berkhof, *Systematic Theology*, pp. 148-49, 220-21.

31. Bavinck, *Dogmatiek*, 3:52-53. Some have even suggested that the fact that man's first sin originated in a temptation from the outside provides the reason why fallen man can be saved from sin whereas fallen angels, whose sin originated in themselves, cannot. Whatever might be the value of this bit of speculation, the difference between the way sin originated in the angelic world and in the human race is an important one, which should neither be ignored nor forgotten.

32. Note, e.g., references to the so-called Book of Jashar in Josh. 10:13 and 2 Sam. 1:18, and cf. Luke 1:1-4.

from Adam's rib. Also, it seems highly unlikely that there was an oral tradition going all the way back to Adam from which the writer of Genesis 1–3 could draw information about the events described in those chapters. According to recent scientific evidence it seems that human beings have been on this earth for possibly hundreds of thousands of years, making it extremely improbable that there could be a dependable oral tradition going all the way back to the beginning. Further, according to Joshua 24:2 and 14, the true knowledge of God had been lost by Abraham and his father before they left Ur of the Chaldees;[33] hence the chain of a true tradition about these early events, if there was such a tradition, would seem to have been broken. Since the writer of Genesis 1–3, therefore, could not consult eyewitnesses to the events he described, and since there was apparently no dependable oral tradition to which he could appeal, we must conclude that the literary genre of these chapters is different from that of other historical sections of the Bible.[34]

This does not mean, however, that what was written in Genesis 3 is not history. The narrative of the Fall in Genesis 3, as we have seen, must be understood as describing an event that happened in history. But the narrative involves a different kind of history-writing than is found, say, in Kings or Chronicles. This raises the question about the literal or nonliteral interpretation of the various aspects of the narrative of the Fall. Must we interpret the serpent literally? How about the speaking of the serpent? How about the two trees: the tree of the knowledge of good and evil (Gen. 2:17) and the tree of life (Gen. 3:22, 24)?

There have been and are theologians standing in the Reformed tradition who, while agreeing that the narrative of the Fall in Genesis 3 describes a historical fall, believe that such details do not necessarily have to be taken literally but may be understood in a symbolic or figurative way. For example, this is the position of the signers of the Majority Report of the study committee dealing with the doctrinal pronouncement of the Synod of Assen of the Gereformeerde Kerken in the Netherlands (1926)—a report presented to the General Synod of the Gereformeerde Kerken held in Amsterdam and Lunteren in 1967-68. This committee was asked to give advice on the question of whether the Gereformeerde Kerken should continue to uphold and

33. "Joshua said to all the people, 'This is what the LORD, the God of Israel, says: "Long ago your forefathers, including Terah the father of Abraham and Nahor, lived beyond the River and worshiped other gods" ' " (Josh. 24:2).
34. On this matter see J. L. Koole, "Het Litterair Genre van Genesis 1–3," *Gereformeerd Theologisch Tijdschrift* 63, no. 2 (May 1963):81-122.

enforce the binding character of the following doctrinal pronouncement of the Synod of Assen:

> That the tree of the knowledge of good and evil, the serpent and his speaking, and the tree of life, according to the evident intention of the scriptural narrative of Genesis 2 and 3, are to be understood in a non-symbolic or literal sense, and were therefore realities perceptible to the senses [*zintuiglijk waarneembare werkelijkheden*].[35]

While not denying the historicity of the Fall, the majority of this committee recommended that the synod should repeal the binding character of this doctrinal pronouncement; this recommendation was adopted by the synod. Those who signed this majority report were G. C. Berkouwer, W. H. Gispen, K. G. Idema, J. L. Koole, A. D. R. Polman, N. H. Ridderbos, D. Van Swigchem, and S. Van Wouwe.[36]

Another Reformed theologian who has taken a similar position is the professor of Old Testament at the Theological Seminary of the Christelijke Gereformeerde Kerken in the Netherlands, B. J. Oosterhoff. In a book published in 1972 he stated that, while the Fall should be understood as a historic event, and while the serpent in the Paradise story should be understood to have been an actual animal, the speaking of the serpent should be conceived of as a symbolic reproduction of something that was historically real.[37]

We must grant, of course, that the most important question in connection with the narrative of the Fall is that of the historicity of man's fall into sin, and that therefore the question of the precise interpretation of the details of the story of the Fall is of lesser importance. Nevertheless, I am convinced that we should interpret the above-mentioned details of the Genesis narrative (the serpent, the speaking of the serpent, and the two trees) literally and not symbolically or figuratively. The reasons why I take this position will become evident as we examine some of the arguments advanced by those who affirm the historicity of the Fall but believe that we need not understand literally the details of the Genesis narrative.

We have already mentioned the first of these arguments: that scholars are now expressing doubts about whether there was an unbroken chain of tradition from Adam's time to the time of the writer of Genesis 3 (presumably Moses). As we have seen, two reasons are

---

35. *Bijlagen bij de Acta van de Generale Synode van de Gereformeerde Kerken in Nederland,* Amsterdam en Lunteren, 1967-68, p. 249 [trans. mine].

36. For the text of this majority report, as well as that of the minority report signed by J. Schelhaas (which favored retaining the binding character of Assen 1926), see ibid., pp. 248-66.

37. *Hoe Lezen Wij Genesis 2 en 3?* (Kampen: Kok, 1972), p. 174.

given to support these doubts: the age of mankind, and the statements in Joshua 24:2 and 14 that Abraham and his fathers served gods other than Yahweh. In the light of recent scholarship, both in the natural sciences and in biblical studies, we must conclude that, though such a chain of tradition is not totally impossible, it now seems extremely unlikely.

However, the fact that there probably was no such unbroken chain of tradition does not necessarily mean that the four items mentioned above are not to be interpreted literally. Actually, we do not know how the writer of Genesis came to know the narrative that he wrote down in Genesis 3. It seems most likely that there was a particular divine revelation to this author about these events at the very beginning of human history.[38] If God revealed the narrative of Genesis 3 to Moses— a narrative that depicts a historical fall—what basis do we have for saying that the above-mentioned four items ought not to be understood literally?[39]

A second argument is that the many anthropomorphisms found in these early chapters of Genesis are not to be interpreted literally. An anthropomorphism is the ascription of human characteristics to nonhuman things or beings—in this case, to God. For example, in Genesis 2:7 we are told that "the LORD God formed man from the dust of the ground and breathed into his nostrils the breath of life." About this passage G. Ch. Aalders, the late professor of Old Testament at the Free University in Amsterdam, makes the following comment:

> It is definitely not necessary to hold that, on the basis of this passage, man was formed out of dust or clay into some kind of clay doll. It is far more likely that these words must be understood as meaning that the body of man is entirely built up of basic substances similar to those found in the earth.[40]

Another example is found in Genesis 3:21, "The LORD God made garments of skin for Adam and his wife and clothed them." About this passage Aalders says,

---

38. See J. L. Koole, "Litterair Genre," p. 110.
39. We may note, however, that the seed of the serpent mentioned in Gen. 3:13 should not be interpreted as referring to the literal animal offspring of the serpent, but rather as referring to those human beings who will share the purpose of the evil power behind the serpent, namely, the devil. Yet even this does not require the denial of the literal interpretation of the serpent.
40. G. Ch. Aalders, *Genesis*, trans. W. Heynen, vol. 1 (1949; Grand Rapids: Zondervan, 1981), p. 85.

When we read the words, "God made garments" and "clothed them," we must understand these statements as anthropomorphisms. As Calvin suggests, it would be entirely in conflict with the spiritual nature of God to envision Him coming down to slaughter animals, skinning them, converting their skins into clothes, and then putting these garments on the man and the woman, all with His own hands.[41]

Since, so the argument goes, statements such as these are not to be taken literally, neither should the speaking serpent and the two trees mentioned in these chapters be understood literally.

Yet anthropomorphisms occur not only in these chapters but in other parts of Scripture as well. Elsewhere in the Old Testament God is said to have feet (Ex. 24:10), a hand (Isa. 50:11), a heart (Hos. 11:8), and eyes (Ps. 34:15). Anthropomorphisms occur in connection with the story of Abraham (God comes to Abraham in the form of a man, Gen. 18), of Jacob (who wrestles with God in the form of a man, Gen. 32:24-32), and of Moses (the Lord meets Moses and seeks to kill him, Ex. 4:24-26). The fact that there are such anthropomorphisms in the narratives dealing with Abraham, Jacob, and Moses does not imply that the history that these narratives describe is to be dismissed as merely figurative or symbolic.

Obviously, to interpret literally the anthropomorphic expressions about God found in Genesis 2 and 3 would distort the biblical description of God as a spirit (John 4:24) and bring him down to the level of a mere man. But this by no means necessarily implies that statements about the serpent or about the trees found in the Garden of Eden are not to be understood literally.

A third argument is that certain aspects of the narrative of the Fall have a symbolic meaning. The two trees, for example, are a case in point. The tree of the knowledge of good and evil stands for the possibility of temptation, of learning about what was good and what was evil in the wrong way. The tree of life stands for the possibility of everlasting and unbroken fellowship with God. The serpent also has a symbolic meaning: obviously, an evil power behind the serpent desired to cause man to sin against God. Since the two trees and the serpent have symbolic meanings, so it is argued, why should we not understand the serpent and the trees as being symbolic or figurative *in toto*?

In reply, however, we may say that the fact that these trees had symbolic significance does not prove that they were not real trees.[42]

---

41. Ibid., p. 112. See Calvin, *Comm. on Genesis*, vol. 1, trans. John King (Grand Rapids: Eerdmans, 1948), *ad loc.*
42. E. J. Young, *In the Beginning*, p. 90.

Further, the fact that an evil power was behind the serpent does not prove that there was not a real serpent.

In fact, we may put it even more strongly. If we say that the serpent, the speaking of the serpent, the tree of the knowledge of good and evil, and the eating of the forbidden fruit were not actual but only symbolic or figurative, then we really know nothing about how man fell into sin. Then we must conclude that Adam and Eve did not actually eat the forbidden fruit, but that they sinned against God in some other way—a way of which we are totally ignorant. As we have seen, however, Genesis 3 gives us God's revelation of how sin came into the world. That revelation was not intended to leave us in the dark but to instruct us. I conclude that to understand the details of the narrative of the Fall nonliterally and symbolically is to fail to do justice to the purpose for which God gave us this revelation.

Both in Genesis 3 and elsewhere the Bible gives clear evidence that the serpent—to mention only one of the details discussed above—is to be understood literally. In Genesis 3:1 the serpent is considered as belonging to the animals God had created: "Now the serpent was more crafty than any of the wild animals the LORD God had made." From the same chapter (v. 14) we learn about God's punishment of the serpent, a punishment that indicates that an actual serpent was being described, not just a symbolic serpent:

> *Cursed are you above all the livestock*
> *and all the wild animals!*
> *You will crawl on your belly*
> *and you will eat dust*
> *all the days of your life.*

There is also a clear reference to an actual serpent in 2 Corinthians 11:3, "But I am afraid that just as Eve was deceived by the serpent's cunning, your minds may somehow be led astray from your sincere and pure devotion to Christ." That Paul is thinking here of Genesis 3 is obvious from his references to the serpent, his cunning, and the deception he practiced. The way Paul alludes to this passage indicates that he understood Genesis 3 not as referring to some totally unknown transgression depicted by veiled symbols, but as describing the deception of Eve by an actual serpent.

As was said, however, it is obvious that there was an evil power or being behind the serpent. The serpent in Genesis 3 is described as doing things that no mere serpent could do—talk—and as knowing things that no mere serpent could know—what God had said to Adam. In his conversation with Eve, the serpent contradicted God ("You will not surely die," v. 4), and attributed unworthy motives to God ("For

God knows that when you eat of it [the forbidden fruit] your eyes will be opened, and you will be like God," v. 5). The serpent's purpose in this conversation was to induce Eve to sin against God. So this was no mere serpent. Behind him was an evil being of some sort, who knew what God had said, who hated God, and who wished to tempt the woman to sin against God.

From the New Testament we learn that the evil power behind the serpent was the devil or Satan. In John 8:44 we hear Jesus saying to the Jews who were disputing with him,

> You are of your father the devil, and your will is to do your father's desires. He was a murderer from the beginning, and has nothing to do with the truth, because there is no truth in him. When he lies, he speaks according to his own nature, for he is a liar and the father of lies. (RSV)

The words "he was a murderer from the beginning" obviously refer to the story of the Fall, where the devil through the serpent brought about the fall into sin and the subsequent death of our first parents. The description of the devil as "the father of lies" again reminds us of the lying words of the serpent in Genesis 3: "You will not surely die." Behind the serpent, Jesus is implying, was the devil.

The identification of the serpent of Genesis 3 with Satan or the devil is explicit in two passages in the Book of Revelation. The first of these is 12:9, "The great dragon was hurled down—that ancient serpent called the devil or Satan, who leads the whole world astray." The second passage is 20:2, "He [the angel] seized the dragon, that ancient serpent, who is the devil, or Satan, and bound him for a thousand years."

We must therefore understand the serpent in Genesis 3 as an actual serpent who really talked (through the malicious power of the devil) but who was an instrument of Satan. Satan, in other words, used the serpent as his tool in leading our first parents to sin against God.[43]

The serpent did not direct himself to the man but to the woman—perhaps because the woman had not directly received God's command

---

43. The position that the serpent of Genesis 3 was an actual serpent Satan used as his instrument in the temptation of Adam and Eve is held by the following theologians: H. Bavinck, *Dogmatiek*, 3:9; Geerhardus Vos, *Biblical Theology*, p. 44; John Calvin, *Comm. on Genesis*, 1:142; L. Berkhof, *Systematic Theology*, p. 224; E. J. Young, *Genesis 3* (London: Banner of Truth, 1966), pp. 22-23; G. C. Aalders, *De Goddelijke Openbaring in de Eerste Drie Hoofdstukken van Genesis* (Kampen: Kok, 1932), pp. 485-88; Keil and Delitzsch, *Comm. on the Old Testament*, vol. 1, *The Pentateuch*, trans. James Martin (1861; Grand Rapids: Eerdmans, 1951), pp. 92-93; Johannes Fichtner, *"ophis,"* TDNT, 5:573.

about eating the forbidden fruit, but had heard about it from Adam. Possibly for this reason the woman would be the more susceptible to argumentation and doubt.

It is obvious that sin began in the heart of Eve already before she actually ate the forbidden fruit. One may note the following stages: The first thing that happened was that Satan, through the serpent, aroused *doubt* in Eve's mind when he said, "Did God really say, 'You must not eat from any tree in the garden'?" (v. 1). In the woman's reply we note the beginning of *resentment*: "The woman said to the serpent, 'We may eat fruit from the trees in the garden, but God did say, "You must not eat fruit from the tree that is in the middle of the garden, and you must not touch it, or you will die" ' " (vv. 2-3). Actually, God had not said that Adam and Eve could not touch this tree; Eve's mentioning this seems to suggest the beginning of resentment against what she now deemed to be an unfair restriction of their activities.

Doubt and resentment soon led to *unbelief*. When the serpent went on to say, "You will not surely die" (v. 4), Eve began to believe the serpent and to disbelieve God. Next the serpent aroused *pride*: "For God knows that when you eat of it your eyes will be opened, and you will be like God, knowing good and evil" (v. 5). Feeling that some greater height of God-likeness than she had previously attained had so far been denied her, and wanting in pride to reach that height, the woman was now ready for the final step. As she looked intently at the tree, *evil desire* was aroused. There was an appeal to the appetite ("the fruit of the tree was good for food"), to the eyes (it was "pleasing to the eye"), and once again to her pride (the fruit was "desirable for gaining wisdom"). The final step was outright *disobedience*: "she took some [of the fruit] and ate it. She also gave some to her husband, who was with her, and he ate it" (v. 6). Through these various stages, therefore, Satan succeeded in leading our first parents to sin against God.[44]

## THE RIDDLE OF SIN

The fact that we can discern these stages in the temptation and fall of our first parents, however, does not mean that we have in the Genesis narrative an explanation for the entrance of sin into the human world. What we have here is the biblical narrative of the origin of sin, but not an explanation for that origin. One of the most important things we must remember about sin, both in the life of man and in

---

44. Cf. H. Bavinck, *Dogmatiek*, 3:8; L. Berkhof, *Systematic Theology*, p. 223.

that of the angels, is that it is inexplicable. The origin of evil is, as Herman Bavinck puts it, one of the greatest riddles of life.[45]

One could say, of course, that the possibility of sinning was present in our first parents when they were created. Augustine put it negatively: Man as he was first created could be described as *posse non peccare*—that is, as a being who was able not to sin.[46] This statement implies, however, that the possibility of sinning was present in Adam and Eve at the beginning. But how this possibility became actuality is a mystery that we shall never be able to fathom. We shall never know how doubt first arose in Eve's mind. We shall never understand how a person who had been created in a state of rectitude, in a state of sinlessness, could begin to sin.

We can find no reason for sin in God's good creation or in the gifts he gave to man. Those gifts were of such a nature that Adam and Eve should have been able to resist the devil's temptation and remain obedient to God. We must acknowledge that they could not have remained standing in their moral integrity apart from the strength of the Holy Spirit who was dwelling within them.[47] But the point is: Adam and Eve could have and should have remained standing. Why they did not is not to be found in God's creation.

Neither can we say that God was the cause of the falling into sin of our first parents. How could God cause them to do what was contrary to his will? The very thought goes counter to everything the Bible teaches us about God. As James says, "Each one is tempted [to sin] when, by his own evil desire, he is dragged away and enticed" (1:14). Adam and Eve were enticed by their own desires to sin, but we shall never understand how or why.

We could say that the sinful deed had as its cause a sinful will, but what was the origin of this sinful will? How could a sinless will begin to will sinfully? Augustine expressed it well:

> Let no one, therefore, look for an efficient cause of the evil will; for it is not efficient, but deficient. . . . Now, to seek to discover the causes of these defections,—causes, as I have said, not efficient but deficient,—is as if someone sought to see darkness or to hear silence.[48]

One may speak, further, of the senselessness and "motivelessness" of sin. Every effort to view man's sin as part of a rational system

45. *Dogmatiek*, 3:33. For a more extensive discussion of this point, see Berkouwer's chapter, "The Riddle of Sin," in his *Sin*, pp. 13-48.
46. *On Rebuke and Grace*, 33.
47. Bavinck, *Dogmatiek*, 2:600-601.
48. *The City of God*, vol. 2 in *Nicene and Post-Nicene Fathers*, First Series (rpt.; Grand Rapids: Eerdmans, 1983), p. 230 (Bk. 12, Chap. 7).

must be repudiated.[49] One cannot make sense out of the senseless. Sin is simply inexplicable, and we have to leave it at that.

It remains true, of course, that the fall into sin of our first parents did not occur outside of God's providential permission. God did not cause man's fall—but he did permit it. This raises the difficult question of how God can permit things to happen that are against his will. Many years ago Augustine put it this way:

> This is the meaning of the statement, "The works of the Lord are great, well-considered in all his acts of will"—that in a strange and ineffable fashion even that which is done against his will [*contra eius voluntatem*] is not done without his will [*praeter eius voluntatem*].[50]

Sin is therefore against God's will but never outside of or beyond (*praeter*) God's will. God permitted the Fall to occur because in his omnipotence he could bring good even out of evil. But the fact that man's sin does not occur outside of the will of God neither excuses it nor explains it. Sin will always remain a riddle.

49. Berkouwer, *Sin*, p. 146. Cf. Bavinck, *Dogmatiek*, 3:54-55, where he calls sin foolish, absurd, unlawful, and irrational.
50. *Enchiridion*, ed. and trans. Albert C. Outler, vol. 7 in the Library of Christian Classics series (Philadelphia: Westminster Press, 1955), p. 399 (chap. 26.100). Cf. Calvin, *Inst.*, I.18.3.

# CHAPTER 8

# *The Spread of Sin*

## THE RESULTS OF THE FIRST SIN

After Adam and Eve had eaten of the forbidden fruit, the first result was great disappointment. Instead of feeling that they were like God, as the serpent had predicted, they were overwhelmed by a deep *sense of shame*: "Then the eyes of both of them were opened, and they realized they were naked; so they sewed fig leaves together and made coverings for themselves" (Gen. 3:7). Previously they had been aware of their nakedness, but had not been ashamed (2:25). Their sense of shame was the immediate response of a guilty conscience. Now, however, Adam and Eve both realized that they had done wrong, and so they contrived to cover themselves by sewing fig leaves together. "That the sense of shame should concentrate itself on that portion of the body which is marked by the organs of generation, no doubt has its deeper reason in this that man instinctively feels that the very fountain and source of human life is contaminated by sin."[1]

The next result of the first sin was *fear*. The man and his wife now hid from God; when God called, "Where are you?" Adam answered, "I was afraid . . ." (3:10). Consciousness of guilt had now brought fear—fear of what God might do to them as punishment for their sin.

But along with the fear came *evasion of responsibility.* What Adam actually said to God was, "I was afraid because I was naked; so I hid" (v. 10). What Adam should have said was that he was afraid because he knew that he had done wrong; instead, he attempted to cover up his guilt. Adam continued this evasion by blaming Eve (v. 12), who in turn blamed the serpent (v. 13). Neither the man nor the woman was willing to own up to personal responsibility in the guilt of this first sin.

1. H. C. Leupold, *Exposition of Genesis,* vol. 1 (Grand Rapids: Baker, 1953), p. 154.

**133**

We learn further from Genesis 3 that God *passed sentence* upon all three of the parties directly involved in the Fall (serpent, woman, man). According to the account, God cursed the serpent (v. 14), and, for Adam's sake, he also cursed the ground (v. 17); but the word *curse* is not used of the man and woman themselves. So, though we may speak of God's *curse* upon the serpent, we must refer to God's *sentence* or *judgment* upon the man and the woman.

Because the serpent was instrumental in the fall of man, a curse now rested upon him, indicating God's displeasure and wrath against man's first sin. God cursed the serpent above all cattle and wild animals: "You will crawl on your belly and you will eat dust all the days of your life" (v. 14). The words "You will crawl on your belly" may mean that the serpent had previously had a different mode of locomotion, but we cannot be sure of this. "You will eat dust" does not refer to the kind of food the serpent was to eat, but rather to the fact that when he is creeping on his belly the serpent is certain to get some dust into his mouth. However, the expression "to eat dust" is also intended to indicate that the serpent would now occupy the position of a defeated enemy.[2]

The words to the serpent now continue with what is often called the *Protevangelium* (the first gospel message) or the Mother Promise:

> *I will put enmity between you and the woman,*
> *    and between your seed and her seed;*
> *he shall bruise your head,*
> *    and you shall bruise his heel.* (v. 15, RSV)

Though these words occur as part of the curse upon the serpent, they clearly indicate the redemptive grace of God toward fallen man. This passage, in fact, bursts upon us like a rising sun dispelling darkness, gloom, and misery.

The words of this text lead us beyond the serpent to the evil power that was behind him: the devil or Satan. When Eve followed the advice of the serpent, she had, in effect, made a league of friendship with the devil. God now graciously substituted enmity for that friendship, in effect saying to Eve, Though you have just turned your back on me by eating of the forbidden fruit, I will still continue to be a friend to you; I will continue to be on your side. God's first response to human sin, therefore, is a response of grace.

This enmity between the woman and the serpent (or, rather, the

---

2. Note the references to enemies having "licked the dust" in Ps. 72:9, Isa. 49:23, and Mic. 7:17. The last-named passage specifically ties in this type of humiliation with that of a serpent: "They [the nations] will lick dust like a snake."

devil who was behind the serpent) is to continue into the future: "and between your seed and her seed." "Your seed" does not mean the literal animal offspring of the serpent, but rather those human beings who will share the devil's purpose and will therefore, like him, be enemies of God. This reminds us of Jesus' words to the Jews who were opposing him: "You belong to your father, the devil, and you want to carry out your father's desire" (John 8:44). "Her seed," on the other hand, means those of the woman's descendants who will be God's people—people who will believe God's promises and will live in harmony with his purposes. So in this part of the text the enmity between the woman and Satan is broadened to include enmity between two groups of people. The history of the world from now on will be a history of antithesis, of opposition, between the people of God (the seed of the woman) and the opponents of God (the seed of the serpent).

In the last part of the passage God seems to turn from the collective to the individual understanding of the two types of seed. "He ['her seed,' now thought of as an individual] shall bruise your head [the head of the serpent—or, rather, of the devil who stands behind the serpent]." Since we should understand "bruise" as meaning "crush" (NIV), this individual is said to be one who will totally defeat Satan or the devil. Though Adam and Eve, we presume, did not fully or clearly understand all this, from the rest of Scripture we learn that the one who was to give Satan the deathblow would be none other than our Lord Jesus Christ. So here already, in Genesis 3, we have the promise of the coming Redeemer.

"And you [the serpent—or, rather, the devil] shall bruise his heel [the heel of the woman's seed—that is, of Christ]." The imagery here is of a man stepping on a serpent's head to crush it, but getting his heel hurt in the process. So the coming Redeemer will have to suffer in the process of winning the victory over Satan (we think of the sufferings of our Lord, particularly on the cross), but he will conquer in the end.

In this beautiful passage we see the wonders of God's grace. Genesis 3:15, which is actually part of God's curse on the serpent, contains in seed form all that God intends to do for the redemption of those whose first parents fell into sin. All the rest of the Bible will be an unfolding of the contents of this marvelous promise.

The judgment of God on the woman is found in verse 16. One of the results of the first sin for the woman is pain in giving birth to children: "I will greatly increase your pains in childbearing; with pain you will give birth to children." The bearing of children will, of course, be a blessing—a fulfillment of the mandate given to our first parents to be fruitful and increase in number (Gen. 1:28). But the pain and discomfort involved in childbirth is a result of the Fall. The second half of the judgment reads, "Your desire will be for your husband, and he will rule over you." "Desire" here probably means the wife's longing for sexual fellowship with her husband; this will continue despite the pains that can be expected at the time of childbirth.

The statement "he will rule over you" tells us that one of the results of the Fall for the woman is that she will be in a position of subordination to her husband. The word translated "will rule" (*māshal*) is also used to describe the governing authority of a monarch. Because of the fall into sin, the harmonious relationship between husband and wife has become distorted. In place of the proper relationship in which, though the husband is the head of the wife and though he occupies a leadership role in the marriage, his wife still stands next to him in a position of equality as a "suitable helper" (Gen. 2:20), now the wife will stand under the husband as someone who is to be subjugated by him or subservient to him. Because of sin the ruling of the husband over the wife will tend to become tyrannical and domineering. In the cultures of many Oriental peoples, where wives have been treated by their husbands as not much more than slaves, we see one of the worst forms of this "ruling."[3] In the Christian community, needless to say, we must try to overcome this result of the Fall, and seek to restore the relationship between husband and wife to that which God originally intended.

We come now to the judgment of God on the man, found in Genesis 3:17-19. Though the judgment pronounced in these verses is addressed to the man, it is significant to note that all the elements of this judgment apply to the woman as well as to the man. First, God says to Adam, "Cursed is the ground because of you" (v. 17). This is the second curse: nature suffers along with humanity; it must share with humankind the results of sin. In this way human beings will be continually reminded of their transgressions against God, and of their need for repentance. The cursing of the ground means that there is a sense in which God will withdraw his favor from the earth—though, as Calvin reminds us, this will not be a total withdrawal;[4] such passages as "the earth is full of the goodness of the Lord" (Ps. 33:5, KJV) and "his [the Lord's] tender mercies are over all his works" (Ps. 145:9, KJV) assure us of that. Scripture describes the result of this cursing of the ground in three ways, which we will look at in turn.

3. Cf. G. Ch. Aalders, *Genesis,* vol. 1, trans. W. Heynen (Grand Rapids: Zondervan, 1981), pp. 108-9.
4. Calvin, *Comm. on Genesis,* trans. John King (Grand Rapids: Eerdmans, 1948), *ad loc.*

1. "Through painful toil you will eat of it [the ground] all the days of your life" (v. 17). The word translated "painful toil" (*'it-sābōn*) is the same word that was rendered "pains" in verse 16, which described the judgment on the woman. As the woman will bear children with pain, so the man will eat the produce of the ground with a painful kind of toil. Whereas Adam's work in the garden before the Fall had been most pleasant and delightful, from now on his work and the work of his descendants will be unpleasant, accompanied by toil and trouble.[5] Though this painful toil is one of the results of sin, these words still imply a blessing. For human beings will continue to eat what the ground brings forth; their lives will still be sustained. We may therefore note two elements in this judgment: (1) a continuity with the original arrangement—the man must continue to till the ground and the ground will continue to provide food for him; (2) a discontinuity from the original arrangement—the man's work will now be attended by hardship. We noted a similar situation in connection with the judgment on the woman, which had a continuity with the original arrangement—the woman would continue to bring forth children—but also a discontinuity—childbearing would now become very painful. In the judgments on the man and the woman, therefore, we can see both blessing and punishment.

2. "It [the ground] will produce thorns and thistles for you" (v. 18). Undesirable types of plants will now begin to spring up, and weeds will multiply, making the task of tilling the soil much more difficult than before. We note that only such aspects of the curse as apply to agriculture are here mentioned. But surely other types of results must be included as well, such as natural disasters—floods, earthquakes, and the like—and disease germs, viruses, and disease-spreading insects. Calvin put it this way: "The whole order of nature was subverted by the sin of man."[6] And we remember that Paul spoke of the "frustration" and "bondage to decay" to which the whole creation has been subjected because of sin (Rom. 8:20-21).

3. "By the sweat of your brow you will eat your food" (v. 19). Here we have a restatement of the "painful toil" of verse 17. Hard labor will now be the man's lot. Life will not be easy.

We come now to the last part of the judgment on the man: God tells him he will return to the ground from which he was taken—"for dust you are and to dust you will return" (v. 19). Since man had been

---

5. This does not mean, of course, that work as such will now become accursed. Work in itself is a blessing, as is evident from the fact that man worked in the garden before the Fall. But because of the Fall work will now become difficult and toilsome.
6. Calvin, *Comm. on Genesis*, 1:177.

formed from the dust of the ground (2:7), it is obvious that these words describe physical death. Though some theologians taught that man would have died anyway, whether he had sinned or not,[7] the fact that these words occur as part of God's judgment on man because of the first sin indicates that physical death is one of the results of sin. God warned that death would be one of the results of Adam's transgression in the so-called Probationary Command: "But you must not eat from the tree of the knowledge of good and evil, for when (or in the day that) you eat of it you will surely die" (Gen. 2:17). Though more than physical death was intended here,[8] physical death was certainly included, since this would be the obvious and primary meaning of the Hebrew verb *mûth* used in this passage.

The question might be asked: since God had said, "in the day that you eat of it you shall die" (KJV, NASB, RSV; Heb. *b^eyōm 'ªkāl^ekā mimmennû*), why did not Adam and Eve die in the physical sense on the very day that they ate the fruit? Some Reformed theologians, who understood this passage to mean precisely this, suggest that the execution of the death sentence was postponed because of God's grace, that is, his common grace.[9] It is not necessary, however, to understand the words of the Probationary Command in this way. Geerhardus Vos calls attention to the fact that the expression "in the day that you eat of it" is simply a Hebrew idiom meaning "as surely as you eat of it."[10] Therefore the fact that Adam and Eve did not die on the day they committed the first sin does not need to cause us difficulty.

The words of Genesis 3:19 indicate that from now on death in the physical sense would be inevitable for the human race. From the state of being "able not to die" (*posse non mori*) humankind had now entered upon the state of "not able not to die" (*non posse non mori*).[11]

We should add that since, according to Scripture, the deepest meaning of life is fellowship with God, the deepest meaning of death must be the disruption of the fellowship with God that man enjoyed

7. E.g., Celestius, Socinus, and Karl Barth (see my *The Bible and the Future*, rev. ed. [Grand Rapids: Eerdmans, 1982], p. 80).
8. Spiritual death—the disruption of man's fellowship with God—must also have been included. And, ultimately, unless God's grace should intervene, eternal death would result—that is, eternal separation from God's favor in the life to come (see ibid., p. 82).
9. E.g., Herman Bavinck, *Dogmatiek*, 3:159; Abraham Kuyper, *De Gemeene Gratie*, vol. 1 (Amsterdam: Höveker & Wormser, 1902), pp. 209-17; G. Ch. Aalders, *Genesis*, 1:93, 110-11; L. Berkhof, *Systematic Theology*, rev. and enl. ed. (Grand Rapids: Eerdmans, 1941), p. 670.
10. Geerhardus Vos, *Biblical Theology* (Grand Rapids: Eerdmans, 1948), pp. 48-49. Other biblical examples of this use of the phrase cited by Vos are 1 Kings 2:37 and Ex. 10:28.
11. Augustine, *On Rebuke and Grace*, 33.

before the Fall, and this disruption is spiritual death. Hence the death that came upon man and woman at the Fall must have included spiritual death—in this sense one could say that our first parents died immediately when the first sin occurred. As a further consequence, every human being since the Fall is born in a state of spiritual death (cf. Eph. 2:1-2). At the time of the Fall humankind also became subject to what we call eternal death—that is, eternal separation from the loving presence of God.

If the grace of God had not intervened, death in all three senses—physical, spiritual, and eternal—would have been the lot of every human being, including our first parents. But we thank God that his grace did intervene, beginning with our first parents. For already to them, as we have seen, God gave his gracious Mother Promise—and we have no reason to doubt that Adam and Eve accepted and believed that promise.

Something remains to be said about the last result of sin mentioned in this chapter: the expulsion of our first parents from the Garden of Eden. We find this described in verses 22-24:

> (22) And the LORD God said, "The man has now become like one of us, knowing good and evil. He must not be allowed to reach out his hand and take also from the tree of life and eat, and live forever." (23) So the LORD God banished him from the Garden of Eden to work the ground from which he had been taken. (24) After he drove the man out, he placed on the east side of the Garden of Eden cherubim and a flaming sword flashing back and forth to guard the way to the tree of life.

Some Bible scholars believe that God's statement, "The man has now become like one of us, knowing good and evil," is a kind of holy irony.[12] Webster defines irony as "the use of words to express something other than and especially the opposite of the literal meaning."[13] That is, God, in a kind of sarcastic way, is telling Adam and Eve that they have indeed attained what the serpent promised them: they have become like God; while saying this, however, God means exactly the opposite. Other interpreters, however, feel—and rightly so—that one should not speak of irony here, since such an understanding of God's words is to fail to honor the majesty and holiness of God.[14]

What God is saying here is this: "Man wished to be like 'one of

---

12. Calvin, *Comm. on Genesis*, 1:182; Vos, *Biblical Theology*, p. 43.
13. *Webster's Ninth New Collegiate Dictionary* (Springfield: Merriam-Webster, 1983), p. 639.
14. Keil and Delitzsch, *Biblical Commentary on the Old Testament*, vol. 1, *The Pentateuch*, trans. James Martin (Grand Rapids: Eerdmans, 1951), pp. 106-7; Aalders, *Genesis*, 1:112-13; Leupold, *Genesis*, 1:180.

us.'[15] Man desired to be so by assuming a divine prerogative: that of determining for himself what was good and what was evil. But this is something only I may do. And I had told man what was good and evil in my sight. But he refused to obey my command. Instead, he took it into his own hands to determine what was good. Thus he became, as it were, his own god. He became like me in the wrong way, in the way of sin and rebellion.[16] Man now knows good and evil in the way that I forbade."[17]

For this reason Adam and Eve were banished from the Garden of Eden. By their sin they had forfeited the privilege of remaining in the garden, and eating of the tree of life. God therefore now said, "He [man] must not be allowed to reach out his hand and take also from the tree of life and eat, and live forever" (v. 22). The fruit of the tree of life would have enabled human beings, in a way that is not further described here, to continue to live forever, without dying. Since Adam and Eve had now become sinners, and since one of the results of sin, as we saw, is physical death, they could not be allowed to stay in the Garden of Eden and to eat of this tree. And so they—and their children—were permanently banished from Paradise.

Yet even here we may see evidence of the grace of God. For if fallen man had continued to eat of the tree of life, he would have lived forever in a sin-torn and sin-defaced body, which would have been a great calamity. We thank God that through the work of Christ we may be delivered from "the body of our humiliation" and may look forward to receiving from Christ at the final resurrection a new body that will be conformed to "the body of his glory" (Phil. 3:21, ASV). And we who are in Christ also thank God that on the new earth, in the life to come, we may look forward to eating once again of that tree of life from which our first parents were driven away (Rev. 22:2).

## THE UNIVERSALITY OF SIN

As a result of the Fall, sin has become universal; except for Jesus Christ no person who ever lived on this earth has been free from sin.

15. Many biblical scholars, both ancient and modern, see in this reference to both the singularity ("God said") and the plurality ("one of us") of God a hint of what will later be developed as the doctrine of the Trinity, finding here an analogy to the words of Gen. 1:26, "Then God said, 'Let us make man....'"

16. One could say that in listening to the serpent our first parents were accepting Satan's perversion of the image of God. They were trying to become "like God" in Satan's way.

17. Man should have known good and evil in the way God knows it: namely, by abstaining from evil. Instead, he now knew good and evil in the wrong way: by committing evil.

This sad fact is acknowledged even by those who are neither adherents of Christianity nor believers in the Bible.

The recognition that there is something wrong with the moral nature of man is found in all religions. In primitive religions many offerings, some of them even human sacrifices, are made to propitiate the gods for man's wrongdoing. The Koran, the sacred book of Islam, admits the universal sinfulness of man, understanding this sinfulness as being a violation of the will of a personal god. In Hinduism no personal god is recognized, and therefore sin is considered to be an illusion; yet the sacred books of Hinduism have much to say about sin, and prescribe many penances by which sin may be removed. Buddhism totally denies the existence of God; yet it affirms the universality of sin—for the Buddhist sin consists essentially of desire, either any desire or particularly selfish desire.

Most philosophers also affirm that the tendency to evil is found in all human beings. Plato, for example, taught that people do wrong when they follow their appetites and passions instead of being ruled by their intellects. Immanuel Kant believed that there is in all human persons a radical evil (*das radikale Böse*), which invariably leads them to do wrong.

Man's inevitable drift toward wrongdoing is also recognized in literature. Such well-known writers of fiction as Fyodor Dostoyevski, Aldous Huxley, George Orwell, William Faulkner, Albert Camus, Graham Greene, and William Golding all describe human nature as basically flawed, as imperfect, as inclined to various types of evil, hypocrisy, and sin. Two recent volumes of nonfiction have made a similar point. In *Whatever Became of Sin?*[18] Dr. Karl Menninger affirms that, though the word *sin* has largely disappeared from our vocabulary, sin, both individual and collective, is still very much in evidence in our present-day culture. Still more recently, M. Scott Peck, like Menninger a psychiatrist, has written an unsettling book entitled *The People of the Lie*.[19] Peck's main thesis is that evil is far more widespread than most of us think. Evil, he affirms, is not found only among criminals, whose atrocious deeds are widely publicized by the media; it is found in the lives of most people who want to be thought good but whose "goodness" is mere pretense. These are people—and many of us are among them—whose lives are filled with various devices for covering up and refusing to acknowledge their sins; hence Peck calls them "the people of the lie."

Granted, many of the groups and individuals described above

18. New York: Hawthorn Books, 1973.
19. New York: Simon and Schuster, 1983.

would not call this moral deficiency *sin* in the biblical sense; namely, transgression of the will of a holy God. Yet they do recognize that there is something radically wrong with human nature today.

The Bible clearly teaches the universality of sin—in the sense of rebellion against God's commandments. After the fall of man has been recorded in Genesis 3, the narrative goes on to describe the first murder: Cain's killing of his brother Abel. As the history continues, we learn how sin spread and increased among humankind until it finally reached such an intensity that the judgment of the flood became necessary. At the time of the flood "the LORD saw how great man's wickedness on the earth had become, and that every inclination of the thoughts of his heart was only evil all the time" (Gen. 6:5). The flood, however, did not basically change the human heart, for even afterward God said, "Never again will I curse the ground because of man, even though every inclination of his heart is evil from childhood" (Gen. 8:21).

Many other Old Testament passages convey the thought of the universality of sin, but I will mention only a few. An incidental reference is found in Solomon's prayer at the dedication of the temple: "When they [the people of Israel] sin against you [God]—for there is no one who does not sin . . ." (1 Kings 8:46). In the Book of Job we find these words: "Who can bring a clean thing out of an unclean? There is not one" (Job 14:4, RSV). Many references to the universal sinfulness of man are found in the Psalms. Note, for example, the following: "If you, O LORD, kept a record of sins, O LORD, who could stand?" (Ps. 130:3); "Do not bring your servant into judgment, for no one living is righteous before you" (Ps. 143:2). From the Book of Proverbs we glean this passage: "Who can say, 'I have kept my heart pure; I am clean and without sin'?" (Prov. 20:9). And from Ecclesiastes: "There is not a righteous man on earth who does what is right and never sins" (Eccl. 7:20).

The New Testament also clearly teaches that sin is universal. When Jesus said to Nicodemus, "I tell you the truth, unless a man is born again, he cannot see the kingdom of God" (John 3:3), he was implying that man's nature is now so evil that a spiritual rebirth is necessary. In the opening chapters of his Epistle to the Romans, Paul describes the universality of sin in vivid strokes; his indictment culminates in these words:

> Now we know that whatever the law says, it says to those who are under the law, so that every mouth may be silenced and the whole world held accountable to God. Therefore no one will be declared righteous in his sight by observing the law; rather, through the law we become conscious of sin. (Rom. 3:19-20)

In fact, says Paul, "All have sinned and fall short of the glory of God" (Rom. 3:23). Not only are unbelievers "children of wrath"—that is, objects of God's wrath because of their sin—but believers are also in this state by nature: "We all once lived in the passions of our flesh, following the desires of body and mind, and so we were by nature children of wrath, like the rest of mankind" (Eph. 2:3, RSV). James recognizes the universal sinfulness of man: "We all stumble in many ways" (Jas. 3:2). And the language of the apostle John on this point is crystal clear: "If we claim to be without sin, we deceive ourselves and the truth is not in us. . . . If we claim we have not sinned, we make him [God] out to be a liar and his word has no place in our lives" (1 John 1:8, 10).

## ORIGINAL SIN

We must now consider the question of original sin, which has always been an essential aspect of the Christian doctrine of man. First, I should point out that we must distinguish original sin from actual sin. Original sin is the sinful state and condition in which every human being is born; actual sin, however, is the sins of act, word, or thought that human beings commit. Later we shall come back to a fuller consideration of actual sin.

We use the expression "original sin" for two reasons: (1) because sin had its origin at the time of the origin of the human race, and (2) because the sin that we call "original" is the source of our actual sins (though not in such a way as to take away our responsibility for the sins we commit).

Before I set forth the doctrine of original sin, we should note that many recent theologians reject that doctrine in the traditional sense. The Christian church has traditionally taught that the Fall was a historical event in which Adam and Eve rebelled against God by eating from the forbidden tree. Because of this first sin, all of Adam and Eve's descendants are now born with a corrupt nature and are under a sentence of condemnation because of their connection with Adam, who, in committing the first sin, acted as their head and representative. However, recent theologians have taught otherwise.

I have previously mentioned Karl Barth (1886–1968), whose denial of the historical Fall was discussed earlier,[20] but quote here two statements that clearly show his position:

---

20. See above, p. 50.

In the matter of human disobedience and depravity there is no "earlier" in which man was not yet a transgressor and as such innocent.[21]

There was never a golden age. It makes no sense to look back longingly to one. Primordial man was a sinner "from the beginning."[22]

G. C. Berkouwer summarizes Barth's view as follows: "Original sin does not involve a transfer (in time) from integrity to corruption, but Adam is *exemplarily* the representative of all who followed him."[23]

Emil Brunner (1889–1966) similarly denies the historicity of the Fall.[24] In *The Christian Doctrine of Creation and Redemption* he says that the Augustinian teaching on original sin is "a perversion of the Biblical doctrine of Sin, and of the genuine Christian truth about sin."[25] Though Brunner wishes to maintain the idea that sin is a dominant force in human life and that all human beings are connected in the solidarity of sin, he clearly rejects the traditional view of original sin. In fact, he says of Romans 5:12 that

> it does not refer to the transgression of Adam in which all his descendants share; but it states the fact that "Adam's" descendants are involved in death, because they themselves commit sin.[26]

Rudolf Bultmann (1884–1976), well known for his program of demythologization, believes that the traditional doctrine of original sin should be eliminated as mythological and therefore unacceptable to modern man.[27]

Reinhold Niebuhr (1893–1971) also rejects the historicity of the Fall.[28] Theodore Minnema says that in Niebuhr's view

> original sin is defined within the structure of self-consciousness. . . .
> The interpreting of original sin with respect to the complexities of the moral consciousness of man substantially alters the traditional and evangelical doctrine of original sin. By original sin Niebuhr does not mean evil in its entire sweep of history beginning with the fall of Adam.[29]

21. *Die Kirchliche Dogmatik*, IV/1 (Zürich: Zollikon, 1953), p. 551, quoted in G. C. Berkouwer, *The Triumph of Grace in the Theology of Karl Barth*, trans. Harry Boer (Grand Rapids: Eerdmans, 1956), p. 83.
22. *Kirchliche Dogmatik*, IV/1, p. 567, quoted in Berkouwer, *Triumph*, pp. 83-84.
23. Berkouwer, *Triumph*, p. 84.
24. See above, pp. 52, 57-58.
25. P. 103.
26. Emil Brunner, *The Christian Doctrine of Creation and Redemption*, trans. Olive Wyon (Philadelphia: Westminster Press, 1952), p. 104.
27. Philip E. Hughes, *Scripture and Myth* (London: Tyndale Press, 1956), p. 7.
28. *The Nature and Destiny of Man*, vol. 1 (New York: Scribner, 1941), pp. 267-68.
29. "Reinhold Niebuhr," in *Creative Minds in Contemporary Theology*, ed. Philip E. Hughes (Grand Rapids: Eerdmans, 1966), pp. 386-87.

The question of original sin has stirred some recent developments in Roman Catholic theology as well. "Since the early fifties," says George Vandervelde, "Roman Catholic publications on the subject of original sin have been issued in a constant stream, and as yet the discussion shows no signs of abating."[30] The immediate occasion for this proliferation of literature, he continues, is

> the gradual erosion of the framework that seems indispensable for the traditional doctrine of original sin, a framework that was never at issue until modern times. This framework consists essentially of a static view of man and his world: the world and man proceed ready-made from God's hands; all men originate from a single human pair; historical development is orientated to and bound by its beginning; a primordial fall has catastrophic and historically irreversible consequences for all men.
> . . . The contemporary discussion of the doctrine of original sin presupposes that this stable framework has been eroded and finally washed away by a dynamic, evolutionary world view.
> The "good creation" lies not at the beginning, but at the end of history. Within this view there is hardly room for a pristine paradise, much less for a primordial fall with catastrophic consequences for all men. Thus the mainstays of the traditional doctrine of original sin have crumbled.[31]

Vandervelde goes on to discuss the reinterpretations of the doctrine of original sin found in the writings of A. Vanneste and U. Baumann, two contemporary Roman Catholic theologians who reject the historicity of the Fall.

Three recent Roman Catholic publications have defended this new and radically different interpretation of the doctrine of original sin. One is the *New Catechism,* subtitled "Catholic Faith for Adults," published originally in Dutch in 1966 and issued in an English translation in 1967. Denying that there was a historical Fall and that creation was different before man sinned, the authors of this catechism maintain that "original sin is the sin of mankind as a whole (including myself) insofar as it affects every man."[32]

Another Dutch book, translated into English in 1968 as *Evolution and the Doctrine of Original Sin,* was written by S. Trooster, a professor in a Roman Catholic theological seminary. According to the author, "evolution has utterly destroyed the Eden-myth and the Adam-myth." Further, "acceptance of the modern viewpoint . . . eliminates the possibility of accounting for the genesis of evil in the world on the basis

---

30. *Original Sin* (Amsterdam: Rodopi, 1975), p. 42.
31. Ibid., pp. 42-43.
32. *A New Catechism: Catholic Faith for Adults,* trans. Kevin Smyth (New York: Herder and Herder, 1967), pp. 267, 269.

of sin committed by the first man."[33] Yet, while he rejects the historicity of the Fall, Trooster wishes to preserve the "reality" of original sin.

Shortly afterward, another Roman Catholic theologian, Herbert Haag, wrote in German a book that was translated *Is Original Sin in Scripture?*[34] From the introduction by Bruce Vawter we learn that the Darwinian revolution lies in the background of this book (p. 11). Here again we have a complete reinterpretation of the doctrine of original sin:

> The idea that Adam's descendants are automatically sinners because of the sin of their ancestor, and that they are already sinners when they enter the world, is foreign to Holy Scripture.
> No man enters the world a sinner. . . . Consequently, he is not at birth, as is often maintained, an enemy of God and a child of God's wrath. A man becomes a sinner only through his own individual and responsible action.[35]

Given such a reinterpretation, this doctrine, even under the label of "original sin," no longer describes original sin. What the authors mentioned above understand by original sin is really actual sin: the following of "Adam's" example, or the deliberate sinning of the members of the human race from the very beginning. We could then ask, But why do human beings invariably sin? How can we then account for the sad situation recognized even by Emil Brunner, namely, that sin is "a dominant force [in human life], and . . . that all men are connected in the solidarity of sin . . ."?[36]

Earlier I dealt with the question of the historicity of the Fall and the interpretation of the narrative of the Fall found in Genesis 3. In that discussion I took the position that the narrative of the Fall does indeed describe an event that happened in history, and that the details of the narrative should not be allegorized but should be understood literally. I based this interpretation, following the well-known dictum that Scripture best interprets Scripture, primarily on New Testament

33. Glen Rock: Newman Press, 1968, trans. John A. Ter Haar (orig. pub. in Dutch in 1965), jacket, p. 18.
34. New York: Sheed and Ward, 1969, trans. Dorothy Thompson (orig. pub. in German in 1966).
35. Ibid., pp. 106-7. We should note, however, that the reinterpretation of the doctrine of original sin found in these recent authors is not all that new. It is found already, e.g., in F. R. Tennant's *The Origin and Propagation of Sin* (Cambridge: Cambridge Univ. Press, 1902). Tennant, like the authors just quoted, rejects the historicity of the Fall and the traditional doctrine of original sin on the basis of the evolutionary view of the origin of man.
36. *Doctrine of Creation*, p. 103.

teachings, particularly those found in the writings of Paul, which clearly point to a historical Fall.

The authors mentioned above, however, base their reinterpretation of the doctrine of original sin primarily on evidence from the natural sciences about the age of the earth, the age of man, and the nature of primitive man. Over against this method of interpreting Scripture, the historic Reformed position has been that the content of the Christian faith may not be determined by the results of natural science, valuable though these results may be, but must be drawn primarily from the Bible itself.

It is, of course, very important that we keep informed about the growing results of scientific investigation in the areas of paleontology, geology, biology, and physical anthropology. And there have been times when our understanding of the Bible has indeed been modified by conclusions derived from natural science—witness the Copernican revolution of the sixteenth century. One result of recent scientific research that most Christian scholars would now concede is that the earth is much older than was formerly believed, and that man has been on the earth for a much longer time than was previously thought.[37] But this does not at all mean that these conclusions (obviously tentative in nature) about the age of the earth and the age of man contradict the teachings of the Bible. As John Jefferson Davis puts it, "the conceptions of human origins as presented by Genesis and by [physical] anthropology, when both are properly understood, are not in contradiction, but form a complementary whole."[38]

Since the New Testament clearly teaches that the fall of man was an event in history, and that there was indeed a first human pair whose sin affected all subsequent history, we must continue to maintain the historic doctrine of original sin. The difficulties that recent scientific research has placed before us in connection with the Genesis narrative[39] must therefore be considered problems with which we must live,

37. Estimates of the age of man vary from 30,000 to 50,000 years or more. See Bernard Ramm, *Offense to Reason* (San Francisco: Harper & Row, 1985), p. 113. See also William Smalley and Marie Fetzer, *Modern Science and Christian Faith* (Wheaton: Van Kampen, 1950), pp. 185-87.

38. "Genesis, Inerrancy, and the Antiquity of Man," in *Inerrancy and Common Sense,* ed. Roger Nicole and J. Ramsey Michaels (Grand Rapids: Baker, 1980), pp. 158-59.

39. One such problem, e.g., is that "of the transition from Genesis 3 to Genesis 4, where the immediate descendants of Adam already exhibit a highly developed level of culture" (ibid., p. 143). One answer is that Moses described "the environment of the first man using the picture of ancient man common in Moses' day" (David Holwerda, "The Historicity of Genesis 1-3," *Reformed Journal* 17, no. 8 [Oct. 1967]:13). See the rest of the article for a further development of this point.

in the hope that some day adequate solutions will be found, rather than information that overthrows what the Bible clearly teaches.[40]

As we proceed, then, to set forth the doctrine of original sin, we need to remember Herman Bavinck's comment: "The doctrine of original sin is one of the most important but also one of the most difficult topics in dogmatics."[41] The reason why this doctrine is so important is twofold: (1) the Bible teaches it, and (2) it is only when we understand man's condition by nature (that is, apart from God's grace) that we can appreciate his need for the rebirth and total renewal that redemption in Christ brings about.

The doctrine of original sin tells us what are the results of Adam's sin for us.[42] Because of Adam's sin, every human being is now born in a sinful state. The question of how sin is transmitted from Adam to us will be taken up later in this chapter.

Original sin includes both *guilt* and *pollution*. Guilt is a judicial or legal concept describing one's relationship to the law—in this case, specifically to God's law. Guilt is the state of deserving condemnation or of being liable to punishment because the law has been violated. When we say that original sin includes guilt, we do not mean that each of us is considered personally responsible for what Adam did. You and I cannot be held directly responsible for something someone else has done. But the doctrine of original sin does mean that we are involved in the guilt of Adam's sin because he acted as our representative when he committed the first sin. Earlier[43] I mentioned that though we can no longer hold to the doctrine that God made a covenant of works with man before the Fall, we must maintain the truth that Adam was our head and representative.

The apostle Paul, in particular, teaches that Adam is our representative. In 1 Corinthians 15 Paul draws a contrast between Adam and Christ—a contrast, however, that also involves a certain similarity. Though the results of our connections with Adam and Christ are diverse, yet both Adam and Christ are described as heads through whom the woe or weal involved comes to us: "For as in Adam all die, so in Christ all will be made alive" (v. 22). Paul focuses the parallel between Adam and Christ in verse 45: "So it is written: 'The first

---

40. On this topic see also Bernard Ramm, *Christian View*, and Philip E. Hughes, *Christianity and the Problem of Origins* (Philadelphia: Presbyterian and Reformed, 1964).
41. *Dogmatiek*, 3:89 [trans. mine].
42. Though Eve sinned in Paradise as well as Adam, original sin is particularly associated with Adam's sin because he was the first head of the human race. When Adam sinned, he acted as our representative. Later the question of the headship of Adam will be taken up in greater detail.
43. See above, p. 121.

man Adam became a living being'; the last Adam, a life-giving spirit."
When Paul here calls Christ "the last Adam" (*eschatos Adam*), he
implies that Adam stands toward us in a relationship analogous to
that of Christ. Adam is our head in one sense, while Christ is our
head in another sense.

The fact that Adam was our head and representative is most fully
developed in Romans 5:14-18. In verse 14 Paul calls Adam "a type
[*typos*] of the one who was to come" (RSV). How could Adam be a
type of Christ? Obviously not in the sense that he acted as a deliverer
of his people (as did, for example, Moses, who was also a type of
Christ), nor in the sense that Adam was an example after whom we
should pattern our lives. Adam was a type of Christ in the sense that
he, like Christ, was our head and representative; what he did affected
all of us who are in him—and that includes all human beings. In
verse 16 Paul says, "For the judgment following one trespass [the sin
of Adam] brought condemnation" (RSV). Here again it becomes crystal clear that Adam acted as our representative when he sinned, since
we all have been placed under condemnation (*katakrima*) because of
his sin. Verse 18 reads as follows: "Then as one man's trespass [or,
one trespass] led to condemnation for all men,[44] so one man's act of
righteousness [or, one act of righteousness] leads to acquittal and life
for all men" (RSV). In this passage it is clearly said that condemnation
rests upon all human beings because of Adam's sin. But Paul here
draws a parallel between what happens to us because of our relation
to Adam and what happens to us because of our relation to Christ:
through Christ we receive "acquittal and life" (lit., "justification of
life," *dikaiōsin zōēs*). As we have received condemnation through Adam,
so we receive justification through Christ. Again we see the analogy
between Adam and Christ. If Christ acted representatively for us, so
did Adam. If Christ was and is our head, Adam must also have been
our head.

By *original guilt*, then (the guilt involved in original sin), we mean
that we deserve condemnation because Adam, our head and representative, broke God's law.

Another aspect of original sin is *pollution*. Pollution, in distinction from guilt, is a moral concept; it has to do with our moral condition rather than with our status before the law. We can define *original
pollution* (the pollution involved in original sin) as the corruption of

---

44. The Greek text here is difficult to render into English. Translated literally, it reads:
"So then, therefore, as through one trespass to all men to condemnation. . . ." The ASV
adds the words "the judgment came" to make the meaning clear: "So then as through
one trespass *the judgment came* unto all men to condemnation."

our nature that is the result of sin and produces sin.[45] As a necessary implication of our involvement in Adam's guilt, all human beings are born in a state of corruption. We should distinguish between two aspects of original pollution: *pervasive depravity* and *spiritual inability.*

What I prefer to call *pervasive depravity* has been traditionally known in Reformed theology as "total depravity"—a term that has often been misunderstood. Negatively, the concept does not mean: (1) that every human being is as thoroughly depraved as he or she can possibly become; (2) that unregenerate people do not have a conscience by means of which they can distinguish between good and evil; (3) that unregenerate people will invariably indulge in every conceivable form of sin; or (4) that unregenerate people are unable to perform certain actions that are good and helpful in the sight of others.[46] Since to many people "total depravity" suggests these misunderstandings, I prefer "pervasive depravity."

*Pervasive depravity,* then, means that (1) the corruption of original sin extends to every aspect of human nature: to one's reason and will as well as to one's appetites and impulses; and (2) there is not present in man by nature love to God as the motivating principle of his life.

What is the scriptural proof for the doctrine of pervasive depravity? Actually, this doctrine underlies all of New Testament teaching. Jesus' insistence that unless one is born again he cannot see the kingdom of God (John 3:3) implies that human beings are unable, in their natural, unregenerate state, even to see the kingdom of God, let alone enter it. The entire New Testament message is addressed to sinners who do not love God by nature, who do not love one another, and who need to be radically changed by the Holy Spirit before they will be able to do what is pleasing in God's sight.

But let us look at some specific passages. An Old Testament text that comes to mind in this connection is Jeremiah 17:9, "The heart [the innermost aspect of man] is deceitful above all things, and desperately corrupt; who can understand it?" (RSV). Two passages from the Gospels are relevant to this issue. Jesus, in a dispute with the Pharisees about the necessity of washing one's hands before eating, explains that it is not what goes into a man but what comes out of a man that defiles him: "For from within, out of men's hearts, come evil thoughts, sexual immorality, theft, murder, adultery, greed, malice, deceit, lewdness, envy, slander, arrogance and folly. All these evils

---

45. Augustine called the pollution involved in original sin both the daughter and the mother of sin (*On Marriage and Concupiscence,* I.27).

46. We must remember that there is such a thing as common grace, by which God restrains sin in unregenerate people to a certain extent (see Chap. 10).

come from inside and make a man 'unclean' " (Mark 7:21-23). In a disputation with the Jews in connection with the healing of a man on the Sabbath day, Jesus said, "I know that you do not have the love of God in your hearts" (John 5:42).

A number of passages in the Pauline epistles teach the doctrine of pervasive depravity. One is Romans 7:18, "For I know that nothing good dwells within me, that is, in my flesh. I can will what is right, but I cannot do it" (RSV). We should note here that although Paul does not always use the word *flesh* in a bad sense, it is characteristic of his writing that he often uses it to denote the willing instrument of sin. In this passage and the one next quoted, therefore, *flesh* does not refer to man's physical body, but rather designates his total nature when it is under the domination or enslavement of sin. This concept of *flesh*, in other words, is precisely the biblical way of describing what I have called pervasive depravity.

The other passage that speaks of the flesh is Romans 8:7a, "For the mind that is set on the flesh is hostile to God" (RSV). Note that this text confirms the second point made under the definition of pervasive depravity, namely, that man by nature does not love God but is hostile toward him.

Another vivid description of pervasive depravity is found in Ephesians 4:17-19:

> So I tell you this, and insist on it in the Lord, that you must no longer live as the Gentiles do, in the futility of their thinking. They are darkened in their understanding and separated from the life of God because of the ignorance that is in them due to the hardening of their hearts. Having lost all sensitivity, they have given themselves over to sensuality so as to indulge in every kind of impurity, with a continual lust for more.

To the same effect are Paul's words in Titus 1:15-16:

> To the pure, all things are pure, but to those who are corrupted and do not believe, nothing is pure. In fact, both their minds and consciences are corrupted. They claim to know God, but by their actions they deny him. They are detestable, disobedient, and unfit for doing anything good.

In another epistle, however, Paul tells us that even those who are now believers were at one time in the same state of depravity as these wicked Gentiles:

> And you [the believers in Ephesus, or, possibly, throughout Asia Minor] he made alive, when you were dead through the trespasses and sins in which you once walked, following the course of this world, following the prince of the power of the air, the spirit that is now at work in the sons of disobedience. Among these we all once lived in the passions of our

flesh, following the desires of body and mind, and so we were by nature children of wrath, like the rest of mankind. (Eph. 2:1-3, RSV)

"Children of wrath," as was observed earlier, means the objects of God's wrath. In other words, Paul is saying, even believers are by nature, apart from God's renewing grace, so evil and depraved that they are rightly the objects of the wrath of God.

It is important to remember that the passages just quoted describe not the believer who through the working of God's Holy Spirit is now in Christ but the human being as he is by nature, unregenerate man. The doctrine of pervasive depravity, in other words, is not a description of the regenerate person or of the Christian believer, but of the natural man.[47]

The second aspect of original pollution is *spiritual inability*, traditionally called "total inability." That every person is born in a state of spiritual inability is another result of Adam's sin. This inability does not mean that the unregenerate person by nature is unable to do good in any sense of the word.[48] Because of God's common grace, as we shall see later, the development of sin in history and society is restrained. The unregenerate person can still do certain kinds of good and can exercise certain kinds of virtue. Yet even such good deeds are neither prompted by love to God, nor done in voluntary obedience to the will of God.

When we speak about man's *spiritual inability*, we mean two things: (1) the unregenerate person cannot do, say, or think that which totally meets with God's approval, and therefore totally fulfills God's law; and (2) the unregenerate person is unable apart from the special working of the Holy Spirit to change the basic direction of his or her life from sinful self-love to love for God. "Spiritual inability" is really only another way of describing the doctrine of "pervasive depravity," this time with an emphasis on the spiritual impotence of the will. Needless to say, these two concepts overlap in meaning.

What is the scriptural proof for the doctrine of spiritual inability? This doctrine, too, underlies all of New Testament teaching. The New Testament's insistence on man's need for rebirth, spiritual renewal, and sanctification underscores man's inability by nature to turn to God in repentance and faith and to live a life that totally pleases God. But let us again look at some specific passages.

47. On the question of whether the believer should still be called "totally depraved," see my *The Christian Looks at Himself*, rev. ed. (Grand Rapids: Eerdmans, 1977), pp. 47-48.
48. Since the expression "total inability" suggests to many people that the unregenerate person cannot do any kind of good whatsoever, and since this is not what the expression means, I prefer the term "spiritual inability."

We turn first to the Gospels, specifically the Gospel of John. Here Jesus said to Nicodemus, "I tell you the truth, unless a man is born again, he cannot see the kingdom of God. . . . Unless a man is born of water and the Spirit, he cannot enter the kingdom of God" (3:3, 5). Nicodemus needed to be told that a person can neither see nor enter the kingdom of God that Jesus founded unless a radical change should have taken place in him, a change here called a new birth. In John 6:44 Jesus said to some Jews who were arguing with him, "No one can come to me unless the Father who sent me draws him," thus expressing in vivid terms the inability of human beings to turn to Christ in their own strength. In the allegory of the vine and the branches Jesus further described the inability of man to bear spiritual fruit apart from him:

> Remain in me, and I will remain in you. No branch can bear fruit by itself; it must remain in the vine. Neither can you bear fruit unless you remain in me.
> I am the vine; you are the branches. If a man remains in me and I in him, he will bear much fruit; apart from me you can do nothing. (15:4-5)

We find more evidence for the doctrine of spiritual inability in Paul's writings. In Romans 7:18-19 Paul highlights in graphic terms the impotence of men and women by nature, telling us that even if such persons wish to do what is good and right, they still are not able to do it:

> For I know that nothing good dwells within me, that is, in my flesh. I can will what is right, but I cannot do it. For I do not do the good I want, but the evil I do not want is what I do. (RSV)

Romans 8:7-8 sets forth man's spiritual inability in bold relief: "For the mind that is set on the flesh is hostile to God; it does not submit to God's law, indeed it cannot; and those who are in the flesh [that is, under the enslavement of the flesh] cannot please God" (RSV).

Other Pauline passages stress the same thought. Just as Jesus said that apart from spiritual rebirth man cannot even see the kingdom of God, Paul says that the natural man[49] can neither understand nor accept what God's Spirit teaches: "The man without the Spirit does not accept the things that come from the Spirit of God, for they are foolishness to him, and he cannot understand them, because they are spiritually discerned" (1 Cor. 2:14). In a passage in which he speaks about the ministry of the apostles and other Christian workers, Paul further describes the inability of man apart from God's strength to

---

49. The term "natural man" as used here means the unregenerate person.

fulfill his calling as a Christian worker: "We dare to say such things because of the confidence we have in God through Christ. Not that we are in any way confident of doing anything by our own resources— our ability comes from God" (2 Cor. 3:4-5, Phillips). No more striking way of expressing our spiritual impotence could be found than to say that we are by nature spiritually dead; this is precisely what Paul says about the former state of believers in Ephesians 2:4-5: "But because of his great love for us, God, who is rich in mercy, made us alive with Christ even when we were dead in transgressions."

As we have seen, Scripture has a lot to say about original sin. Yet, even as believers, we often fail to emphasize this teaching. We need to recognize the necessity of a thorough understanding of the doctrine of original sin. As Philip Hughes says,

> Original sin, however mysterious its nature may be, tells us that the reality of sin is something far deeper than the mere outward commission of sinful deeds. ... It tells us that there is an inner root of sinfulness which corrupts man's true nature and from which his sinful deeds spring. Like a deadly poison, sin has penetrated to and infected the very center of man's being: hence his need for the total experience of rebirth by which, through the grace of God in Christ Jesus, the restoration of his true manhood is effected.[50]

## THE TRANSMISSION OF SIN

Earlier in this chapter we discussed the headship of Adam and the fact that we all stand under condemnation because of our involvement in Adam's sin. But now the question arises, What is the precise nature of the relationship between Adam and his descendants? In what way has Adam's sinfulness and guilt been transmitted to us?

To this difficult question various answers have been given. Some theologians deny that there is any connection between Adam's sin and our own sins. The most prominent advocate of this view was Pelagius, a British monk and theologian who settled in Rome about the year 400 A.D. According to Pelagius and his followers there is no necessary connection between Adam's sin and the sins of his descendants. Adam was created neutral: neither good nor bad. Man today is born in the same condition. There is no such thing as original sin; there is no transmission of guilt from Adam to us, and neither is there any transmission of pollution. Sin is not a condition into which one is born;

---

50. "Another Dogma Falls," *Christianity Today* 13, no. 17 (May 23, 1969):13. This need is also affirmed in Thomas M. Gregory, "The Presbyterian Doctrine of Total Depravity," in *Soli Deo Gloria*, A Festschrift for John H. Gerstner, ed. R. C. Sproul (Philadelphia: Presbyterian and Reformed, 1976), pp. 36-54.

there are only sinful deeds, and these deeds always have a personal character. Human beings today have wills that are totally free; they can do either good or bad as they please. When man does something wrong, his nature is not affected; afterwards he is just as capable of doing the right as he was before he did the wrong. Like a "spring" doorstop, after every movement in either direction, man springs back to a neutral position. Pelagius even said that a person can, if he or she will, keep God's commandments without sinning; Scripture, so he claimed, points to many examples of blameless lives.

How, then, does Pelagius account for the universality of sin? By means of imitation. Adam set before his descendants a bad example. We all tend to imitate the bad examples of our parents, brothers, sisters, wives or husbands, friends and associates. This is the way sin is transmitted from one generation to another, and from one person to another.

In other words, human persons do not need to be regenerated or born again in order to do what is pleasing to God; they have that ability by nature. Pelagius's view of divine grace was purely external. Grace, for him, is not an inward-working influence of the Holy Spirit inclining our wills toward the good, but it consists only of external gifts and natural endowments, such as man's rational nature and free will, the revelation of God's law in Scripture, and the example of Christ.[51]

Pelagius's view of man was quite unsatisfactory; in fact, the church decisively rejected it.[52] We can refute his view by making several observations.

First, Pelagius's view is contrary to Scripture. Romans 5:12-21 clearly indicates that there is a very real connection between Adam's sin and that of his descendants (the exact nature of this connection will be discussed later in this chapter). In Ephesians 2:3 Paul, writing to believers, affirms, "Like the rest, we [who are now believers] were by nature objects of wrath." Why should anyone be an object of wrath by nature if all human beings have been born in a morally neutral state?

51. On Pelagius see J. N. D. Kelly, *Early Christian Doctrines* (London: A. & C. Black, 1958), pp. 357-61; Joseph C. Ayer, *A Source Book for Ancient Church History* (New York: Scribner, 1913), pp. 457-60; B. B. Warfield, *Two Studies in the History of Dogma* (New York: Christian Literature Co., 1897); John Ferguson, *Pelagius: A Historical and Theological Study* (Cambridge: Heffer, 1956); and Robert F. Evans, *Pelagius; Inquiries and Reappraisals* (New York: Seabury Press, 1968).
52. Pelagianism, which includes the views of Pelagius's disciple Celestius, who became the leader of the movement, was condemned by the Council of Carthage in 418 and by the Council of Ephesus in 431.

Second, Pelagius's position is contrary to our experience. Sin does not leave our nature untouched but intimately affects it. After a sinful act we are no longer the same. Sinful deeds spring up out of a bad nature, and, when unchecked, lead to sinful habits and, ultimately, to sinful enslavement. One is reminded of Jesus' words, "I tell you the truth, everyone who sins is a slave to sin" (John 8:34).

Third, bad examples do not invariably corrupt. Think of Joseph in Egypt and of Daniel at the court of Nebuchadnezzar. The environment may occasion sin but it does not cause it. The root of sin lies deeper: in the corrupt human heart.

Another unsatisfactory view of the transmission of sin from Adam to us is that called "mediate imputation." Imputation, as the word is commonly used in theology, is a legal or judicial term that means "to reckon something to someone's account." The term is used in three senses in Christian theology: "To denote the judicial acts of God (1) by which the guilt of Adam's sin is imputed to his posterity, (2) by which the sins of Christ's people are imputed to Him, and (3) by which the righteousness of Christ is imputed to his people."[53] At this point we shall be dealing with the first of these three meanings.

The view of mediate imputation was first advanced by Josué De La Place (or Placeus; 1596–1655) of the School of Saumur in France. His views were condemned by the Synod of Charenton held in 1645, and by the *Formula Consensus Helvetica*, a Swiss confession of faith issued in 1675.[54] However, Placeus's views found wide acceptance in France, England, Switzerland, and America; in the last-named country such New England theologians as Samuel Hopkins, Timothy Dwight, and Nathanael Emmons taught this doctrine.[55]

Placeus taught that the imputation to us of the guilt of Adam's sin was not immediate but mediate—that is, not direct but mediated by something else. We all derive sinful corruption from Adam through our parents. On the basis of this corruption we are also considered to be involved in the guilt of Adam's fall. We are considered guilty be-

---

53. C. W. Hodge, "Imputation," ISBE, vol. 2 (Grand Rapids: Eerdmans, 1982), p. 812. Cf. also R. K. Johnston, "Imputation," in *Evangelical Dictionary of Theology,* ed. Walter A. Elwell (Grand Rapids: Baker, 1984), pp. 554-55.
54. An English translation of this confession can be found in A. A. Hodge, *Outlines of Theology* (Grand Rapids: Eerdmans, 1957), pp. 656-63.
55. H. Bavinck, *Dogmatiek,* 3:88-89. Further discussions of Placeus's doctrine of imputation may be found in G. F. Karl Müller, "Placeus," *Realencyklopädie für Protestantische Theologie und Kirche,* ed. J. J. Herzog, vol. 15 (Leipzig: Hinrichs, 1904), pp. 471-72; John Murray, *The Imputation of Adam's Sin* (Grand Rapids: Eerdmans, 1959), pp. 42-64; G. C. Berkouwer, *Sin,* trans. P. Holtrop (Grand Rapids: Eerdmans, 1971), pp. 454-58.

cause we have been born in a state of corruption. The imputation of Adam's guilt to us is therefore *mediate*: mediated through the corruption in which we have been born.

It is easy to understand the motivation for this view. Placeus and his followers wanted to avoid the suggestion that God imputes guilt to people who are not guilty. To justify the seeming arbitrariness of the imputation of Adam's sin on humankind, then, Placeus posited the view that the corruption in which we are born makes us guilty, and that therefore the imputation of Adam's guilt to us rests upon a "guiltiness" that we have from birth.

We may object to this view for three reasons. 1. The corruption into which we are born is an implication, and thus a result, of Adam's sin; it cannot therefore be considered the basis on which we are regarded as guilty of Adam's sin. To affirm this is almost like saying that we are guilty of Adam's sin because we all have to die.

2. If Adam's guilt is mediated to us through the corruption in which we are born, why does not God impute to us the guilt of all the sins of all our ancestors?

3. There is no indication in the key passage on which the doctrine of the imputation of Adam's guilt is based (Rom. 5:12-21) that the imputation of the guilt of Adam's sin is mediated through our corruption. In verses 16 and 18 Paul clearly states that condemnation came upon us because of the one trespass of Adam; so to say that that condemnation was grounded upon the sinful depravity in which we were born is to introduce an element into the text that is not there.

We now take up two additional views dealing with the transmission of sin from Adam to us—those called "realism" and "immediate imputation"—which do greater justice to the biblical data than do the views just treated. Before we do so, however, it may be well to remind ourselves that we are dealing here with something deeply mysterious. We simply cannot understand how we sinned in Adam; the Bible does not tell us. Nor can we understand how the guilt of Adam's sin is imputed to us; the Bible does not answer this question either. What the Bible does tell us is *that* we sinned in Adam, and *that* the guilt of Adam's first sin is imputed to us; further than that we should not go. Sin remains a mystery, not only in its commission but also in its transmission.

The view of the relation between Adam's sin and the sin of his descendants commonly called "realism" is by no means a new one. In the early church Tertullian and Augustine held it; more recently,

William G. T. Shedd, Augustus H. Strong, S. Greijdanus, and K. Schilder have championed it.[56]

Briefly stated, according to this view God originally created one generic human nature, which in the course of time was divided into many separate individuals. Adam, however, possessed the whole of this human nature. Thus, when he sinned, all of human nature sinned. Therefore we are all guilty of Adam's sin, since we, as part of this generic human nature, actually committed the first sin in him and with him. Augustine put it this way:

> For we were all in that one man, since we all were that one man who fell into sin. . . . For not yet was the particular form created and distributed to us in which we as individuals were to live, but already the seminal nature was there from which we were to be propagated; and this being vitiated by sin, and bound by the chain of death, and justly condemned, man could not be born of man in any other state.[57]

One can understand the motivation behind this view. Both Shedd and Greijdanus make the point that the sin in which we are involved through our relationship with Adam must be actually *our* sin. It is not fair, so they contend, to think of God as imputing to us the guilt of a sin that we have not committed. If God is to hold us guilty because of this sin, there must be a real sense in which it *is* our sin. And this it is on the basis of the realistic view: we were all in Adam when he sinned; hence Adam's sin is actually the sin of us all.[58]

One reason why the realistic view developed in the early church may be the translation of the last clause of Romans 5:12, *eph' hō pantes hēmarton*, in the Vulgate[59] by these words: *in quo omnes peccaverunt* ("in whom all sinned"). This was the way Augustine rendered the passage, and one can readily see how this translation led to his realistic view. *Eph' hō*, however, does not mean *in whom*; it is a Greek idiom meaning *because* or *since*. The proper translation of this clause, therefore, is "because all sinned." The realistic understanding of our relationship to Adam's sin, however, does not stand or fall with the Vulgate translation; even when rendered "because all sinned," these words can still convey the realistic view.

56. W. G. T. Shedd, *Dogmatic Theology*, vol. 2 (1888–94; Grand Rapids: Zondervan, n.d.), pp. 181-92; A. H. Strong, *Systematic Theology*, vol. 2 (Philadelphia: Griffith and Rowland, 1907–1909), pp. 619-37; S. Greijdanus, *Toerekeningsgrond van het Peccatum Originans* (Amsterdam: Bottenburg, 1906); K. Schilder, *Heidelbergsche Catechismus*, vol. 1 (Goes: Oosterbaan and Le Cointre, 1947), pp. 331-58.
57. *City of God*, trans. M. Dods, Bk. 13, Chap. 14, vol. 2 in *Nicene and Post-Nicene Fathers*, First Series (rpt.; Grand Rapids: Eerdmans, 1983), p. 251.
58. An expression commonly used by those who hold this view is that we were all "in the loins of Adam" when he sinned.
59. Jerome's Latin translation of the Bible, completed in A.D. 404.

A number of difficulties involved in this view have been advanced. Let us look at some of these, and see whether these objections can be answered.

Opponents of realism hold that this view does not really solve the problem of the relation between Adam's sin and ourselves. We do not solve the problem by agreeing that we were all present in Adam when he sinned, for we were not present in him as *individuals*, but as "parts" of an undifferentiated total human nature. This certainly does not make clear our personal responsibility in the commission of Adam's first sin.

This objection, however, can be answered. Hebrews 7:9-10 explains that Levi paid tithes to Melchizedek through Abraham, since he was "still in the loins of his ancestor" (v. 10, RSV; Gk.: *en tē osphui tou patros*) when Abraham met Melchizedek. Obviously Levi, Abraham's great-grandson, was not aware of his having paid tithes to Melchizedek 180 or more years before he was born; yet the author of Hebrews says that Levi, in effect, did pay tithes to Melchizedek. If we accept the fact that Adam was the father of the human race, as the Bible says he was, then we all were in a sense "in the loins of Adam" when Adam committed the first sin.[60] Though we cannot understand how we then sinned in Adam, any more than we can understand how Levi paid tithes to Melchizedek before the former had been born, there must be some sense in which we did actually do so.

A second difficulty is that the realistic view does not make clear why we are involved only in the guilt of Adam's first sin, and not also in the guilt of Adam's other sins, or of the sins of our parents, or of the sins of all our ancestors.

This objection, too, can be answered. As many theologians have pointed out, Adam was a "public person" when he committed the first sin. He was then acting as our head—something that could not be said about him when he committed subsequent sins, nor about our parents and ancestors when they sinned.

Third, the analogy between Adam and Christ found in Romans 5:12-21 presents an obstacle to the realistic interpretation. For there is no generic human nature in Christ that is individualized in all who believe in him. The parallelism between Adam and Christ found in

---

60. The proponents of realism are not the only ones to use this expression ("in the loins of Adam") to describe the position of all human beings at the time of Adam's first sin. Cf. the *Formula Consensus Helvetica* (1675), Par. 11; Zacharias Ursinus, *Schatboek over den Heidelbergsche Catechismus*, 3rd ed., vol. 1, trans. F. Hommius (Gorinchem: Goetzee, 1736), p. 92; *Synopsis Purioris Theologiae* (Lugduni Batavorum: Donner, 1881), 15, 11; H. Bavinck, *Dogmatiek*, 3:91.

this passage, therefore, seems to rule out the relationship between Adam and us that is affirmed by the realistic view.

In response to this objection, we should remember a very important point: though Romans 5:12-21 does point to a parallelism between Adam and Christ, that parallelism is not total. There are significant differences between the headship of Adam and that of Christ, not only in the sense that we receive bad things from Adam and good things from Christ, but also in the manner in which we are related to each. The proponents of realism point out[61] that these differences in our relationship to Adam and Christ include two matters: (1) We were never "in the loins of Christ" but we were "in the loins of Adam"; and (2) since we were in Adam's loins when he sinned, we did in a sense sin in him, so that our being regarded as sinners by God because of our relationship to Adam is not something that does not comport in any way with our actual status. In the case of Christ, however, his righteousness is imputed to us in such a way that God now looks upon us "*as if* [we] had never sinned . . . and *as if* [we] had been as perfectly obedient as Christ was obedient for [us]."[62] Though our righteousness in Christ is an "as if" righteousness—not our own but someone else's—our sinfulness in Adam is not "as if"; it is indeed our own.

I believe that the insights embodied in the realistic view of the transmission of Adam's sin to us are important, and reflect significant scriptural teachings. They are, however, not sufficient; they need to be supplemented by a view that does greater justice than does the realistic view to the representative character of Adam's headship. Herman Bavinck, in fact, had this to say about the matter: "Federalism [the view of immediate or direct imputation, which will be discussed below] does not exclude the truth which lies hidden in realism; on the contrary, it fully accepts this truth; it proceeds from that truth, but does not remain standing there."[63] In general, Reformed theologians have separated these two lines of interpretation (realism and immediate imputation). It is my conviction, however, that they ought to be combined. In other words, the decision we should make about these two understandings of the transmission of sin is not an either-or but rather a both-and.

Another view of the nature of the transmission of sin from Adam to us, usually called "immediate imputation," teaches that the impu-

---

61. Cf. S. Greijdanus, *Toerekeningsgrond*, pp. 44-45; K. Schilder, *Catechismus*, 1:353-54.
62. Heidelberg Catechism, Answer 60 (1975 trans., Christian Reformed Church) [italics mine].
63. *Dogmatiek*, 3:93 [trans. mine].

tation of Adam's guilt to us is not mediated by anything else (like the presence of corruption in us), but is immediate and direct. Because the term *immediate* suggests immediacy in time, and is therefore somewhat confusing, I prefer to designate this view as that of *direct imputation*. Such Reformed theologians as Herman Bavinck, J. Gresham Machen, A. D. R. Polman, John Murray, and Louis Berkhof have held this view.[64]

According to the proponents of the "direct imputation" view, Adam stands in a twofold relationship to his descendants: he is both their natural or physical head (in the sense of being their progenitor) and their representative.[65] When he sinned, he did so as our representative, and therefore we are all involved in the guilt of that sin, and in the condemnation that results from it. We may call this involvement in guilt and condemnation *imputation*. God imputes to us the guilt of Adam's first sin. This imputation is not mediated by our innate corruption, but is direct and unmediated.

As an implication, and therefore a result, of our involvement in Adam's guilt, all human persons are born in a state of corruption.[66] This corruption (also called pollution or depravity) is transmitted to us through our parents. Our involvement in and identification with Adam's sin carries with it the perversity apart from which sin does not exist. We are born in a state of corruption because we are in solidarity with Adam in his sin.[67] We do not understand how this corruption can be transmitted from parents to children; the laws of human heredity can provide no explanation for this process. But both Scripture and experience tell us that the pollution of sin is indeed passed on from parents to their offspring.

*Direct* imputation, therefore, refers only to the transmission of

64. Bavinck, *Dogmatiek,* 3:96-102; J. G. Machen, *The Christian View of Man* (New York: Macmillan, 1937), pp. 255-62; A. D. R. Polman, *Woord en Belijdenis* (Franeker: Wever, 1957), 1:268-70; John Murray, *The Imputation of Adam's Sin,* pp. 36-41, 64-70; L. Berkhof, *Systematic Theology,* pp. 242-43.

65. Many proponents of direct imputation also support the doctrine of the covenant of works. Although in the previous chapter (see above, pp. 117-21) I rejected the doctrine of the covenant of works, this does not imply the rejection of direct imputation, as long as we maintain that Adam was indeed the head and representative of the human race. It is significant that John Murray, one of the strongest protagonists of direct imputation, likewise rejects the doctrine of the covenant of works.

66. The only exception to this, of course, is Jesus Christ. But since he is a divine person who assumed a human nature, he can hardly be called a "human person."

67. At this junction the realistic view helpfully supplements the view of direct imputation. According to the realistic view, we are born in a state of corruption not just because Adam was our representative and thus brought imputed guilt upon us, but also because we were actually in Adam when he sinned, at which time our human nature became corrupt.

guilt, not to the transmission of corruption. In other words, there is a *direct* imputation of guilt, and a *mediate* transmission of corruption.

Probably the greatest difficulty with this view is that it seems to suggest that God imputes to us the guilt of a sin that we did not commit. Note, for example, Berkouwer's comment: "In federalism [the view of direct imputation] the idea of a 'representation' is linked together with imputation in a manner which leaves the impression that the unguilty are merely 'declared' to be guilty."[68] Theologians who voice this objection usually quote passages like the following to show that God does not consider children guilty of the sins of their fathers:[69]

> Fathers shall not be put to death for their children, nor children put to death for their fathers; each is to die for his own sin. (Deut. 24:16)
>
> In those days people will no longer say, "The fathers have eaten sour grapes, and the children's teeth are set on edge." Instead, everyone will die for his own sin; whoever eats sour grapes—his own teeth will be set on edge. (Jer. 31:29-30)
>
> The soul who sins is the one who will die. The son will not share the guilt of the father, nor will the father share the guilt of the son. The righteousness of the righteous man will be credited to him, and the wickedness of the wicked will be charged against him. (Ezek. 18:20)

Though we do stand before a most difficult problem, and though we can in no way understand fully what is involved here, at this point we must again remember the truth that is stressed by the proponents of the realistic view: we were all in Adam when he sinned. If this is so, then we cannot say that the guilt that is imputed to us because of Adam's sin is totally foreign to us. In a very real sense, in other words, Adam's sin was our sin.

Since we have surveyed these various views on the transmission of sin, we should now take a careful look at the Scripture passage that is foundational to this discussion: Romans 5:12-21. We must grant at the outset that Paul's primary purpose in this section is not to describe the transmission of sin and its results, but rather to unfold the amazing benefits we receive through Christ, and thus to glorify the abounding grace of God toward sinful humanity. But in order to bring out the splendor of Christ's gifts, Paul sketches them against the dark background of man's sinful and condemned state. And we need to understand that background.

Verse 12 is the key verse: "Therefore, just as sin entered the world

68. *Sin*, p. 524.
69. Ibid., pp. 427, 518-20; S. Greijdanus, *Toerekeningsgrond*, p. 43; K. Schilder, *Catechismus*, 1:340.

through one man, and death through sin, and in this way death came to all men, because all sinned. . . ." The first half of the verse obviously refers to Adam (though his name is not mentioned until v. 14), and tells us why death came upon him. The second half deals with "all men," and answers the question, Why did death come upon all human beings? The answer is: "because all sinned." Some scholars[70] have interpreted these words as pointing to *actual sin,* that is, the sin we commit, in distinction from the sin in which and with which we were born. In other words, to these interpreters "because all sinned" means "because all human beings committed sins after they were born."

In my judgment, however, this interpretation is incorrect. Paul is not referring here to *actual sin*; he is saying that death came upon all human beings because they all *sinned in Adam*. Note what he says in verses 15 and 17: "the many died by the trespass of the one man"; "by the trespass of the one man, death reigned." These clauses clearly tie in the death of the many, not with the actual sins of those who died but with the one sin of the one man, Adam.

Further, verses 13 and 14 read as follows:

> For before the law was given, sin was in the world. But sin is not taken into account when there is no law. Nevertheless, death reigned from the time of Adam to the time of Moses, even over those who did not sin by breaking a command, as did Adam.

"Who did not sin by breaking a command, as did Adam," is a paraphrase of a clause that, translated literally, reads: "even over those who had not sinned according to the likeness of Adam's transgression." The thrust of these verses is this: the people who lived between Adam and Moses were not given a clear command with a clear threat of death in case of disobedience, as was Adam. Nevertheless, they all died. Since this fact is adduced as an argument to support verse 12, it is apparent that Paul's point is that these people did not die because of their own personal, actual sins, but because of their connection with Adam.

Finally, the fact that humans may die in infancy also militates against the view that Paul means *actual sin,* for on the basis of this interpretation, infants ought not to die, since they are incapable of actual sin.

We should, therefore, understand the clause "because all sinned" as referring not to actual sin but to original sin. We should not under-

---

70. E. F. Harrison, *Romans,* in the Expositor's Bible Commentary series (Grand Rapids: Zondervan, 1976), p. 62; William Hendriksen, *Romans,* vol. 1 (Grand Rapids: Baker, 1980), pp. 178-79.

stand it to mean "because we all were *accounted to be* sinners in Adam," but rather "because we all *sinned* in Adam," since we were all "in his loins" when he sinned. This, Paul is saying, is why death has come to all human beings because of Adam's transgression.[71]

We should consider, for a moment, the last clause of verse 14: "Adam, who was a type [*typos*] of the one who was to come" (RSV). A *type* in the Bible is a figure, model, or pattern of something or someone else—in this case, of a person who was still to come, namely, Jesus Christ. Earlier we discussed the sense in which Adam was a type of Christ.[72] As Christ represented us and functioned for us, so did Adam; like Christ, Adam was both our head and our representative. Herman Bavinck puts it this way: "There have been only two men whose life and works have reached out to the very boundaries of humankind, whose influence and dominion extend to the ends of the earth and even into eternity. They are Adam and Christ."[73] F. F. Bruce quotes a statement made by Thomas Goodwin, a seventeenth-century British theologian: "In God's sight there are two men—Adam and Jesus Christ—and these two men have all other men hanging at their girdle strings."[74]

We have already dealt briefly with verses 16 and 18, in connection with the headship of Adam.[75] However, we should add here that the language of these verses is legal or judicial language. Condemnation (pronouncing someone guilty) is contrasted with justification (acquitting someone from guilt). From both verses we learn that one trespass (the sin of Adam) brought or led to condemnation for all people.

To be sure, Paul does not here use the word *impute* (the Greek word *logizomai*, sometimes rendered *impute* in the KJV, is not found

---

71. In connection with the concept of "all through one" that dominates Romans 5:12-21, attention is called to the Hebrew idea of "corporate personality." In the Old Testament a group is often portrayed as functioning through and/or represented by a leader, so that the leader becomes identified with the group (i.e., the use of names like Jacob, Israel, Judah, and Ephraim to stand for both the individuals involved and the people who descended from them). The idea that Adam represents and functions for all his descendants, therefore, is not foreign to the Scriptures. On the concept of corporate personality, see H. Wheeler Robinson, *The Christian Doctrine of Man* (Edinburgh: T. & T. Clark, 1911), pp. 27-30; idem, *Inspiration and Revelation in the Old Testament* (Oxford: Clarendon Press, 1946), pp. 70-71, 82-83; H. H. Rowley, *The Re-discovery of the Old Testament* (Philadelphia: Westminster Press, 1946), pp. 216-17.
72. See above, p. 149.
73. *Dogmatiek*, 3:95-96 [trans. mine].
74. F. F. Bruce, *Romans*, in the Tyndale New Testament Commentary series (Grand Rapids: Eerdmans, 1963), p. 127. Cf. A. Oepke, "*en*," TDNT, 2:542.
75. Above, p. 149.

in these verses). What he tells us here is that all human beings are under condemnation because of Adam's sin, but he does not say exactly how this condemnation is transmitted to us. Since the language of these verses is legal, and since imputation is a legal concept, we may, if we wish, interpret these verses as teaching the direct imputation of guilt and condemnation from Adam to us. But we must remember that when we do so, the concept of imputation is an inference from the scriptural data.[76]

The question could be raised: Does this teaching mean that all infants who die are eternally lost? Not necessarily. To be sure, all infants are under the condemnation of Adam's sin as soon as they are born. But the Bible clearly teaches that God will judge everyone according to his or her works.[77] And those who die in infancy are incapable of doing any works, whether good or bad. One cannot be dogmatic about this question. But we may find wise counsel in the words of a highly respected Reformed theologian, Herman Bavinck:

> With respect to the salvation . . . of children who die in infancy, we can on the basis of Scripture go no further than to refrain from uttering a determinative and decisive judgment [*beslist en stellig oordeel*] either in a positive or negative sense. Only it deserves to be mentioned that as regards these momentous questions Reformed theology is in a much more favorable position than any other theology. . . . For the Reformed did not wish, in the first place, . . . to determine the grade or extent of the knowledge that was considered indispensable for salvation. And, in the second place, they maintained that the means of grace were not absolutely necessary for salvation, but that God could also regenerate to eternal life outside of or without Word and sacraments.[78]

Finally, we should take a close look at verse 19, which reads as follows in the Revised Berkeley Version: "For as through the disobedience of one man many were placed in the position of sinners, so through the obedience of the One many will be placed in the position

---

76. Even John Murray, a staunch proponent of the doctrine of direct imputation, admits this: "When we speak of the sin of Adam as imputed to posterity, it is admitted that nowhere in Scripture is our relation to the trespass of Adam expressly defined in terms of imputation" (*Imputation of Adam's Sin*, p. 71).

77. Cf. such passages as Matt. 16:27; Rom. 2:6; Rev. 20:12; 22:12. See my *The Bible and the Future*, pp. 261-62.

78. *Dogmatiek*, 4:810 [trans. mine]. Bavinck refers here to Calvin, *Inst.*, IV.16.19. Bavinck's statement concerns all those who die in infancy. With respect to the children of believers, however, the promise of the covenant of grace, that God will be the God not only of us who are believing adults but also of our children, should give Christian parents assurance that their infants who die are not lost (cf. Canons of Dort, I.17: "godly parents ought not to doubt concerning the election and salvation of those of their children whom God calls out of this life in infancy" [trans. mine]).

of righteous ones." The key word in this passage is the verb *kathistēmi,* which occurs twice in this verse. Among the meanings of *kathistēmi* listed in the Greek-English Lexicon of Arndt and Gingrich, the choice here is between two groups of meanings: *ordain* or *appoint* and *make* or *cause.* Most English translations render the two occurrences of *kathistēmi* in this verse by the word *made*: "were made sinners," and "will be made righteous." Only the Berkeley version, quoted above, renders this as "were placed in the position of" sinners and righteous ones (a rendering that is close to *ordain* or *appoint*). Which is the better translation?

The second half of the verse uses legal or forensic language: *dikaioi katastathēsontai* refers to justification—a legal or judicial act of God whereby he declares us to be righteous in Christ. That these words do not refer to sanctification (the renewing work of the Holy Spirit whereby he makes us more holy) is evidenced by the frequent references to justification as a judicial act in both the remote (vv. 1 and 9) and the nearer context (vv. 16, 17, and 18). Further, it is not until chapter 6 that Paul begins to discuss in depth the topic of sanctification. Therefore, since we must understand the second half of verse 19 in a legal or forensic sense, the Berkeley translation, "placed in the position of righteous ones," is a more accurate rendering of this half of the text than that found in the other English translations.

If the second half of the verse is to be understood in a legal sense, by way of analogy the first half of the verse should be similarly understood. Here again the form of *kathistēmi* that is used does not mean *made* but *ordain* or *appoint.* Again the Berkeley translation is to be preferred: "through the disobedience of one man many [lit., the many] were placed in the position of sinners." Albrecht Oepke, writing about Romans 5:19, comments as follows: "Here . . . the emphasis is on the judicial sentence of God, which on the basis of the act of the head determines the destiny of all."[79] According to the first half of this verse, therefore, Adam's disobedience placed all human beings[80] in the position of sinners, in the category of sinners, so that they were considered to be guilty in Adam.

In the above interpretation of Romans 5:12-21 I have combined the approaches of direct imputation and realism. Because Adam was our head and representative when he sinned, the guilt of his sin is reckoned to our account (direct imputation). And because we were in

---

79. *"Kathistēmi,"* TDNT, 3:446.
80. Here the expression *the many (hoi polloi)* obviously means *all,* since all (with the exception of Christ) are in Adam.

Adam when he sinned, we were involved in his sin, and therefore we have been born with a corrupt nature (realism).

It needs to be said again, however, that all this is but the background for the glorious message of the abundant grace of God. The first eleven verses of Romans 5 celebrate the marvels of God's love: "But God demonstrates his own love for us in this: While we were still sinners, Christ died for us" (v. 8). The second half of Romans 5, verses 12-21, continues to celebrate that love, this time against the background of what came upon us because of our relationship to Adam, our first head. Twice in these later verses Paul uses the expression "much more" when he describes the grace of God (in vv. 15 and 17). In verse 20, in fact, he puts it this way: "where sin increased, grace increased all the more." His point in this section of the chapter is that the grace of God fills our lives to overflowing with blessings that are abundantly greater than the evil results of Adam's fall.

Note the contrasts found in these verses: Through Adam came death, but through Jesus Christ came everlasting life. Because of Adam's sin we are regarded as sinners, but because of Christ's obedience we are regarded as righteous. Because of Adam we are subject to condemnation; because of Christ we receive justification, and are permanently reconciled to God.

What is said about Adam in this passage is like the dark background of Rembrandt's painting of the presentation of Christ in the temple: the mysterious darkness dramatizes the heavenly brilliance of the Christ-child, on whom the shaft of light falls. Ultimately, therefore, Romans 5:12-21 should move us to a ringing doxology:

> *O for a thousand tongues to sing*
> *My great Redeemer's praise,*
> *The glories of my God and King,*
> *The triumphs of His grace.*

# CHAPTER 9

# The Nature of Sin

In the preceding two chapters we have discussed the origin of sin—how sin came into the world—and the spread of sin—how it has been transmitted to us through the ages. But what is the *nature* of sin? How should we define and describe it? In this chapter we will consider these questions.

## THE ESSENTIAL CHARACTER OF SIN

*Sin has no independent existence.* In this connection mention should first be made of the views of Matthias Illyricus Flacius, a German Lutheran theologian who lived from 1520 to 1575. Flacius claimed that sin was not just an "accident" of man's condition (that is, a perversion of his essence), but that it was now the *essence* and *substance* of man. Flacius's views remind us of those associated with Manichaeism, a third-century dualistic religious movement which taught that good and evil are two eternal principles that continue to exist side by side, and that evil is to be associated particularly with the body. The *Formula of Concord,* a Lutheran confession that appeared in 1577, took issue with Flacius's view, tying it in with Manichaeism, in these words:

> But, on the other hand, we reject also the false dogma of the Manichaeans, where it is taught that original sin is, as it were, something essential and substantial, infused by Satan into the nature, and mingled with the same, as wine and poison are mixed.[1]

Over against the view that sin is a separate substance, Christian theologians from Augustine on have maintained that sin should be thought of as a defect in something that is good. This is what Flacius's

---

1. Art. I, Negative VII, found in P. Schaff, *Creeds of Christendom,* vol. 3 (New York: Harper, 1877), p. 102. On Flacius, see Berkouwer, *Man,* pp. 130-36.

opponent, Victorinus Strigel, meant when he called sin "accidental" to human nature. Many years before, Augustine had called sin *privatio boni,* that is, a deprivation or loss of the good.[2] Sin is like the blindness that robs a previously sighted person of his or her sight. Or, to use a different figure, sin is like a wounded hand. The fact that the hand is only wounded implies that it can be healed. On the basis of this understanding, man's sin can ultimately be overcome and done away with. If sin were a substance, if it were indeed now part of the essence of human nature, how could it ever be conquered? The fact that sin is not part of the essence of our nature made it possible for Christ to assume a human nature that was not totally other than that of fallen man and still to be without sin.

This understanding implies that sin has not changed our essence but has changed the direction in which we are moving. In connection with the discussion of the image of God I pointed out that human beings after the Fall still retain that image in the structural sense but have lost it in the functional sense.[3] That is, though fallen man still bears the image of God, he now functions wrongly as an image-bearer of God. This, in fact, makes sin all the more heinous. Sin is a perverse way of using God-given and God-reflecting powers.[4]

Sin, therefore, is not something physical but something ethical. It was not given with creation but came after creation; it is a deformation of what is. To call sin *privatio boni* may not be a totally satisfactory definition of sin, since sin is more than a deprivation of the good and is also active rebellion against God. Nevertheless, this definition does convey an important truth about the nature of sin.

*Sin is always related to God and his will.* Many people consider what Christians call *sin* mere imperfection—the kind of imperfection that is a normal aspect of human nature. "Nobody's perfect," "everybody makes mistakes," "you're only human," and similar statements express this type of thinking. Over against this we must insist that, according to Scripture, sin is always a transgression of the law of God.

---

2. *Enchiridion,* 11 and 12, ed. and trans. Albert C. Outler, vol. 7 in the Library of Christian Classics series (Philadelphia: Westminster Press, 1955).
3. Above, pp. 68-73.
4. C. S. Lewis has expressed this point in an unforgettable way:

> Is it still God speaking when a liar or a blasphemer speaks? In one sense, almost Yes. Apart from God he could not speak at all. . . . And indeed the only way in which I can make real to myself what theology teaches about the heinousness of sin is to remember that every sin is the distortion of an energy breathed into us. . . . We poison the wine as He decants it into us; murder a melody He would play with us as the instrument. We caricature the self-portrait He would paint. Hence all sin, whatever else it is, is sacrilege. (*Letters to Malcolm, Chiefly on Prayer* [London: Collins, Fontana Books, 1966], pp. 71-72)

Though there are many laws in the Bible, particularly in the first five books of the Old Testament, what is meant here by *law* is the small group of commands that we recognize as containing a brief summary of what God requires of man, namely, the Ten Commandments.

Though this law was given by God to the Israelites at Mount Sinai, it did not contain moral standards that were totally foreign to man. Lewis Smedes puts it this way:

> What Moses brought from Sinai endorsed a morality that was endemic to the human race, affirmed in conscience as much as it was violated in practice. People who know little and care less about what the Bible tells us to do tend nevertheless to know in spite of themselves what the Bible actually requires in the moral life. Paul assumed that, as far as morality was concerned, people who never heard of God's commands were somehow familiar with his will.[5]

By way of proof for his last statement, Smedes goes on to quote Romans 2:14-16:

> When Gentiles who have not the law do by nature what the law requires, they are a law to themselves, even though they do not have the law. They show that what the law requires is written on their hearts, while their conscience also bears witness and their conflicting thoughts accuse or perhaps excuse them on that day when, according to my gospel, God judges the secrets of men by Christ Jesus. (RSV)

What is "written on the hearts" of people who have never seen a Bible, however, is specifically set forth in the Decalogue or Ten Commandments found in Exodus 20 and Deuteronomy 5. From that same Bible the believer learns that to break God's commandments is sin. In other words, as the Heidelberg Catechism puts it, the Christian learns to know his sin from the law of God.[6] The following Scripture passages confirm this: "Through the law we become conscious of sin" (Rom. 3:20b); "Indeed I would not have known what sin was except through the law. For I would not have known what it was to covet if the law had not said, 'Do not covet' " (Rom. 7:7b); "If you show favoritism, you sin and are convicted by the law as law-breakers" (Jas. 2:9); "Every one who sins breaks the law; in fact, sin is lawlessness" (1 John 3:4).

That all sin, even sin against our neighbors, is ultimately sin against God is shown by the familiar words of Psalm 51:4. David had sinned flagrantly and grievously against Bathsheba and Uriah; yet when he finally confessed his sin he said to God, "Against you, you

---

5. *Mere Morality* (Grand Rapids: Eerdmans, 1983), p. 10.
6. Heidelberg Catechism, Q. and A. 3.

only, have I sinned and done what is evil in your sight." David did not mean that he had not sinned against people, but in the depth of his repentance he had come to the conviction that all sin is finally sin against God. The sin of our first parents was one of disobedience to God's command, and the same thing can be said about every subsequent sin.

Sin is therefore fundamentally opposition to God, rebellion against God, which roots in hatred of God. To quote the Heidelberg Catechism again, "I have a natural tendency to hate God and my neighbor."[7] By way of proof, the catechism refers to Romans 8:7: "The sinful mind [the mind of man by nature] is hostile to God. It does not submit to God's law, nor can it do so."

Before we leave this point, however, something else should be said. To be fully understood, sin must be seen not only in the light of the law but also in the light of the gospel. The gospel—the good news about what Christ has done to save us from sin—is necessary precisely because we have broken God's law. When we see what Christ had to go through to save us from sin, when we look to Calvary and hear Christ's heart-rending cry, "My God, my God, why have you forsaken me?" (Matt. 27:46), we see the awful magnitude of sin. The revelation of God's wrath against sin displayed at the cross of Christ, who was made sin for our sake (2 Cor. 5:21), speaks volumes about the unfathomable gravity of our iniquity. Anselm put it well when he responded to the question, "Why could God not simply wipe out man's sin without requiring an atonement?" by saying, "You have not yet considered how great is the weight of sin."[8] The gospel, however, not only reveals the enormity of our sin; it also proclaims the way in which we can be delivered from our sin, thus calling us to repentance.

*Sin has its source in what Scripture calls "the heart."* Augustine used to say that sin has its source in man's will: "Either, then, the will itself is the first cause of sin, or there is no first cause of sin."[9] What we commonly call "the will," however, is simply another name for the total person in the act of making decisions. We never exercise an isolated "will"; what we call *willing* always involves other aspects of the self, like intellect and emotion. Behind willing is the person who wills.

Therefore, using scriptural language, I prefer to say that sin has its source in the *heart*. I here use the concept *heart* as it is used in

7. Answer 5 (1975 trans., Christian Reformed Church).
8. *Cur Deus Homo (Why God Became Man)*, Bk. I, Chap. 21: "Nondum considerasti quanti ponderis sit peccatum."
9. *De Libero Arbitrio,* III.17.

Scripture: as a description of the inner core of the person; the "organ" of thinking, feeling, and willing; the point of concentration of all of our functions.[10] In other words, sin has its source not in the body nor in any one of man's various capacities, but in the very center of his being, in his *heart*. Since sin has poisoned the very fountain of life, all of life is bound to be affected by it.

Biblical support for this point can be found in the following passages: "Keep your heart with all vigilance; for from it flow the springs of life" (Prov. 4:23, RSV); "The heart is deceitful above all things, and desperately corrupt; who can understand it?" (Jer. 17:9, RSV); "For out of the heart come evil thoughts, murder, adultery, sexual immorality, theft, false testimony, slander" (Matt. 15:19); "The evil man brings evil things out of the evil stored up in his heart. For out of the overflow of his heart his mouth speaks" (Luke 6:45b).

*Sin includes thoughts as well as acts.* According to human law, wrongdoing only concerns what one does or leaves undone, not what one thinks; no one is ever jailed for wrong thoughts (unless those thoughts have been expressed). But God's law goes much deeper than this. That thoughts may be sinful as well as words or deeds is evident from the tenth commandment, which forbids coveting. Jesus clearly taught that even should an adulterous thought not be carried out into action, it is still sin: "But I tell you that anyone who looks at a woman lustfully has already committed adultery with her in his heart" (Matt. 5:28). Paul, in fact, speaks of the "lust of the flesh" in Galatians 5:16, 17, and 24 (KJV). *Flesh* here means man's total nature under the enslavement of sin; the New International Version translates *epithumian sarkos* in verse 16 by "desires of the sinful nature." Obviously, in these passages the Greek word *epithumia* (desire) means bad desire, desire for what is forbidden. So perhaps the King James rendering, "lust of the flesh," in these passages is really more accurate as well as more vivid than the RSV's "desires of the flesh." When Paul says in verse 17, "for the flesh lusteth against the Spirit" (KJV), he is underscoring the fact that there are sinful desires as well as sinful deeds.

*Sin includes both guilt and pollution.* Earlier we discussed original

10. This understanding of the "heart" as the concentration point of all one's temporal functions has been developed in recent years particularly by D. H. Th. Vollenhoven (*Het Calvinisme en de Reformatie van de Wijsbegeerte* [Amsterdam: H. J. Paris, 1933]) and Herman Dooyeweerd (*De Wijsbegeerte der Wetsidee*, 3. vols. [Amsterdam: H. J. Paris, 1935]). A brief summary of their view can be found in K. J. Popma, "Het Uitgangspunt van de Wijsbegeerte der Wetsidee en het Calvinisme," in *De Reformatie van het Calvinistisch Denken*, ed. C. P. Boodt (The Hague: Guido de Bres, 1939). See also the discussion of the biblical words for "heart" in Chap. 11 below.

guilt and pollution.[11] Now the point must be made that not only original sin but also actual sin involves both guilt and pollution.

In the earlier discussion of pervasive depravity and total inability[12] we saw that the pollution of original sin also attaches itself to our actual sins. Actual sin not only springs forth from the pollution involved in original sin, it also intensifies that pollution. Sinful deeds often lead to sinful habits, and sinful habits may eventually bring about a totally sinful kind of life. As Augustine put it, the pollution involved in original sin is both the mother and the daughter of sin.[13]

Actual sin, however, also involves guilt—namely, the state of deserving condemnation or of being liable to punishment because the law has been violated. In the fifth petition of the Lord's Prayer, for example, our Lord taught us to pray, "Forgive us our debts, as we also have forgiven our debtors" (Matt. 6:12).[14] Paul says in Romans 3:19, "Now we know that whatever the law says, it says to those who are under the law, so that every mouth may be silenced and the whole world held accountable to God."[15] And in Romans 1:18 Paul puts it quite vividly: "The wrath of God is being revealed from heaven against all the godlessness and wickedness of men who suppress the truth by their wickedness." That God is here said to be wrathful against men because of their sin must imply that the objects of his wrath are considered guilty.

*Sin is at root a form of pride.* We have already seen this in the narrative of the Fall: the serpent aroused pride in Eve's heart when he said, "For God knows that when you eat of it [the forbidden fruit] your eyes will be opened, and you will be like God" (Gen. 3:5). We have also noted that the root sin of the fallen angels was pride.[16] What was true of the first sin of man and of the first sin of the angels is still true of every sin today. Augustine put it this way:

> And what is the origin of our evil will but pride? For "pride is the beginning of sin" (Ecclus. 10:13). And what is pride but the craving for undue exaltation? And this is undue exaltation, when the soul abandons Him to whom it ought to cleave as its end, and becomes a kind of end to itself.[17]

11. See above, pp. 148-54.
12. See above, pp. 150-54.
13. *On Marriage and Concupiscence*, I.27.
14. The Greek word for debts, *opheilēmata*, literally means "things which are owed to someone." Failure to give what is owed implies guilt.
15. The Greek word translated "accountable" is *hypodikos*, which means "liable to judgment or punishment," obviously implying guilt.
16. See above, p. 122.
17. *City of God*, trans. M. Dods, Bk. 14, Chap. 13, vol. 2 in *Nicene and Post-Nicene Fathers*, First Series (rpt.; Grand Rapids: Eerdmans, 1983), p. 273.

At root sin means refusing to recognize our total dependence on God, and wanting to be on our own. In other words, sin is basically self-interest: wanting things our way instead of God's way. As C. S. Lewis said, pride is the basic sin behind all particular sins.

> From the moment a creature becomes aware of God as God and of itself as self, the terrible alternative of choosing God or self for the centre is opened to it. This sin . . . is the fall in every individual life, and in each day of each individual life, the basic sin behind all particular sins: at this very moment you and I are either committing it, or about to commit it, or repenting it. We try, when we wake, to lay the new day at God's feet; before we have finished shaving, it becomes *our* day and God's share in it is felt as a tribute which we must pay out of "our own" pocket, a deduction from the time which ought, we feel, to be "our own."[18]

*Sin is usually masked.* This is one of the most baffling characteristics of sin. Sin is a pervasive aspect of our lives, and yet all too often we fail to realize it. In this connection three observations are in order:

1. Sin is always committed for "some good reason." Eve ate the forbidden fruit because she thought that this was a way of becoming more like God. A person steals because he thinks he needs this money more than the owner does, and it is only fair that in this way the rich should contribute to the welfare of the poor. A murderer kills because his victim is considered to be a menace to society, which would be better off without him. A person might even commit adultery as a way, so he imagines, of showing love to a lonely person.

Since we are "rational" creatures, we always want to have reasons for doing things. Whether the reasons we give when we sin are the real reasons is another story. Psychologists call this process "rationalization"—people tend to invent reasons for doing what they know they should not do, but nevertheless want to do.

2. We often fail to recognize our own sin. We see sin very clearly in others, but very dimly in ourselves. It was David who prayed in Psalm 19:12, "Who can discern his errors? Forgive my hidden faults." Moses admitted to God in Psalm 90:8, "You have set our iniquities before you, our secret sins in the light of your presence." Jesus spoke of this same problem when he said that we are able to see the speck of sawdust in the brother's eye but fail to notice the plank in our own eye (Matt. 7:3). Our sins, as someone has said, are like notes pinned to our backs; we just don't see them.

> Error and sin both have this property, that the deeper they are the less their victim suspects their existence; they are masked evil. . . . We can rest contentedly in our sins.[19]

18. *The Problem of Pain* (New York: Macmillan Paperbacks Edition, 1983), p. 75.
19. Ibid., pp. 92, 93.

3. We often tend to cover up our sins. The well-known story of David before the prophet Nathan (2 Sam. 12:1-15) illustrates this point. Previous to his confession to Nathan, the guilty king had been hiding his sin. In Psalm 32 David describes his state of mind during the cover-up:

> When I kept silent,
>     my bones wasted away
>     through my groaning all day long.
> For day and night
>     your hand was heavy upon me;
> my strength was sapped
>     as in the heat of summer. (vv. 3-4)

The Pharisee in Jesus' parable, his eyes totally closed to his own hypocrisy, prayed, "God, I thank you that I am not like all other men— robbers, evildoers, adulterers—or even like this tax collector" (Luke 18:11). Though most of us would not express ourselves as bluntly as did this Pharisee, there is enough of this kind of pride in each of us to make the shoe pinch.

The universal tendency we have to fail to recognize our sins is vividly and unforgettably portrayed in Dorothy Sayers's play, *The Zeal of thy House*.[20] The play deals with the rebuilding of Canterbury Cathedral, a part of which had been destroyed by fire. The members of the cathedral chapter have engaged an architect from France, William of Sens, to rebuild the damaged structure. William has a consuming passion to construct the most beautiful cathedral ever built, presumably for the glory of God. Before the rebuilding has been completed, however, William has an accident: he falls fifty feet from a traveling cradle, and is severely injured. Feeling the need to confess his sins, William asks a priest to come to his sickbed; to the priest he confesses all the sins he can remember. But now the angel Michael comes to him, saying, "God is condemning you for your great sin." "What sin?" William asks. "Didn't I just confess all my sins? What sin is left?" "The cathedral!" is Michael's reply. What William thought he was doing for the glory of God he was really doing to exalt himself.

## BIBLICAL WORDS FOR SIN

We learn some important things about the nature of sin by looking at the various biblical words used for this concept. The most commonly used term in the Old Testament is *chattā'th*. Basically, it means "to miss the mark," conveying the thought that all wrongdoing is a falling short of the way God intends his children to live. Sin, this word is saying, means failing to fulfill the purpose for which God created us.

20. In Dorothy Sayers, *Four Sacred Plays* (London: Victor Gollancz, 1948), pp. 7-103.

Other Old Testament words include '*āwōn*, iniquity or guilt; *pesha'*, rebellion, revolt, refusal to be subject to authority; '*ābhar*, transgression (lit., "crossing over"); *resha'*, wickedness or ungodliness; *ra'*, evil or wickedness; *ma'al*, trespass or act of treachery; and '*āwen*, idolatry, iniquity, or vanity.

Among the New Testament words for sin, the most common one is *hamartia*, which is the Greek equivalent of the Hebrew word *chattā'th*, and, like it, means "to miss the mark"—or, putting it into New Testament language, to "fall short of the glory of God" (Rom. 3:23). Less commonly used are the following: *anomia*, lawlessness or the breaking of the law; *paraptōma*, derived from *parapiptō* (to fall aside) and therefore meaning trespass or false step; *parabasis*, derived from *parabainō* (to overstep) and therefore meaning transgression or stepping over the boundary of what is right; *asebeia*, godlessness or impiety; *parakoē* (lit., disobedience to a voice), failing to listen when God is speaking; and *adikia*, unrighteousness, injustice, or wrongdoing. Each of these words sheds light on the way the Bible understands sin.

## VARIOUS TYPES OF SIN

There are as many different kinds of sin as there are commandments of God. Sins can be classified in many ways; I will mention only some of these classifications here.

One ancient classification, which goes back to the early history of Christian monasticism, refers to the so-called "seven deadly sins" (also sometimes called the capital sins). These seven sins were thought to be the roots from which many other sins could arise. Traditionally, the seven deadly sins were listed as follows: (1) vainglory or pride; (2) covetousness; (3) lust, usually understood as inordinate or illicit sexual desire; (4) envy; (5) gluttony, which usually included drunkenness; (6) anger; and (7) sloth.[21]

Other ways of classifying sins include the following: Sins against God, the neighbor, or ourselves; sins of thought, word, or deed; sins that have their roots in "the lust of the flesh," "the lust of the eyes," or "the pride of life" (1 John 2:16, RSV);[22] sins of weakness, ignorance, or malice; sins of omission or commission; secret sins or open sins; private sins or public sins.[23]

21. The classical discussion of these seven sins is found in Thomas Aquinas, *Summa Theologica*, I-II, Q. 84, Art. 4.
22. Cf. the NEB translation: "everything the world affords, all that panders to the appetites or entices the eyes, all the glamour of its life."
23. Sometimes sins committed in private may later become public, as when sexual intercourse outside of marriage results in pregnancy.

## GRADATIONS IN SIN

All forms of sin are displeasing to God and entail guilt. Not every sin, however, is equally serious. We may and should recognize certain gradations in the seriousness of sin.

We take up first the traditional Roman Catholic distinction between *mortal* and *venial* sins—a distinction already made by Tertullian and Augustine,[24] and further worked out by such scholastic theologians as Lombard and Aquinas.[25] This distinction still plays an important part in the Roman Catholic understanding of their sacrament of penance, the purpose of which is the forgiveness of sins committed after baptism.

The following descriptions have been culled from Roman Catholic sources. Mortal sin is defined as

> a complete turning from God which results in the death (thus the term "mortal") of sanctifying grace in the soul. Three conditions are generally laid down as necessary in order that an offense be judged a mortal sin: (1) The offense in itself must be gravely wrong, either objectively (such as murder or adultery) or subjectively (that is, the offender considers the offense to be gravely wrong); (2) the offender must know that the offense is gravely wrong; (3) the offender must be free in the commission of the offense.[26]

Another Roman Catholic source describes mortal sin as follows:

> The transgression in a grave matter of law which is made with full advertence [attention] and full consent. It is called mortal (bringing death) because it cuts the sinner off from sanctifying grace and in a sense brings death to the soul. Since it is a grave rebellion against God, a person who dies in mortal sin dies cut off from God.[27]

In the *Maryknoll Catholic Dictionary* venial sin (the term is derived from a Latin word meaning "pardon") is defined as

> an offense against God not serious enough to cause the loss of sanctifying grace. Venial sin is likened to an illness of the soul, and not its death. A sin is venial when its matter is not grave (e.g., stealing a nickel, a jocose lie), or when there is wanting full advertence or full consent to grave matter. Venial sins can become mortal sins through an erroneous conscience, through malicious intent and through the accumulation of matter, as in theft.[28]

24. Tertullian, *On Modesty*, chaps. 2, 3, 19; *Against Marcion*, IV.9. Augustine, *Enchiridion*, 44, 71; *City of God*, Bk. 21, Chap. 27.
25. Lombard, *Sentences*, II, Dist. 42; Aquinas, *Summa Theologica*, I-II, Qq. 88, 89.
26. *The New Catholic Peoples' Encyclopedia*, vol. 3, rev. ed. (Chicago: The Catholic Press, 1973), p. 639.
27. Albert J. Nevins, ed., *The Maryknoll Catholic Dictionary* (New York: Grosset and Dunlap, 1956), p. 529.
28. Ibid., p. 530.

When a Roman Catholic goes to confession and receives the sacrament of penance, all mortal sins must be confessed, since, if one dies in mortal sin, he or she will be lost. Although venial sins do not result in the loss of salvation, it is highly desirable (though not absolutely necessary) that they be confessed as well.[29]

Calvin rejected this distinction, not because he recognized no gradations in the seriousness of sin, but because, in his judgment, all sins are mortal in the sense that they all deserve damnation.

> Let the children of God hold that all sin is mortal. For it is rebellion against the will of God, which of necessity provokes God's wrath, and it is a violation of the law, upon which God's judgment is pronounced without exception. The sins of the saints are pardonable, not because of their nature as saints, but because they obtain pardon from God's mercy.[30]

Calvin is right. The Bible clearly rejects the distinction between mortal and venial sin. As Paul says in Galatians 3:10, quoting from Deuteronomy 27:26, "All who rely on observing the law are under a curse, for it is written: 'Cursed is everyone who does not continue to do everything written in the book of the law.' " If this is so, how can anyone say that certain sins, that is, certain ways of breaking God's law, do not bring one under this curse? James further reminds us that "whoever keeps the whole law, and yet stumbles at just one point, is guilty of breaking all of it" (Jas. 2:10). Certainly a "venial sin" would be a "stumbling at one point." A practical difficulty with the above-mentioned distinction is the danger either of keeping believers in a continual state of anxiety and fear ("have I perhaps committed a mortal sin, and am I therefore lost?") or of bringing about an attitude of lighthearted carelessness about sin, by suggesting the thought that most sins are venial and are therefore not too serious.

Rejecting the distinction between mortal and venial sins, however, does not imply that there are no differences or gradations in the seriousness of sin. Four such differences may be noted.

*The distinction based on "sins of the spirit" over against "sins of the body."* Earlier[31] I pointed out that according to Augustine the root sin of man is pride; he further taught that what he called "concupiscence," which we would call "sensuality" or "carnal appetite," was secondary to and a result of pride.[32] What Augustine meant was that rebellion against God, which is primarily a "sin of the spirit" (though, of course, the body is also involved), is a more weighty transgression of God's

---

29. *New Catholic Peoples' Encyclopedia,* 3:718.
30. *Inst.,* II.8.59.
31. See above, p. 173.
32. *Enchiridion,* 24.

will than a so-called sin of the body like adultery (though in such a sin the "spirit" is also involved).

Luther made a similar point. He taught that many people pursue virtue only for the sake of their own honor, thus revealing their "fleshliness" even in their "noblest" pursuits.[33] Luther, in fact, distinguished between two kinds of fleshly people: *sinistrales* (those on the left) and *dextrales* (those on the right). The former, he said, show their fleshliness in yielding to their passions and lusts (like drunkards and adulterers); the latter show their fleshliness even while they are subduing their lusts and ostensibly practicing virtue. The latter, Luther added, are the worse of the two.[34] One is reminded of Jesus' denunciation of the Pharisees, who were so wretchedly evil precisely because they thought they were righteous.

C. S. Lewis, a Christian layman with deep insights into the faith, once put it this way:

> If anyone thinks that Christians regard unchastity as the supreme vice, he is quite wrong. The sins of the flesh are bad, but they are the least bad of all sins. All the worst pleasures are purely spiritual: the pleasure of putting other people in the wrong, of bossing and patronising and spoiling sport, and backbiting; the pleasures of power, of hatred. . . . That is why a cold, self-righteous prig who goes regularly to church may be far nearer to hell than a prostitute. But, of course, it is better to be neither.[35]

I believe that the Bible confirms this point. In Romans 1:24-32 we read that God gave up those who refused to acknowledge him, who "although they knew God . . . neither glorified him as God nor gave thanks to him" (v. 21), to all kinds of unmentionable bodily lusts. And in Matthew 21 Jesus is reported as having said to the chief priests and Pharisees who in their pride had rejected him and his message,

> I tell you the truth, the tax collectors and the prostitutes are entering the kingdom of God ahead of you. For John came to you to show you the way of righteousness, and you did not believe him, but the tax collectors and the prostitutes did. And even after you saw this, you did not repent and believe him. (vv. 31-32)

*The distinction based on the degree of knowledge the sinner has.* Both the Old and the New Testament teach that the sin of a person who knows the will of the Lord but goes against it is greater than that of someone who breaks God's law without full knowledge of what that

---

33. Carl Stange, "Luther und das Sittliche Ideal," in *Studien zur Theologie Luthers* (Gütersloh: Bertelsmann, 1928), pp. 183-84.
34. Erdmann Schott, *Fleisch und Geist nach Luthers Lehre* (Leipzig: Scholl, 1928), p. 6.
35. *Mere Christianity* (New York: Macmillan, 1967), pp. 94-95.

law requires. We know that the Old Testament sometimes speaks about "the curses of the covenant." God had made a covenant with his ancient people, promising them great blessings if they would fear him and walk in his ways. If, however, they disobeyed him, they would be punished all the more severely because of the greater knowledge of God's will that he had given to them. The covenant of grace, therefore, entailed not only blessings but also curses. We see this in Deuteronomy 29:18-28, particularly verses 20-21, where Moses, speaking of a person who has turned away from God in the stubbornness of his heart, says:

> The LORD will never be willing to forgive him; his wrath and zeal will burn against that man. All the curses written in this book will fall upon him, and the LORD will blot out his name from under heaven. The LORD will single him out from all the tribes of Israel for disaster, according to all the curses of the covenant written in this Book of the Law.

Similarly, Jeremiah says:

> The LORD said to me, "Proclaim all these words in the towns of Judah and in the streets of Jerusalem: 'Listen to the terms of this covenant and follow them. From the time I brought your forefathers up from Egypt until today, I warned them again and again, saying, "Obey me." But they did not listen or pay attention; instead, they followed the stubbornness of their evil heart. So I brought on them all the curses of the covenant I had commanded them to follow but that they did not keep.' " (Jer. 11:6-8)

And Amos, addressing the disobedient people of Israel, thunders like a lion, "You only have I [the LORD] chosen of all the families of the earth; therefore I will punish you for all your sins" (Amos 3:2).

The New Testament also teaches that the seriousness or gravity of a person's sin depends on the degree of knowledge that he or she had when the sin was committed. This is evident first of all from Jesus' words about two kinds of servants:

> That servant who knows his master's will and . . . does not do what his master wants will be beaten with many blows. But the one who does not know and does things deserving punishment will be beaten with few blows. From everyone who has been given much, much will be demanded; and from the one who has been entrusted with much, much more will be asked. (Luke 12:47-48)

Jesus made a similar observation about Sodom and Gomorrah, cities whose wickedness had become proverbial: "I tell you the truth, it will be more bearable for Sodom and Gomorrah on the day of judgment than for that town [a town that refuses to heed the gospel message as brought by the disciples]" (Matt. 10:15). The point is clear:

the sins of those who heard the gospel and yet rejected it are more serious in the sight of God than the wrongdoings—notorious though they may be—of those who never heard the gospel.[36]

After Pilate had said that he had power either to free or to crucify him, Jesus answered, "You have no power over me that was not given to you from above. Therefore the one who handed me over to you is guilty of a greater sin" (John 19:11). Jesus was apparently referring to Caiaphas, the ruling high priest, who had condemned him and delivered him up to Pilate. Caiaphas's sin was greater than Pilate's because he had acted with greater knowledge of Christ and his mission than had Pilate.

Paul also makes the point that lack of knowledge reduces the gravity of a sin: "Even though I was once a blasphemer and a persecutor and a violent man, I was shown mercy because I acted in ignorance and unbelief [lit., "ignorantly in unbelief"]" (1 Tim. 1:13).

*The distinction based on the degree of intent involved in the sin.* In the Old Testament a clear distinction is made between sins committed unintentionally and those committed intentionally. From Numbers 15:27-29 we learn about the sacrifice that could be brought to make atonement for a person who had sinned unintentionally. But in verse 30 we read the following: "But anyone who sins defiantly [lit., "with a high or uplifted hand"], whether native-born or alien, blasphemes the LORD, and that person must be cut off from his people." Note that in the case of the second kind of sin no atoning sacrifice was available. Whether this means that a person who sinned defiantly was for that reason always beyond forgiveness and salvation is another question (think of David's adultery and murder, which were yet subsequently forgiven), but it is clear that intentional sin is much more serious than unintentional sin.

From Leviticus 4:22 we learn that when a leader sinned unintentionally, he was indeed guilty; after the proper sacrifice had been brought, however, this sin could be forgiven. A similar distinction between sins is made in Numbers 35, where we read that the Lord instructed Moses to select some towns in the land of Canaan that were to be "cities of refuge,"

> to which a person who has killed someone accidentally [or unintentionally—the same Hebrew word is used here as in Numbers 15:27] may flee. They will be places of refuge from the avenger, so that a person accused of murder may not die before he stands trial before the assembly. (vv. 11-12)

36. Note a similar comment about Tyre and Sidon in Luke 9:13-14.

In verses 20-21 of the same chapter, however, we are told that "if anyone with malice aforethought [lit., "in hatred"] shoves another or throws something at him intentionally so that he dies. . . , that person shall be put to death."

In other words, though an unintentional sin is still a sin that brings guilt on the one who commits it, it is a sin of lesser magnitude than an intentional sin. Criminal law today still recognizes this principle when it distinguishes between first-degree murder and manslaughter.

*The distinction based on the extent to which a person gives in to sin.* Earlier reference was made to Matthew 5:28, where Jesus is quoted as saying, "But I tell you that anyone who looks at a woman lustfully has already committed adultery with her in his heart." A lustful look is therefore sinful. But surely the sin is magnified and intensified when the lustful look is permitted to lead to an adulterous act. Similarly, to have sinful anger in your heart is bad enough, but to give vent to that anger in vitriolic word or violent deed is worse.

Louis Berkhof sums up what the Bible teaches about gradations in sin as follows:

> Sins committed on purpose, with full consciousness of the evil involved, and with deliberation, are greater and more culpable than sins resulting from ignorance, from an erroneous conception of things, or from weakness of character. Nevertheless the latter are also real sins and make one guilty in the sight of God.[37]

## THE UNPARDONABLE SIN

Though all forms of sin are displeasing to God, the Bible speaks of one sin that is unpardonable—not because it is too great for God to forgive, but because by its nature it excludes the possibility of repentance.

We look first at the chief Scripture passages that describe this sin. Probably the most frequently quoted text is Mark 3:28-30 (par. Matt. 12:31-32; Luke 12:10). Matthew tells us that on this occasion Jesus had healed a demon-possessed man who was blind and mute. When the Pharisees heard about this miracle, they countered that Jesus was driving out demons only through Beelzebub, the prince of demons. In his rebuke of these Pharisees Jesus said that he was driving out demons by the Spirit of God, as evidence that the kingdom of God had

---

37. *Systematic Theology,* rev. and enl. ed. (Grand Rapids: Eerdmans, 1941), p. 252. On this point see also H. Bavinck, *Dogmatiek,* 3:148-51; and G. C. Berkouwer, *Sin,* chap. 9, pp. 285-322.

come upon them (Matt. 12:22-28). Jesus then uttered these telling words:

> I tell you the truth, All the sins and blasphemies of men will be forgiven them. But whoever blasphemes against the Holy Spirit will never be forgiven; he is guilty of an eternal sin. He said this because they were saying, "He has an evil spirit." (Mark 3:28-30)

Webster's dictionary defines *blasphemy* as "the act of insulting or showing contempt or lack of reverence for God." According to the above passage, some blasphemies can be forgiven, but blasphemy against the Holy Spirit can never be forgiven. What is the nature of this blasphemy? It would appear that, in the light of Jesus' words, the Pharisees had just committed this sin. They had deliberately attributed to the devil something that Christ, according to his own testimony, had done through the power of the Spirit of God. The imperfect tense of the verb for *saying* in verse 30 (*elegon*) suggests that the Pharisees said this not just once, but continually. This sin, therefore, was not committed in ignorance. The Pharisees saw the miracle and heard Jesus say that he had done this through the power of the Holy Spirit. Nevertheless they persisted in ascribing this marvelous deed to the devil.

What leaps out at us here is the expression Jesus uses to describe this transgression: the person who commits it "is guilty of an eternal sin" (*aiōniou hamartēmatos*, Mark 3:29). This is the only place in the Bible where this expression occurs. An *eternal sin* is one that remains forever—that is, it can never be forgiven.

Another passage that deals with the unpardonable sin is found in 1 John 5:16, where John writes:

> If anyone sees his brother commit a sin that does not lead to death, he should pray and God will give him life. I refer to those whose sin does not lead to death. There is a sin that leads to death. I am not saying that he should pray about that.

In a sense all sin leads to death (Rom. 6:23; Jas. 1:15). But God will forgive a sin that is repented of and confessed (1 John 1:9). Why, then, does John say that this "sin that leads to death" (*hamartia pros thanaton*)[38] need not be prayed for?

John Stott ties in this sin with the blasphemy against the Holy Spirit described by Jesus in the Gospels, and suggests that the death to which this sin leads is, in fact, " 'the second death,' reserved for

---

38. The RSV rendering, "mortal sin," is quite confusing, suggesting the Roman Catholic distinction between mortal and venial sins. In Roman Catholic practice, however, "mortal sins" can be forgiven if they have been properly confessed.

those whose names are not 'written in the book of life' (Rev. xx.15, xxi.8)."[39]

It is interesting to note that John does not forbid prayer for the forgiveness of such a sin but merely abstains from recommending such prayer. If a person has committed the unpardonable sin, we know that God will not grant him or her forgiveness and eternal life in answer to our prayer. But can we know for certain that a person has committed this sin? Alexander Ross's words about this problem are helpful:

> It [the sin against the Holy Spirit] seems to describe rather a *settled state* of sin, in which a man may go so far as to call evil good and good evil (Is. 5:20) . . . ; the character of such a person becomes fixed in evil. But then, how can we mortals, with our limited knowledge and insight, ever be certain that any man has reached that condition of soul? It ought to be observed that John does not say that the *sin unto death* can be definitely recognized as such. The practical conclusion, then, to which this passage leads us, is, possibly, that we ought to go on praying, exercising the judgment of charity.[40]

We turn next to two passages from the Book of Hebrews. The first is from Hebrews 6:4-6:

> It is impossible for those who have once been enlightened, who have tasted the heavenly gift, who have shared in the Holy Spirit, who have tasted the goodness of the word of God and the powers of the coming age, if they fall away, to be brought back to repentance, because to their loss they are crucifying the Son of God all over again and subjecting him to public disgrace.

Without going into detail on this passage, we may observe that the people here described have received some instruction in the truths of salvation, and have after such instruction, and after certain types of religious experiences, fallen away. The writer states specifically that these people cannot be brought back to repentance. The words "crucifying the Son of God all over again" suggest that now, after their defection from the faith, they are expressing a hatred for Christ that is comparable to the hatred of the Pharisees described in Mark 3:29. Since it is clearly stated that these people cannot now repent of their sin, it would seem reasonable to suppose (though we cannot be absolutely sure) that here again we have a description of the unpardonable sin.

The other Hebrews passage is from chapter 10:

39. *The Epistles of John*, Tyndale New Testament series (Grand Rapids: Eerdmans, 1964), pp. 188-89.
40. *The Epistles of James and John* (Grand Rapids: Eerdmans, 1954), p. 221.

If we deliberately keep on sinning after we have received the knowledge of the truth, no sacrifice for sins is left, but only a fearful expectation of judgment and of raging fire that will consume the enemies of God. Anyone who rejected the law of Moses died without mercy on the testimony of two or three witnesses. How much more severely do you think a man deserves to be punished who has trampled the Son of God under foot, who has treated as an unholy thing the blood of the covenant that sanctified him, and who has insulted the Spirit of grace? (vv. 26-29)

Here again there is reference to previous instruction in the faith: "after we have received the knowledge of the truth." The intentional nature of this sin is stressed: "If we deliberately (*hekousios*) keep on sinning." The words "no sacrifice for sins is left" use Old Testament language to express the unpardonableness of this sin.[41]

This sin is described in vivid terms. The person who is committing this sin has totally despised Christ ("trampled [him] under foot"), spurned and repudiated the blood shed by Christ for the purpose of bringing him or her closer to God, and has insulted and spat in the face of the Holy Spirit who is the bringer of grace. Most commentators, therefore, including Calvin, see also in these words a description of the unpardonable sin.

Louis Berkhof has defined the unpardonable sin as

the conscious, malicious, and wilful rejection and slandering, against evidence . . . , of the testimony of the Holy Spirit respecting the grace of God in Christ, attributing it out of hatred and enmity to the prince of darkness.[42]

There are five comments that we should make by way of elucidating this point.

1. The unpardonable sin is not the same as doubt, since it is a deliberate rejection of known truth about God's revelation in Christ, often including defiance of God and ridicule of sacred things.

2. This sin presupposes a revelation of the grace of God, a working of the Holy Spirit, and some illumination of the mind about the truths of salvation. It cannot therefore be committed by one who has no previous knowledge of "saving truth."

3. The unpardonable sin consists of a deliberate turning away from the grace of God in Christ. Calvin describes it as "striving knowingly to extinguish the Spirit dwelling within us," "deliberately and maliciously turning light into darkness," and "changing the one medicine of salvation into a deadly poison."[43]

41. See above, p. 181.
42. *Systematic Theology*, p. 253.
43. *Harmony of the Gospels*, trans. T. H. L. Parker, vol. 2 (Grand Rapids: Eerdmans, 1979), pp. 46-47.

4. This sin excludes the possibility of repentance, and is therefore unpardonable. When he commits it, the sinner has reached a point of no return. As R. Laird Harris puts it, "This sin, by its nature, makes forgiveness impossible, for the only possible light is deliberately shut out."[44] Herman Bavinck, after saying that God has laid down certain laws even for the realm of sin, goes on to affirm that

> the law which is operative in this sin is that it excludes all repentance, sears the conscience, altogether hardens the sinner, and in this way makes his sins unpardonable.[45]

5. Finally, a person who fears that he or she has committed this sin probably has not done so, since such a fear is incompatible with the state of mind of one who has sinned in this way.

44. "Blasphemy," in *Baker's Dictionary of Theology*, ed. E. F. Harrison (Grand Rapids: Baker, 1960), p. 98.
45. *Dogmatiek*, 3:157 [trans. mine]. On the unpardonable sin, see also Berkouwer, *Sin*, chap. 10, pp. 323-53.

# CHAPTER 10

# The Restraint of Sin

We have already discussed the devastating effects of the Fall on man's behavior. First, we saw that the Fall perverted the image of God in which man was created, with the result that the human person now functions sinfully in his relation to God, to others, and to nature.[1] I further described the universality of sin,[2] and went on to show that the condition of human beings after the Fall, apart from God's redemptive grace, is one of pervasive depravity and spiritual inability.[3]

If these descriptions are true, it would seem that life on earth today ought to be virtually impossible. Because of the Fall, every human being is basically self-centered and unloving, hating God, hating others, and exploiting nature. If this is so, it would appear that we have today nothing better than a hell on earth.

It is interesting to note that there has been a shift of thinking in recent years in the assessment of the behavior of human beings. There was a time in Western thought when human nature was described in rosy terms as basically good, and human beings were thought of as capable of noble and unselfish behavior, given the proper training and education. A number of liberal theologians who lived in the early decades of the twentieth century taught this view.[4] But this romantic, optimistic view of human nature is no longer in vogue. Beginning with the works of Walter Rauschenbusch (1861–1918) and continuing with the writings of Karl Barth (1886–1968) and Reinhold Niebuhr (1893–1971), there emerged a much more realistic view of man as basically sinful and self-centered. This sober and uncomplimentary

---

1. See Chap. 5 above, pp. 83-85.
2. See above, pp. 140-43.
3. See Chap. 8 above, pp. 150-54.
4. E.g., Samuel Z. Batten, who wrote *The Social Task of Christianity* in 1911; Washington Gladden (1836–1918); George D. Herron (1862–1925); and Arthur Cushman McGiffert (1861–1933).

view is also echoed by recent novelists, and has surfaced in nonfiction volumes in which human nature is pictured as sinful and hypocritical.[5]

Also illustrative of this shift is a fascinating book published in 1966, *Shantung Compound*, by Langdon Gilkey.[6] Gilkey was a liberal theologian who had been taught in seminary that man was basically good and unselfish. During the Second World War he was interned by the Japanese in a detention camp in China. Having been put in charge of housing, Gilkey tried to improve living conditions in the camp, which contained people from a number of countries, by appealing to the generosity, helpfulness, and good will of his fellow detainees. But it was all in vain. To his amazement, he learned through many frustrating experiences that human beings are all basically self-centered, even though they do not like to admit it. Life had disproved his theory. An unforgettable sentence sums up his conclusion: "Those humanists who insist that men are naturally wise and good enough to be moral seemed to me to be continually refuted by the patent persistence of dangerous selfishness among people whose intentions were good."[7]

We must agree, therefore, in the light of biblical teaching and human observation, that fallen man is indeed basically self-centered. Therefore, men and women need to be regenerated, to have a basic change of commitment and a new center of loyalty before they will be able to live the unselfish life to which God calls them.

But now we face a problem. As we live on this earth, we do not seem to experience consistently the kind of human badness and depravity sketched above. Many of us do have good neighbors. We find that most of the time we can trust people with whom we have business dealings. Often we run into people—and they are not always Christians—who seem to be kind, helpful, and unselfish. How can we account for this? How can we account for the degree of goodness we find in our fellow human beings, for the amount of truth we find in the writings of unbelievers, and for the amount of beauty that has been produced by musicians, painters, poets, and novelists who, as far as we can discern, are not Christians?

Augustine had an answer to this question. When his Pelagian adversaries reminded him of the virtues of the heathen, he called these virtues "splendid vices" (*splendida vitia*), since they were not practiced for God's glory but for self-love and human praise.[8]

---

5. See above, p. 141.
6. New York: Harper and Row, 1966.
7. *Shantung Compound*, pp. 229-30.
8. *City of God*, Bk. 5, Chaps. 12-20, vol. 2 in *Nicene and Post-Nicene Fathers*, First Series (rpt.; Grand Rapids: Eerdmans, 1983); *On Marriage and Concupiscence*, I.4.

Calvin, however, though basically agreeing with Augustine, was not totally satisfied with this answer. The former was just as deeply convinced of the sinfulness and corruption of fallen man as was the latter. But, Calvin went on to ask, how can we account for the elements of truth, goodness, beauty, civilization, and order that we find in this fallen, sinful world? Surely we cannot ascribe them to man's native ability, since he is unable to do any good in his own strength. We must, therefore, attribute these good things to the grace of God— a grace that restrains sin in fallen humankind even though it does not take away man's sinfulness. This type of grace Calvin distinguished from the particular or saving grace whereby man's nature is renewed and whereby he is enabled to turn to God in faith, repentance, and grateful obedience. Though Calvin used various terms to describe the general grace of God that restrains sin without renewing human beings, later theologians in the Reformed tradition were to call this *common grace.*

## THE DOCTRINE OF COMMON GRACE

We note now some of the ways in which Calvin described how this common grace functions:

> But here it ought to occur to us that amid this corruption of nature there is some place for God's grace; not such grace as to cleanse it, but restrain it inwardly. . . . Thus God by his providence bridles perversity of nature, that it may not break forth into action; but he does not purge it within.[9]

> Then follow the arts, both liberal and manual. The power of human acuteness also appears in learning these because all of us have a certain aptitude. . . . Hence, with good reason we are compelled to confess that its beginning [that is, the beginning of aptitude or talent in the arts] is inborn in human nature. Therefore this evidence clearly testifies to a universal apprehension of reason and understanding by nature implanted in men. Yet so universal is this good that every man ought to recognize for himself in it the peculiar grace of God.[10]

> Whenever we come upon these matters [valuable contributions in art and science] in secular writers, let that admirable light of truth shining in them teach us that the mind of man, though fallen and perverted from its wholeness, is nevertheless clothed and ornamented with God's excellent gifts. If we regard the Spirit of God as the sole fountain of truth, we shall neither reject the truth itself, nor despise it wherever it shall appear, unless we wish to dishonor the Spirit of God. For by holding the gifts of the Spirit in slight esteem, we contemn and reproach the Spirit himself.[11]

9. *Inst.,* II.3.3.
10. *Inst.,* II.2.14.
11. *Inst.,* II.2.15.

We can summarize here what Calvin is saying in this last quotation: (1) unbelievers may have the light of truth shining in them; (2) unbelievers may be clothed with God's excellent gifts; (3) all truth comes from the Spirit of God; (4) therefore to reject or to despise the truth when it is uttered by unbelievers is to insult God's Holy Spirit.

In another place Calvin says this:

> I do not deny that all the notable endowments that manifest themselves among unbelievers are gifts of God. . . . For there is such a great difference between the righteous and the unrighteous that it appears even in the dead image thereof. For if we confuse these things, what order will remain in the world? Therefore, the Lord has not only engraved such a distinction between honorable and wicked deeds in the minds of individual men but often confirms it also, by the dispensation of his providence. For we see that he bestows many blessings of the present life upon those who cultivate virtue among men. . . . All these virtues—or rather, images of virtues—are gifts of God, since nothing is in any way praiseworthy that does not come from him.[12]

Calvin, therefore, did pioneer work in this area of theological thought. Though he did not develop a full-blown doctrine of common grace, he did clearly teach that there is a grace of God that restrains the manifestation of sin in human life without taking away man's sinfulness, permitting unbelievers to utter many truths (even though they do not know *the truth*) and to produce many cultural products that are good.[13]

One of the later Reformed theologians who has made significant contributions to the doctrine of common grace is Herman Bavinck. On his assumption of the presidency of the Theological Seminary of the Gereformeerde Kerken in the Netherlands at Kampen in 1894, he delivered a presidential address (*rectorale rede*) entitled *Common Grace* (*De Algemeene Genade*). In this address he showed that the doctrine of common grace is grounded in Scripture, was first taught by Calvin, and is still of great significance and value. The following quotations will indicate how important Bavinck considered this doctrine to be:

> From this common grace proceeds all that is good and true that we still see in fallen man. The light still shines in the darkness. The Spirit of God lives and works in everything that has been created. Therefore there still remain in man certain traces of the image of God. There is still intellect and reason; all kinds of natural gifts are still present in him. Man still has a feeling and an impression of divinity, a seed of religion. Reason is a priceless gift. Philosophy is an admirable gift from God. Music is also a gift of God. Arts and sciences are good, profitable, and

12. *Inst.*, III.14.2.
13. For a fuller treatment of Calvin's views on this topic, see Herman Kuiper, *Calvin on Common Grace* (Grand Rapids: Smitter Book Co., 1928).

of high value. The state has been instituted by God. . . . There is still a desire for truth and virtue, and for natural love between parents and children. In matters that concern this earthly life, man is still able to do much good. . . . Through the doctrine of common grace the Reformed have, on the one hand, maintained the specific and absolute character of the Christian religion, but on the other hand they have been second to none in their appreciation for whatever of the good and beautiful is still being given by God to sinful human beings.[14]

Sin is a power, a principle, which has penetrated deeply into all forms of created life. . . . It would, if left to itself, have devastated and destroyed everything. But God has interposed with his grace. Through his common grace he restrains sin in its disintegrating and destructive working. But this [kind of grace] is still not sufficient. It subdues, but does not change; it restrains, but does not conquer.[15]

Ten years after Bavinck delivered this lecture, his illustrious contemporary, Abraham Kuyper, published the first volume of the most extensive treatment of common grace ever written, *De Gemeene Gratie (Common Grace)*.[16] Volume I, called the historical section, is a biblical-theological study that traces the history of common grace from the covenant with Noah through the New Testament era, with concluding chapters about the significance of common grace for the life to come. Volume II, the doctrinal volume, discusses the relation between common grace and creation, predestination, world history, the church, providence, the curse, and culture. Volume III, the practical section, applies the concept of common grace to such topics as government, church and state, the family, education, and society.

G. C. Berkouwer, who deals with the doctrine of common grace in chapter 5 of *Man: the Image of God* ("Corruption and Humanness"), recognizes Kuyper's contribution to the study of common grace. Kuyper, he says,

follows in Calvin's footsteps in his view of God's general grace or common grace. . . . According to Kuyper, this teaching . . . forms an indispensable part of Reformed doctrine. It arises from the confession of the deadly character of sin, and not from an attempt to relativize the extent of corruption. Kuyper, like Calvin, is enthralled by the beautiful and imposing achievements of men outside the church. This undeniable fact, says Kuyper, puts us before the apparent dilemma of either denying all these achievements or else viewing man as after all not completely fallen. But Reformed doctrine refuses to choose either horn of the dilemma. On the one hand, this good may not and can not be denied; and on the other

14. H. Bavinck, *De Algemeene Genade* (Grand Rapids: Eerdmans-Sevensma, 1922), p. 17 [trans. mine].

15. Ibid., p. 27 [trans. mine]. See also Bavinck's chapter, "Calvin and Common Grace," in *Calvin and the Reformation*, ed. Wm. P. Armstrong (New York: Revell, 1909).

16. This work eventually comprised three volumes. It was published by Höveker and Wormser in Amsterdam from 1902 to 1904.

hand, the completeness of corruption may not be diminished. There is only one solution: that grace is at work even in fallen man, to check the destruction which is inherent in sin.[17]

Those who acknowledged that there is such a thing as common grace, Berkouwer goes on to say,

> wished to reckon with the fact that in real life we do not encounter an antithesis between fullgrown badness and perfect holiness, but that even in the lives of unbelievers deeds become visible which reveal an undeniable likeness to the good works of believers.[18]

Not all Reformed theologians, however, agreed with Calvin, Bavinck, and Kuyper on the question of common grace. In the United States, Christian Reformed pastors Herman Hoeksema and Henry Danhof rejected the concept of common grace as unbiblical. Their position, briefly stated, was as follows: (1) God's grace is always particular and never common. Only the elect (those chosen for salvation from eternity) receive grace from God; those who are not elect, called "the reprobates," receive no grace from God whatever. (2) There is no such thing as a gracious restraint of sin on the part of God in the lives of "reprobate" persons. (3) The unregenerate cannot do any kind of good. Even the so-called virtues of the unregenerate, because they are wrongly motivated, are really sins.[19]

A heated discussion of this issue ensued within the Christian Reformed Church, reflected by the publication of many articles, pamphlets, and books on the subject. Taking issue with Hoeksema and Danhof, the 1924 Synod of the Christian Reformed Church of North America adopted the following three points: (1) There is, besides the saving grace of God shown only to those chosen to eternal life, also a certain favor or grace of God that he shows to his creatures in general. (2) God restrains sin in the life of the individual and in society. (3) The unregenerate, though incapable of "saving good" [the kind of good of which a regenerate person is capable], can perform "civil good" (*burgerlijk goed*) [a relative kind of good that meets certain external norms of social behavior].[20]

---

17. *Man*, pp. 152-53.

18. *De Mens het Beeld Gods* (Kampen: Kok, 1957), p. 166 [trans. mine].

19. These views were set forth in the following volumes: H. Danhof and H. Hoeksema, *Van Zonde en Genade* (Kalamazoo: Dalm, 1923); H. Hoeksema, *A Triple Breach in the Foundation of Reformed Truth* (Grand Rapids: C. J. Doorn, 1924); H. Hoeksema, *The Protestant Reformed Churches in America*, Part II (1936; Grand Rapids: [the author], 1947); H. Hoeksema, *Reformed Dogmatics* (Grand Rapids: Reformed Free Publishing Association, 1966).

20. [Trans. and abbrev. mine.] The full text of these three points may be found in the 1924 *Acts of Synod of the Christian Reformed Church*, pp. 145-47.

The Christian Reformed Church, therefore, by means of these decisions, endorsed the concept of common grace and rejected the views of Hoeksema and Danhof. These pastors, together with their followers, then proceeded to form a new denomination, the Protestant Reformed Churches in America.

There were also discussions of the doctrine of common grace in the Netherlands. In the 1930s and '40s Klaas Schilder, Professor of Dogmatics at the Theological Seminary of the Gereformeerde Kerken of the Netherlands in Kampen, publicly criticized the doctrine as Kuyper had defended it. Schilder's position was, in fact, quite similar to that of Herman Hoeksema. Schilder objected to the term *common grace* (*algemeene genade*) on the ground that, in his judgment, the term *grace* as used in Scripture always implies the forgiveness of sins. That the effects of God's curse on fallen mankind are being somewhat alleviated, Schilder does not see as an evidence of God's grace. The prolongation of human history after the Fall is not due to divine grace. There is no grace of God that restrains sin in the unregenerate. The doctrine of common grace, he maintains, weakens biblical teaching about human depravity and tends to introduce a "two-territory concept"—that is, the idea that, in addition to the fallen world in which sin reigns, there is a kind of neutral territory in which the effects of sin are minimized, and in which the antithesis between faith and unbelief is denied.[21]

Schilder's views gave rise to widespread discussion and debate. The General Synod of the Gereformeerde Kerken that met from 1940 to 1943 took issue with Schilder and his followers on the question of common grace, and adopted the following four-point pronouncement on the matter: (1) That God, despite his wrath against the sinfulness of men, still endures this fallen world in his longsuffering, doing good to all human beings. (2) That he has caused to remain in man certain small remnants of the original gifts of creation and a certain light of nature, though this light is insufficient for salvation. (3) That these remnants and blessings serve to restrain sin temporarily, so that possibilities given in the original creation can still come to development in this sinful world. (4) That God in this way shows undeserved goodness to the evil and the good—a goodness we call common grace (*algemeene genade* or *gemeene gratie*), but that is to

21. See K. Schilder, *Is de Term "Algemeene Genade" Wetenschappelijk Verantwoord?* (Kampen: Zalsman, 1947); this volume combined two lectures delivered in 1942 and 1946. Cf. his *Heidelbergsche Catechismus,* vol. 1 (Goes: Oosterbaan en Le Cointre, 1947), pp. 175ff., 116-20, 278, 284, 295, 109-10.

be distinguished from the saving grace that is shown to those who have been given to Christ by the Father.[22]

## BIBLICAL BASIS FOR COMMON GRACE

Does the Bible teach that there is a grace of God that restrains sin in the lives of those who are not his people? I believe it does. Let us look at some relevant Scripture passages.

Genesis 20 tells the story of Abraham's brief sojourn in the country of the Philistines. After he had said that his wife, Sarah, was his sister, the Philistine king Abimelech took Sarah with the intent of adding her to his harem. But one night God told Abimelech in a dream not to touch Sarah on pain of death, since she was a married woman. When Abimelech protested that he had taken Sarah under the impression that she was Abraham's sister, God said to him, "Yes, I know you did this with a clear conscience, and so I have kept you from sinning against me. That is why I did not let you touch her" (Gen. 20:6). Abimelech was obviously not a believer. Yet God restrained him from sinning. The fact that God promised Abimelech that Abraham would pray for him so that he might not die (v. 7) indicates that this restraint of sin was a gracious act on God's part.

In his letter to the Romans, Paul describes what happens to those who, though they knew God, did not glorify him as God:

> Therefore God gave them over [Gk.: *paredōken*] in the sinful desires of their hearts to sexual impurity for the degrading of their bodies with one another. . . . Because of this, God gave them over to shameful lusts. . . . Furthermore, since they did not think it worthwhile to retain the knowledge of God, he gave them over to a depraved mind, to do what ought not to be done. (Rom. 1:24, 26, 28)

In verse 18 of this chapter Paul tells us that the wrath of God is being revealed from heaven against the godlessness and wickedness of men and women who suppress the truth. In this suppression of the truth they are without excuse, "since what may be known about God is plain to them, because God has made it plain to them" (v. 19). Because they refused to glorify God as God, even though he had revealed himself to them in nature, God gave them over to sexual impurity, shameful lusts, and many other types of sinful and arrogant behavior. Three times in these verses Paul uses the aorist form *paredōken*, meaning "he gave them over" or "he abandoned them" to their

---

22. [Trans. and abbrev. mine.] The full text of this pronouncement, which was adopted in 1942, may be found in the *Acta van de Voortgezette Generale Synode van de Gereformeerde Kerken in Nederland*, 1940-43, pp. 95-96.

sins. The aorist tense of the verb *paradidōmi* suggests that there were specific times in the lives of these people when this "giving up" or "giving over" occurred. This clearly implies that previous to the "giving over" God was restraining the manifestation of sin in their lives; at a certain point, however, that restraint was taken away. Charles Hodge, commenting on this passage, puts it this way: "He [God] withdraws from the wicked the restraints of his providence and grace, and gives them over to the dominion of sin."[23]

One of the ways in which sin is restrained in the lives of human beings is through the penalties imposed by the state on criminals and other transgressors of the law—penalties like fines, prison sentences, and even, sometimes, capital punishment. As Paul points out,

> rulers hold no terror for those who do right, but for those who do wrong. Do you want to be free from fear of the one in authority? Then do what is right and he will commend you. For he is God's servant to do you good. But if you do wrong, be afraid, for he does not bear the sword for nothing. He is God's servant, an agent of wrath to bring punishment on the wrongdoer. (Rom. 13:3-4)

When Paul here tells us that every earthly ruler is God's servant, he clearly implies that it is God who by means of such rulers is restraining sin.

Similarly, Peter writes:

> Submit yourselves for the Lord's sake to every authority instituted among men: whether to the king, as the supreme authority, or to governors, who are sent by him to punish those who do wrong and to commend those who do right. (1 Pet. 2:13-14)

The punishment of those who do wrong—surely a means whereby sin is restrained, though imperfect and sometimes counterproductive—is here said to be done by governmental authorities who have been sent by the king. But Peter urges his readers to submit themselves to such governmental authorities "for the Lord's sake," implying that these rulers have been established among humankind by God's providence, and that therefore through their rule God is restraining sin.

In his second letter to the Thessalonians, Paul discusses the time of the Second Coming of Christ. He tells his readers that the Second Coming will not occur until "the man of lawlessness" (whom most interpreters identify with the antichrist mentioned in the Epistles of John) is revealed (2:3). Paul goes on to speak of a power that is now holding back the appearance of this man of lawlessness:

---

23. *Commentary on the Epistle to the Romans* (1886; Grand Rapids: Eerdmans, 1964), p. 40.

> And now you know what is holding him back, so that he may be revealed
> at the proper time. For the secret power of lawlessness is already at work;
> but the one who now holds it back will continue to do so till he is taken
> out of the way. (2:6-7)

Paul does not tell us who or what is holding back the manifestation of the man of lawlessness. What is puzzling here is that Paul
speaks of this restraint or holding back in both impersonal and personal terms: "You know *what* is holding him back" (v. 6), and "*the
one* who now holds it back" (v. 7). We cannot identify the power or
person restraining the man of lawlessness, but it is clear from this
passage that there *is* a power or a person holding him back. Furthermore, since the appearance of the man of lawlessness will usher in
a period of intense wickedness, at which time a man will proclaim
himself to be God (v. 4) and the work of Satan will be evidenced in
every sort of evil (vv. 9-10), it is clear that the holding back of this
incarnation of wickedness is tantamount to a restraint of sin. That
God's gracious control is behind this restraint is so obvious that it
hardly needs to be mentioned.[24]

## The Means by Which Sin Is Restrained

By what means does God restrain sin? It has often been said that it
is through their own reason and will that human beings are enabled
to restrain sin and to practice certain virtues. This position was often
defended by the scholastic theologians; Thomas Aquinas, for example,
believed that man's reason is able to control his lower passions. Though
there may be some truth in this conception, it must be judged deficient
for at least two reasons. First, it is too individualistic—sin is restrained more through social pressure than through the reasoning of
an individual. Second, as was pointed out earlier,[25] we often use our
reason simply to justify the wrong thing we want to do, a process
psychologists call *rationalization*. Reason, therefore, may as often be
used to defend an evil deed as to prevent it. A smart crook is, in fact,
more dangerous than a stupid one.

One important means by which God restrains sin in those who
are not his people is his *general revelation*, which has an impact on
the conscience of every human being. General revelation is the theological term that means God's revelation of himself through nature,
which is addressed to all of humankind, and which has as its goal the

---

24. On the question of the restraint of the man of lawlessness, see my *The Bible and
the Future*, rev. ed. (Grand Rapids: Eerdmans, 1982), pp. 158-62. See also H. Ridderbos,
*Paul*, trans. John R. De Witt (Grand Rapids: Eerdmans, 1975), pp. 521-26.
25. See above, p. 174.

revelation of enough knowledge of God to render men and women inexcusable when they do not serve or glorify God. In his letter to the Romans Paul sets forth the role of general revelation in restraining sin:

> Indeed, when Gentiles, who do not have the law, do by nature things required by the law, they are a law for themselves, even though they do not have the law, since they show that the requirements of the law are written on their hearts, their consciences also bearing witness, and their thoughts now accusing, now even defending them. (2:14-15)

The Gentiles, unlike the Jews who belong to God's covenant people, "do not have the law"—that is, they do not have the law of Moses, and are living outside the sphere of the special revelation of God's saving grace found in the Scriptures. What does Paul mean when he says that at times such Gentiles "do by nature things required by the law" (*ta tou nomou*, lit., "the things of the law")? He does not mean that these Gentiles are able to keep the law from the inner motive of love for God and with the purpose of glorifying God. First, he points out that the Gentiles *do* things required by the law—not stressing an inner motivation but rather their outward actions. Second, Paul does not say that they keep the law (which would require inward as well as outward conformity to it), but only that they *do the things of the law,* that is, that they do certain outward things prescribed by the law. Third, he says that they do the things required by the law *by nature* (*phusei*). *By nature* describes these Gentiles as they are in themselves, apart from God's regenerating and sanctifying grace. But the Scriptures plainly teach that apart from such regenerating grace no one can even begin to keep the law of God in its inward sense (see, e.g., Rom. 8:7-8). Hence what these Gentiles are able to do by nature must preclude the possibility of true inward obedience to the law, and must point to a type of obedience, not motivated by a love for God, that is only outward conformity to certain precepts of the law.

Translated literally, the next words read, "these, not having law, are to themselves law" (*houtoi nomon mē echontes heautois eisin nomos*). In other words, though these Gentiles do not have the law of Moses, there is within them a law that they must recognize—we may call this, if we wish, natural law. This law is the impact of God's general revelation on their consciences. The evidence for this is that "they show that the requirements of the law [*to ergon tou nomou*, lit., "the work of the law"] are written on their hearts" (v. 15). Paul does not say that these Gentiles reveal *the law* written on their hearts, as is said of God's redeemed people (e.g., Jer. 31:33), but that they show *the work of the law* written on their hearts. Whenever Gentiles do by nature things required by the law, Paul says here, they show that there is in their hearts an effect produced by the law that makes them recognize certain types of outward behavior as good and certain other types of outward behavior as bad. What law is this? The law expressed in God's general revelation, which teaches even Gentiles that there is a difference between right and wrong, that wrong is punished and right is rewarded.

In the last part of verse 15 Paul tells us that these Gentiles also have consciences that pass judgment on their deeds in the light of the moral standards they recognize. In this way their consciences reveal the impact upon them of God's general revelation.

We learn from this passage that Gentiles are capable "by nature" of a kind of outward conformity to God's law because of the impact on their consciences of God's general revelation. This outward conformity, to be sure, is not to be confused with the kind of obedience to God's law of which even believers have only a small beginning, but it does indicate that by means of his general revelation God restrains sin in the lives of those who are not his people.

The Canons of Dort, a Calvinistic creed adopted by the Dutch Synod of Dordrecht (1618–1619), recognized this restraint of sin through God's general revelation in a statement that is reminiscent of Romans 2:14-15. Instead of speaking about general revelation, however, the Canons mention "the light of nature," clearly implying that this light is available to every human being. The article affirms not only the fact that even unregenerate persons have some capability for "virtue and outward discipline" (thus implying a certain restraint of sin), but also the spiritual inadequacy of such behavior and the perversion of this natural light by sinful man:

> There is left in man after the fall, to be sure, a certain light of nature [*lumen aliquod naturae*] by means of which he retains certain ideas about God [*notitias quasdam de Deo*], about natural things, about the distinction between what is honorable and what is shameful, and shows some zeal for virtue and outward discipline [*aliquod virtutis ac disciplinae externae studium ostendit*]. But so far is this light of nature from enabling him to arrive at a saving knowledge of God [*ad salutarem Dei cognitionem*] and from converting himself to God that he does not even use it properly in natural and civil matters. Rather, he wholly pollutes it—such as it is— in various ways and suppresses it in unrighteousness. By doing this, he makes himself inexcusable before God.[26]

Another means by which God restrains sin in human life is through the various types of penalties for wrongdoing provided by human government—through laws, codes of behavior, and coercive measures

26. The Canons of Dort, III-IV.4 [trans. mine]. Quotations from the Latin text are from J. N. Bakhuizen Van den Brink, *De Nederlandsche Belijdenisgeschriften* (Amsterdam: Holland, 1940), p. 246.

whereby these laws are enforced. This point has been commented on above.

G. C. Berkouwer mentions a third means whereby sin is restrained in human society by what he calls *mede-menselijkheid*. This term is difficult to translate; literally, it translates as "fellow-humanbeingness," but could perhaps best be rendered as "social relationships." What Berkouwer means is this: since man never exists in isolation, but always in relatedness to fellow human beings, his sin is restrained through this relatedness. For example, we are often kept from doing the wrong we might feel inclined to do because we are married to someone who would be hurt by such action, or because our wrong action would cause our children to suffer and would perhaps bring disgrace to our parents. We are sometimes restrained from sin because we have neighbors and fellow workers who watch our actions closely, and because we have a good reputation among our associates that we wish to maintain. We are restrained from doing bad things because we have friends who would be deeply hurt by such conduct on our part. Still, as Berkouwer warns us, this social relatedness does not always keep us from sinning, since sometimes the entire society in which we live may be so corrupt as to exert a negative influence upon us.[27] We think, for example, of the way in which the German people (with some notable exceptions) blindly followed their *Führer* in his demonic program of murder and destruction during the Nazi war years.

## THE VALUE OF THE DOCTRINE OF COMMON GRACE

The doctrine of common grace, like any other doctrine, can be and sometimes is abused. Belief in common grace could be used as an excuse for softening the antithesis between a Christian world-and-life view and a non-Christian one, or as an excuse for questionable or worldly behavior. The doctrine of common grace could also lead to a toning down of biblical teaching on the depravity of man, and on the absolute necessity of regeneration.

Despite these possible abuses, against which the Christian Reformed Synod of 1924 already warned,[28] the doctrine of common grace has great significance and many values. What are some of these values?

The doctrine of common grace underscores *the destructive power of sin*. When properly understood, it is not a denial of either the antithesis between a Christian and a non-Christian way of looking at culture, or the pervasive depravity of fallen man. This doctrine

27. *Man,* pp. 179-87.
28. *Acts of Synod of the Christian Reformed Church,* 1924, pp. 135-37.

does not intend to create a kind of "neutral territory," where art and science may be pursued without concern for Christian distinctiveness. Actually, as we noted when we looked at Calvin's view of common grace, the affirmation of this doctrine grew out of a recognition of the depravity of man.

The doctrine of common grace recognizes *the gifts we see in unregenerate human beings as gifts from God.* This doctrine reminds us that, as Calvin said, we may appreciate the *truths* uttered by unregenerate philosophers even while recognizing that they do not know the *truth* as it is in Christ. We as Christian believers, therefore, may learn much from great works of literature written by unbelievers, even though we do not share their ultimate commitment. We may appreciate what has been produced by non-Christians in such areas of artistic endeavor as architecture, sculpture, painting, and music, since their gifts are from God. We may therefore enjoy the cultural products of non-Christians in such a way as to glorify God through them—even though such praise of God was not part of the conscious intent of these artists.

The doctrine of common grace also helps us to account for the *possibility of civilization and culture on this earth despite man's fallen condition.* As was said earlier, if God did not restrain sin in the unregenerate world, this earth would be like hell. But because of common grace, and because of the restraint of sin that this grace has brought about, civilization and culture have been possible. In fact, the civilizations of the past and present, despite the imperfections that have adhered to them, have made significant and abiding contributions to human culture.

One of the important implications of the doctrine of common grace for us is that we must continue to work and pray for a better world. The sentiment of many evangelical Christians seems to be, "This world is in the hands of the devil; let's just write it off as a total loss. Why paint the ship when it's sinking? Why vacuum the rug when the floodwaters are rising? This world is bad and it's getting worse; let's just forget about it and concentrate on evangelism."[29] Such a

29. This attitude is especially typical, though not necessarily so, of dispensational types of premillennial eschatology, which teach that when Christ comes again, all believers will be raptured up to heaven with Christ so as to escape the tribulation about to begin on the earth. On the basis of this view, there would seem to be little incentive for working for a better world, since the world is bound to get worse, and since believers will be snatched from it before it gets really bad. See David O. Moberg, *The Great Reversal* (Philadelphia: Lippincott, 1972), pp. 21, 37; also George M. Marsden, *Fundamentalism and American Culture* (New York: Oxford Univ. Press, 1980), pp. 66, 90, 125, 127, 158. For a critique of the dispensational view of the rapture, see *The Bible and the Future*, pp. 164-71.

view of the present world, however, does not reflect a proper, biblically based attitude.

This earth is still God's earth. He created it, maintains it, and directs it in such a way that sin is to some extent restrained, civilization is still possible, and human culture is significant.

So we must continue to concern ourselves with this present world, its politics, its economics, its life, and its culture. Not that we expect to see a totally Christianized world on this side of the new earth; we do not. But we must continue to work for a better world here and now. To that end we must use the resources of education and the printed page. We must be active in the political arena, through the efforts of Christian legislators, judges, and magistrates; through the ballot box, petitions, and referendums; through bringing pressure to bear on elected officials. We must continue to do all we can to alleviate suffering and hunger in the world, and to bring justice to the oppressed. We must keep on opposing the senseless nuclear arms race, and keep on working for world peace. We must continue to try to eliminate the enslavement caused by poverty and the inhumanity of slums. We must persistently oppose all forms of racism.

Our Reformed understanding of Scripture implies that all of life is to be brought under obedience to Christ. This means that Christian missions will involve a deed-ministry as well as a word-ministry. This means that the church should be concerned not only about spiritual problems but also about material needs—of people both in far-distant lands and in the local community. This means that we must be concerned to make our contribution toward a growing Christian culture: Christian art, literature, and education.[30] This means that we must teach our children and young people to see all of life in the light of God's word.

All of this ties in with that branch of theology called *eschatology* (the doctrine of the last things). Our future as believers includes a new earth in which righteousness will dwell (Isa. 65:17-25; 2 Pet. 3:13; Rev. 21:1-4). This new earth will not be totally other than the present earth; it will be the present earth renewed and glorified, purged of all the results of sin. Paul makes this point in Romans 8:19-21:

> The creation waits in eager expectation for the sons of God to be revealed. For the creation was subjected to frustration, not by its own choice, but by the will of the one who subjected it, in hope that the creation itself will be liberated from its bondage to decay and brought into the glorious freedom of the children of God.

30. In this connection, see H. Richard Niebuhr's *Christ and Culture*, esp. chap. 6, "Christ the Transformer of Culture" (New York: Harper and Row, 1951).

The new earth, Paul is saying here, will not be a world that has no continuity whatever with the present earth, but it will be the old creation completely liberated from its present bondage to decay, corruption, and sin. In other words, there will be continuity as well as discontinuity between the present earth and the new earth. This implies that our life and work on this earth will have abiding significance for the new earth that is to come.[31]

According to Revelation 21:24 and 26, "the glory and the honor of the nations" will be brought into the Holy City that will be found on the new earth. These intriguing words suggest that the unique contributions of every nation to the life of the present earth will in some way enrich life on the new earth. How this will be, we do not know. But this statement and the words of Revelation 14:13 that the works or deeds (*erga*) of the dead who die in the Lord will follow them, suggest some sort of continuity between what is done and accomplished on this earth and the life to come. Jean Daniélou puts it this way:

> Each of us will be eternally that which we shall have made ourselves on earth. Likewise, the new heaven and the new earth will be the transfiguration of this world, such as the work of man will have contributed to constitute it. In this sense the history of civilizations as that of the cosmos enters into the total compass of the history of salvation.[32]

Richard Mouw makes a similar point:

> The Holy City [i.e., the new Jerusalem of Revelation 21] is not *wholly* discontinuous with present conditions. The biblical glimpses of this City give us reason to think that its contents will not be completely unfamiliar to people like us. In fact, the contents of the City will be more akin to our present cultural patterns than is usually acknowledged in discussions of the afterlife.[33]

On the basis of this continuity between the present earth and the Holy City of the new earth, Mouw urges his readers to keep active in their cultural, scientific, educational, and political pursuits, knowing that in this way they will be preparing for a fuller and richer life on the new earth that awaits them.

Some day the restraint of sin will be complete. To that day we look forward in faith and hope.

---

31. See chap. 20, "The New Earth," in my *The Bible and the Future*, pp. 274-87. See also Hendrikus Berkhof, *Christ the Meaning of History*, trans. Lambertus Buurman (1962; Grand Rapids: Baker, 1979), pp. 188-93.

32. "The Conception of History in the Christian Tradition," in *The Journal of Religion* 30, no. 3 (July 1950): 176. For a fascinating discussion of the relation between the present world and life on the new earth, see Abraham Kuyper, *De Gemeene Gratie*, 1:454-94.

33. *When the Kings Come Marching In* (Grand Rapids: Eerdmans, 1983), pp. 6-7.

# CHAPTER 11

# *The Whole Person*

One of the most important aspects of the Christian view of man is that we must see him in his unity, as a whole person. Human beings have often been thought of as consisting of distinct and sometimes separable "parts," which are then abstracted from the whole. So, in Christian circles, man has been thought of as consisting either of "body" and "soul," or of "body," "soul," and "spirit." Both secular scientists and Christian theologians, however, are increasingly recognizing that such an understanding of human beings is wrong, and that man must be seen in his unity. Since our concern is with the Christian doctrine of man, we now look anew at the biblical teaching about human beings, to see whether this is so.

What we ought to observe first of all is that the Bible does not describe man scientifically; in fact,

> the general judgment [of theologians] is that the Bible gives us no scientific teaching about man, no "anthropology" that would or could be in competition with a scientific investigation of man in the various aspects of his existence or with philosophical anthropology.[1]

Further, the Bible does not use exact scientific language. It uses terms like *soul, spirit,* and *heart* more or less interchangeably. This is because

> the parts of the body are thought of, not primarily from the point of view of their difference from, and interrelation with, other parts, but as signifying or stressing different aspects of the whole man in relation to God. From the standpoint of analytic psychology and physiology the usage of the Old Testament is chaotic: it is the nightmare of the anatomist when any part can stand at any moment for the whole.[2]

It is therefore not possible to construct an exact, scientific, biblical psychology. Some have attempted to do so; most notable among

---

1. G. C. Berkouwer, *De Mens het Beeld Gods* (Kampen: Kok, 1957), p. 211 [trans. mine]. Cf. Ray S. Anderson, *On Being Human* (Grand Rapids: Eerdmans, 1982), p. 213.
2. John A. T. Robinson, *The Body* (London: SCM Press, 1952), p. 16.

them is Franz Delitzsch, whose *System of Biblical Psychology* was originally published in 1855. But even Delitzsch had to admit that "the Scripture is no scholastic [or didactic] book of science" and that "it is true that on psychological subjects, just as little as on dogmatical or ethical, does Scripture comprehend [or contain] any system propounded in the language of the schools."[3]

In 1920 the Dutch theologian Herman Bavinck wrote a book entitled *Biblical and Religious Psychology.* But he, like Delitzsch, admitted that

> [the Bible] does not furnish us with a popular or scientific psychology, any more than it provides us with a scientific account [*schets*] of history, geography, astronomy, or agriculture. . . . Even if one wished to try it, it would be impossible to draw from the Bible a psychology that would in some way meet our need. For not only would one be unable to give a complete account of all the various data, but the words that the Bible uses, such as spirit, soul, heart, and mind, have been borrowed from the popular language of the Jews of those days, ordinarily have a different content than that which we associate with those terms, and are not always used in the same sense. The Scriptures never use abstract, philosophical concepts, but always speak the rich language of everyday life.[4]

Though we cannot derive an exact, scientific psychology or anthropology from the Bible, we can learn from Scripture many important truths about man. We have, in fact, been doing so in the earlier chapters of this book. We should first of all remind ourselves again that the most important thing the Bible says about man is that he is inescapably related to God. Berkouwer puts it this way: "We may say without much fear of contradiction that the most striking thing in the Biblical portrayal of man lies in this, that it never asks attention for man in himself, but demands our fullest attention for man in his relation to God."[5] We may add that the Bible also focuses our attention on man as he is related to others and to creation.[6] In other words, the Scriptures are not primarily interested in the constituent "parts" of man or in his psychological structure, but in the relationships in which he stands.

## TRICHOTOMY OR DICHOTOMY?

From time to time, however, it has been suggested that man should be understood as consisting of certain specifically distinguishable

---

3. *A System of Biblical Psychology,* 2nd ed., trans. Robert E. Wallis (Edinburgh: T. & T. Clark, 1867), p. 16.
4. *Bijbelsche en Religieuze Psychologie* (Kampen: Kok, 1920), p. 13 [trans. mine].
5. *Man,* p. 195.
6. See above, pp. 75-82.

"parts." One of these understandings is commonly known as *trichotomy*—the view that, according to the Bible, man consists of body, soul, and spirit. One of the earliest proponents of trichotomy, as we saw, was Irenaeus, who taught that whereas unbelievers have only souls and bodies, believers acquire in addition spirits, which have been created by the Holy Spirit.[7] Another theologian who is usually associated with trichotomy is Apollinarius of Laodicea, who lived from approximately 310 to approximately 390 A.D. Most interpreters ascribe to him the view that man consists of body, soul, and spirit or mind (*pneuma* or *nous*), and that the *Logos* or divine nature of Christ took the place of the human spirit in the human nature that Christ took upon himself.[8] Berkouwer, however, points out that Apollinarius first developed his erroneous Christology in a *dichotomistic* context.[9] But J. N. D. Kelly says that it is a question of secondary importance whether Apollinarius was a dichotomist or a trichotomist.[10]

Trichotomy was taught in the nineteenth century by Franz Delitzsch,[11] J. B. Heard,[12] J. T. Beck,[13] and G. F. Oehler.[14] More recently it has been defended by such writers as Watchman Nee,[15] Charles R. Solomon (who states that through his body man relates to the environment, through his soul to others, and through his spirit to God),[16] and Bill Gothard.[17] It is interesting to note that trichotomy is also defended in both the old and the new *Scofield Reference Bible*.[18] In spite of this support, we must reject the trichotomist view of human nature.

---

7. See above, pp. 34-35.
8. E.g., Louis Berkhof, *History of Christian Doctrines* (Grand Rapids: Eerdmans, 1937), pp. 106-7; J. L. Neve, *A History of Christian Thought* (Philadelphia: United Lutheran Publication House, 1943), p. 126; Anderson, *On Being Human*, pp. 207-8.
9. *Man*, p. 209. See also the comment by A. Grillmeier quoted in his n. 20. *Dichotomy* is the view that man is to be understood as consisting of two "parts," body and soul.
10. J. N. D. Kelly, *Early Christian Doctrines* (London: Black, 1958), p. 292.
11. *System of Biblical Psychology*, pp. vii, 247-66.
12. *The Tripartite Nature of Man* (Edinburgh: T. & T. Clark, 1866).
13. *Outlines of Biblical Psychology*, trans. from the 3rd German ed. of 1877 (Edinburgh: T. & T. Clark, 1877), p. 38.
14. *Theology of the Old Testament*, ed. G. E. Day (1873; Grand Rapids: Zondervan, n.d.), pp. 149-51.
15. *The Release of the Spirit* (Indianapolis: Sure Foundation, 1956), p. 6.
16. *The Handbook of Happiness* (Denver: Heritage House Publications, 1971), p. 28; see also pp. 27-58.
17. Wilfred Brockelman, *Gothard, The Man and his Ministry: An Evaluation* (Santa Barbara: Quill Publications, 1976), pp. 85-96.
18. *The Scofield Reference Bible* (New York: Oxford Univ. Press, 1909), n. 1 on 1 Thess. 5:23; *The New Scofield Reference Bible* (New York: Oxford Univ. Press, 1967), n. 2 on 1 Thess. 5:23.

First, it must be rejected because *it seems to do violence to the unity of man.* The very word itself suggests that man can be split up into three "parts": *trichotomy,* from two Greek words, *tricha,* "threefold" or "into three," and *temnein,* "to cut." Some trichotomists, including Irenaeus, even suggest that certain people have spirits whereas others do not.

Second, we must reject it because *it often presupposes an irreconcilable antithesis between spirit and body.* Actually, trichotomy originated in Greek philosophy, particularly in the view of Plato, who also had a tripartite understanding of human nature. Herman Bavinck has a helpful discussion of this point in his *Biblical Psychology.* He points out that in Plato and other Greek philosophers a sharp antithesis was posited between invisible and visible things. The world as a material substance was not created by God, so said the Greeks, but stood eternally over against him. A mediating power was therefore necessary that could bind the world and God together and bring them into fellowship—the so-called world-soul. The view of man found in Greek thought, Bavinck continues, is similar: Man is a rational being who possesses reason (*nous*), but he is also a material being who has a body. Between these two there must be a third reality that acts as a mediator: *the soul,* which is able to direct the body in the name of reason.[19]

The Bible, however, does not teach any such sharp antithesis between spirit (or mind) and body. According to the Scriptures matter is not evil but has been created by God. The Bible never denigrates the human body as a necessary source of evil, but describes it as an aspect of God's good creation, which must be used in God's service. For the Greeks the body was considered "a tomb for the soul" (*sōma sēma*) that man gladly abandoned at death, but this conception is totally foreign to the Scriptures.

We must also reject trichotomy because *it posits a sharp distinction between the spirit and the soul that finds no support in Scripture.* We can see this most clearly when we observe that the Hebrew and Greek words rendered *soul* and *spirit* are often used interchangeably in the Bible.

1. Man is described in the Bible both as someone who is *body and soul* and as someone who is *body and spirit*: "Do not be afraid of those who kill the body but cannot kill the soul" (Matt. 10:28); "An unmarried woman or virgin is concerned about the Lord's affairs: Her aim is to be devoted to the Lord in both body and spirit" (1 Cor. 7:34);

19. *Bijbelsche en Religieuze Psychologie,* p. 53. Cf. TDNT, 6:395.

"As the body without the spirit is dead, so faith without deeds is dead" (Jas. 2:25).

2. Grief is referred to the *soul* as well as to the *spirit*: "In bitterness of soul Hannah wept much and prayed to the LORD" (1 Sam. 1:10); "The LORD will call you back as if you were a wife deserted and distressed in spirit" (Isa. 54:6); "Now is my soul troubled" (John 12:27, RSV); "After he had said this, Jesus was troubled in spirit" (John 13:21); "Now while Paul was waiting for them at Athens, his spirit was provoked within him" (Acts 17:16, RSV); "For by what that righteous man [Lot] saw and heard as he lived among them, he was vexed in his righteous soul day after day with their lawless deeds" (2 Pet. 2:8, RSV).

3. Praising and loving God is ascribed to both *soul* and *spirit*: "My soul magnifies the Lord, and my spirit rejoices in God my Savior" (Luke 1:46-47, RSV); "Love the Lord your God with all your heart and with all your soul and with all your mind and with all your strength" (Mark 12:30).

4. Salvation is associated with both *soul* and *spirit*: "Receive with meekness the implanted word, which is able to save your souls" (Jas. 1:21, RSV); "Hand this man over to Satan, so that the sinful nature may be destroyed and his spirit saved on the day of the Lord" (1 Cor. 5:5).

5. Dying is described as the departure either of the *soul* or of the *spirit*: "And as her soul was departing (for she died), she called his name Ben-oni" (Gen. 35:18, RSV); "Then he stretched himself upon the child three times, and cried to the LORD, 'O LORD my God, let this child's soul come into him again' " (1 Kings 17:21, RSV); "Do not be afraid of those who kill the body but cannot kill the soul" (Matt. 10:28); "Into your hands I commit my spirit" (Ps. 31:5); "And when Jesus had cried out again in a loud voice, he gave up his spirit" (Matt. 27:50); "Her spirit returned, and at once she stood up" (Luke 9:55); "Jesus called out with a loud voice, 'Father, into your hands I commit my spirit' " (Luke 23:46); "While they were stoning him, Stephen prayed, 'Lord Jesus, receive my spirit' " (Acts 7:59).

6. Those who have already died are sometimes referred to as *souls* and sometimes as *spirits*: Matt. 10:28 (quoted above); "When he opened the fifth seal, I saw under the altar the souls of those who had been slain" (Rev. 6:9); "You have come to God, the judge of all men, to the spirits of righteous men made perfect" (Heb. 12:23); "He [Christ] was put to death in the body but made alive by the Spirit, through whom also he went and preached to the spirits in prison who disobeyed long ago when God waited patiently in the days of Noah" (1 Pet. 3:18-20).

Trichotomists often appeal to two New Testament passages, Hebrews 4:12 and 1 Thessalonians 5:23, as specifically supporting their view; but neither of these passages does so.

Hebrews 4:12 reads as follows:

> The word of God is living and active. Sharper than any double-edged sword, it penetrates even to dividing soul and spirit, joints and marrow; it judges the thoughts and attitudes of the heart.

These words describe the penetrating power of the word of God. The author of Hebrews does not intend to say that the word of God causes a division between a "part" of human nature called the soul and another "part" called the spirit, any more than he intends to say that the word causes a division between the joints of the body and the marrow found in the bones. The language is figurative. The next clause indicates the intent of the author: he wishes to say that the word of God judges "the thoughts and attitudes (or intentions) of the heart." God's word (whether understood as meaning the Bible or Jesus Christ) penetrates into the innermost recesses of our being, bringing to light the secret motives for our actions. This passage, in fact, is in many ways parallel to a text from Paul: "He [the Lord] will bring to light what is hidden in darkness and will expose the motives of men's hearts" (1 Cor. 4:5). There is therefore no reason to understand Hebrews 4:12 as teaching a psychological distinction between soul and spirit as two constituent parts of man.

The other passage is 1 Thessalonians 5:23, which reads:

> And the God of peace himself sanctify you wholly [*holoteleis*]; and may your spirit and soul and body be preserved entire [*holoklēron*], without blame at the coming of our Lord Jesus Christ. (ASV)

We should observe first that this passage is not a doctrinal statement but a prayer; Paul prays that his Thessalonian readers may be totally sanctified and completely preserved or kept by God until Christ comes again. The totality of the sanctification prayed for is expressed in the text by two Greek words. The first, *holoteleis*, is derived from *holos*, meaning whole, and *telos*, meaning end or goal; the word means "whole in such a way as to reach the goal." The second word, *holoklēron*, derived from *holos* and *klēros*, portion or part, means "complete in all its parts." It is interesting to note that in the second half of the passage both the adjective *holoklēron* and the verb *tērētheiē* ("may be preserved or kept") are in the singular, indicating that the emphasis of the text is on the whole person. When Paul prays for the Thessalonians that the spirit, soul, and body of each one of them may be preserved or kept, he is obviously not trying to split man into three parts, any more than Jesus intended to split man into four parts when he said, "Love the Lord your God with all your heart and with all your soul and with all your strength and with all your mind" (Luke 10:27). This passage therefore also provides no ground for the trichotomic view of the constitution of man.[20]

The other commonly held view about the constitution of man is that called *dichotomy*—the view that man consists of body and soul. This view has been much more widely held than trichotomy. Does our rejection of trichotomy mean that we must now opt for dichotomy? A number of theologians affirm this belief. Louis Berkhof, for example, believes that "the prevailing representation of the nature of man in Scripture is clearly dichotomic."[21]

It is my conviction, however, that we should reject dichotomy as well as trichotomy. As Christian believers we should certainly repudiate dichotomy in the sense in which the ancient Greeks taught it. Plato, for example, advanced the view that body and soul are to be thought of as two distinct substances: the thinking soul, which is divine, and the body. Since the body is composed of the inferior substance called matter, it is of lower value than the soul. At death the body simply disintegrates, but the rational soul (or *nous*) returns to "the heavens" if its course of action has been just and honorable, and continues to exist forever. The soul is considered a superior substance, inherently indestructible, while the body is inferior to the soul, mortal, and doomed to total destruction. There is in Greek thought, therefore, no room for the resurrection of the body.[22]

But even aside from the Greek understanding of dichotomy, which is clearly contrary to Scripture, we must reject the term *dichotomy* as such, since it is not an accurate description of the biblical view of man. The word itself is objectionable. It comes from two Greek roots: *dichē*, meaning "twofold" or "into two"; and *temnein*, meaning "to cut." It therefore suggests that the human person can be cut into two

20. On the interpretation of Heb. 4:12 and 1 Thess. 5:23, see further Bavinck, *Bijbelsche Psychologie*, pp. 58-59; Louis Berkhof, *Systematic Theology*, rev. and enl. ed. (Grand Rapids: Eerdmans, 1941), pp. 194-95; Berkouwer, *Man*, p. 210. On Heb. 4:12 see also F. F. Bruce, *The Epistle to the Hebrews*, in the New International Commentary on the New Testament series (Grand Rapids: Eerdmans, 1964), pp. 80-83. For a defense of the trichotomic interpretation, see F. Delitzsch, *The Epistle to the Hebrews*, trans. T. Kingsbury (Edinburgh: T. & T. Clark, 1882), pp. 202-14, esp. 212-14.

21. *Systematic Theology*, p. 192. Cf. A. H. Strong, *Systematic Theology*, vol. 2 (Philadelphia: Griffith and Rowland, 1907), pp. 483-88; J. T. Mueller, *Christian Dogmatics* (St. Louis: Concordia, 1934), p. 184; H. C. Thiessen, *Introductory Lectures in Systematic Theology* (Grand Rapids: Eerdmans, 1949), pp. 225-26; Gordon H. Clark, *The Biblical Doctrine of Man* (Jefferson, MD: The Trinity Foundation, 1984), pp. 33-45.

22. Cf. my *The Bible and the Future*, rev. ed. (Grand Rapids: Eerdmans, 1982), pp. 86-87. On this point note also Berkouwer, *Man*, pp. 212-22.

"parts." But man in this present life cannot be so cut. As we shall see, the Bible describes the human person as a totality, a whole, a unitary being.

The best way to determine the biblical view of man as a whole person is to examine the terms used to describe the various aspects of man. Before we do so, however, two observations are in order: (1) As was said, the Bible's primary concern is not the psychological or anthropological constitution of man but his inescapable relatedness to God; and (2) we must always bear in mind what J. A. T. Robinson says about the Old Testament usage of these terms: "Any part can stand at any moment for the whole,"[23] and what G. E. Ladd affirms about the New Testament usage of these words: "Recent scholarship has recognized that such terms as body, soul, and spirit are not different, separable faculties of man but different ways of viewing the whole man."[24]

With this in mind, we will deal first with Old Testament words, and then with those found in the New Testament.

## OLD TESTAMENT WORDS

We begin with the Hebrew word *nephesh,* most commonly rendered "soul." The Hebrew lexicon of Brown, Driver, and Briggs[25] gives ten meanings for this word, of which the following are significant for our purpose: "the inner being of man," "living being" (used of both human beings and animals),[26] "the man himself" (often used as a personal pronoun: myself, himself, etc.; in this sense it may mean man as a whole), "seat of the appetites," "seat of the emotions." The word may sometimes refer to a deceased person, with or without *mēth* ("dead"). The *nephesh* is sometimes even said to die.

It is clear, therefore, that the word *nephesh* may often stand for the whole person. Edmond Jacob puts it this way: "*Nephesh* is the usual term for a man's total nature, for what he is and not just what he has. . . . Hence the best translation in many instances is 'person.' "[27]

The next Hebrew word is *rūach,* commonly translated "spirit."

---

23. *The Body,* p. 16.
24. G. E. Ladd, *A Theology of the New Testament* (Grand Rapids: Eerdmans, 1974), p. 457.
25. Francis Brown, S. R. Driver, and Charles Briggs, *Hebrew and English Lexicon of the Old Testament* (New York: Houghton Mifflin, 1907).
26. Probably the best-known example of the use of this word to refer to man is Gen. 2:7, "And the LORD God formed man from the dust of the ground and breathed into his nostrils the breath of life, and man became a living being [*nephesh chayyāh*]."
27. *"Psychē,"* TDNT, 9:620.

The root meaning of this word is "air in motion"; it is often used to describe the wind. Brown-Driver-Briggs lists nine meanings, including the following: "spirit," "animation," "disposition," "spirit of the living and breathing being dwelling in the flesh of men and animals" (only one instance of the latter: Eccl. 3:21), "seat of emotion," "organ of mental acts," "organ of the will." *Rūach*, therefore, overlaps in meaning with *nephesh*. W. D. Stacey says:

> When reference is made to man in his relation to God, *rūach* is the term most likely to be used. . . , but when reference is made to man in relation to other men, or man living the common life of men, then *nephesh* is most likely, if a psychical term is required. In both cases the whole man was involved.[28]

*Rūach*, it follows, must not be thought of as a separable aspect of man, but as the whole person viewed from a certain perspective.

We look next at the Old Testament words usually translated as "heart": *lēbh* and *lēbhābh*. Brown-Driver-Briggs gives ten meanings for these two words, including the following: "the inner man or soul," "mind," "resolutions of the will," "conscience," "moral character," "the man himself," "seat of the appetites," "seat of the emotions," "seat of courage." F. H. Von Meyenfeldt, in his definitive study of the word, concludes that *lēbh* or *lēbhābh* usually represents the whole person and has a predominantly religious significance.[29]

Not only is the word *heart* in the Old Testament used to describe the seat of thinking, feeling, and willing; it is also the seat of sin (Gen. 6:5; Ps. 95:8, 10; Jer. 17:9), the seat of spiritual renewal (Deut. 30:6; Ps. 51:10; Jer. 31:33; Ezek. 36:26), and the seat of faith (Ps. 28:7; 112:7; Prov. 3:5).

More than any other Old Testament term, the word *heart* stands for man at the deepest center of his existence, and as he is in the depths of his being. Herman Dooyeweerd, the Dutch philosopher, found the heart in Scripture to be "the religious root of man's entire existence";[30] the philosophy he developed stresses that the heart is the center and source of all of man's religious, philosophical, and moral activities. Ray Anderson calls the heart "the center of the subjective self"; it is "the unity of body and soul in their true order—it is the person."[31]

---

28. *The Pauline View of Man* (London: Macmillan, 1956), p. 90.
29. F. H. Von Meyenfeldt, *Het Hart (Leb, Lebab) in het Oude Testament* (Leiden: E. J. Brill, 1950), pp. 218-19.
30. *Wijsbegeerte der Wetsidee*, vol. 1 (Amsterdam: H. J. Paris, 1935), p. 30.
31. *On Being Human*, p. 211.

All three Old Testament terms examined so far, therefore, describe man in his unity and wholeness, though looking at him from slightly different aspects. H. Wheeler Robinson comments: "It is not possible to give any exact differentiation of the provinces covered by 'heart,' *nephesh*, and *rūach*, for the simple reason that such exact differentiation was never made."[32]

We take up next the word *bāsār*, commonly rendered "flesh." Brown-Driver-Briggs lists six meanings, including the following: "flesh" (for the body itself), "blood relatives or kindred," "man over against God as frail and erring," "mankind." N. P. Bratsiotis says that *bāsār* is most frequently used in the Old Testament for "the external, fleshly aspect of man's nature."[33] He goes on to say that when *bāsār* is distinguished as the external aspect of man and *nephesh* is understood as the internal aspect, even then we must never think of these words as describing a dualism of soul and body in the Platonic sense.

> Rather, *bāsār* and *nephesh* are to be understood as different aspects of man's existence as a twofold entity. It is precisely this emphatic anthropological wholeness that is decisive for the twofold nature of the human being. It excludes any view of a dichotomy between *bāsār* and *nephesh* . . . as irreconcilably opposed to each other, and reveals the mutual organic psychosomatic relationship between them.[34]

The word *bāsār* is often used to describe man in his weakness. H. W. Wolff observes that frequently *bāsār* describes human life as frail and weak, giving as an example of this usage Jeremiah 17:5, "Cursed is the one who trusts in man, and depends on flesh for his strength."[35]

*Bāsār* may sometimes denote the entire person, not just the physical aspect.[36] But it may also be joined with *nephesh* in ways that refer to the whole man. Clarence B. Bass, commenting on Old Testament words for "body," states,

> Body and soul are used almost interchangeably, soul to indicate man as a living being, and body (flesh) to denote him as a corporeally visible creature. . . . This unity of body and soul [has] led some writers to conclude that the Old Testament lacks a view of the physical body as a discreet entity. . . . More properly, however, the Old Testament sees body

32. *The Christian Doctrine of Man* (Edinburgh: T. & T. Clark, 1911), p. 26.
33. "*Bāsār*," in G. Johannes Botterweck and Helmer Ringgren, eds., *Theological Dictionary of the Old Testament*, trans. John T. Willis, vol. 2, rev. ed. (Grand Rapids: Eerdmans, 1977), p. 325.
34. Ibid., p. 326.
35. *Anthropologie des Alten Testaments* (Munich: Chr. Kaiser, 1973), p. 55.
36. F. B. Knutson, "Flesh," ISBE, 2:314.

and soul as coordinates interpenetrating each other in function to form a single whole.[37]

*Bāsār*, therefore, also is often used in the Old Testament to denote the whole person, though with an emphasis on his external side.

Thus, the thought-world of the Old Testament totally excludes any kind of dichotomy or dualism that would picture man as made up of two distinct substances. As H. Wheeler Robinson says, "The final emphasis must fall on the fact that the four terms [*nephesh, rûach, lēbh,* and *bāsār*] . . . simply present different aspects of the unity of personality."[38]

## New Testament Words

The first New Testament word we will examine is *psychē*, the Greek equivalent of *nephesh*, most commonly translated "soul." The Arndt-Gingrich lexicon of New Testament Greek lists a number of meanings for this word, some of which are: "life-principle," "earthly life itself," "seat of the inner life of man" (including feelings and emotions), "seat and center of life that transcends the earthly," "that which possesses life: a living creature" (plural, persons).[39]

Eduard Schweizer affirms that *psychē* is often used in the Gospels to describe the whole man,[40] to depict true life in distinction from purely physical life,[41] and to refer to the God-given existence that survives death.[42] Paul, Schweizer continues, uses *psychē* when referring to natural life and true life; he often uses the word to describe the person.[43] In the Book of Revelation *psychē* may be used to denote life after death (as in 6:9).[44] It is clear, therefore, that *psychē*, like *nephesh*, often stands for the whole person.

We turn next to the word *pneuma*, the New Testament equivalent of *rûach*, which when it refers to man is most commonly translated

37. "Body," ibid., 1:528-29. Note also the comment by J. Pedersen, "Soul and body [in Old Testament terminology] are so intimately united that a distinction cannot be made between them. They are more than 'united'; the body is the soul in its outward form" (*Israel: Its Life and Culture,* vol. 1 [London: Oxford Univ. Press, 1926], p. 171).
38. *The Christian Doctrine of Man,* p. 27.
39. William F. Arndt and F. Wilbur Gingrich, *A Greek-English Lexicon of the New Testament and Other Early Christian Literature* (Chicago: Univ. of Chicago Press, 1957).
40. "*Psychē*," TDNT, 9:639.
41. Ibid., p. 642.
42. Ibid., p. 644.
43. Ibid., p. 648.
44. Ibid., p. 654.

"spirit." The Arndt-Gingrich lexicon gives eight meanings, including the following: "the spirit as part of the human personality," "a person's self or ego," "a disposition or state of mind." Schweizer says that Paul uses *pneuma* for the psychical functions of man, that it is often a parallel to *psychē*, and that it can denote man as a whole, with a stronger emphasis on his psychical than on his physical nature.[45]

George Ladd, in a discussion of Pauline psychology, tells us that in Paul's thought man serves God with the spirit and experiences renewal in the spirit. Paul sometimes contrasts *pneuma* with the body as the inner dimension over against the outer side of man (2 Cor. 7:1; Rom. 8:10). *Pneuma* may describe man's self-awareness or self-consciousness (1 Cor. 2:11).[46] W. D. Stacey makes the point that Paul does not see *pneuma* as something only regenerated people have: "All men have *pneuma* from birth, but the Christian *pneuma*, in fellowship with the Spirit of God, takes on a new character and a new dignity (Rom. 8:10)."[47]

It is interesting to note that *pneuma* may also refer to life after death. As we have seen, Hebrews 12:23 describes deceased saints as "the spirits of righteous men made perfect," and both Christ (Luke 23:46) and Stephen (Acts 7:59) as they are dying commit their spirits to God the Father or God the Son. Christ is also said to have preached to the "spirits in prison," obviously referring to deceased persons (1 Pet. 3:19).

*Pneuma* is therefore largely synonymous with *psychē*, the two words often used interchangeably in the New Testament. Ladd does, however, suggest a distinction between them: "Spirit is often used of God; soul is never so used. This suggests that *pneuma* represents man in his Godward side, while *psychē* represents man in his human side."[48] In general, I agree with this, but there are exceptions. For example, the *psychē* is sometimes described as praising or magnifying the Lord (Luke 1:46), and James tells us about the implanted word that is able to save our souls (*psychas*, Jas. 1:21). *Pneuma*, it is clear, may often be used to designate the whole person; it, like *psychē*, describes an aspect of man in his totality.

The next word we will look at is *kardia*, the New Testament equivalent of *lēbh* and *lēbhābh*, usually translated "heart." Arndt-Gingrich gives as the main meaning of this word "the seat of physical, spiritual, and mental life." It is also described as the center and source

---

45. "Pneuma," TDNT, 6:435.
46. Ladd, *A Theology of the New Testament*, pp. 461-63.
47. *The Pauline View of Man*, p. 135.
48. *New Testament Theology*, p. 459.

of the whole inner life of man, with its thinking, feeling, and volition. The heart is also said to be the dwelling place of the Holy Spirit.

Johannes Behm similarly describes the heart in the New Testament as the main organ of psychic and spiritual life, the place in the human being at which God bears witness to himself. The heart is the center of the person's inner life: of his or her feelings, understanding, and will. Heart means the whole inner being of man, the innermost part of him; it stands for the ego, the person. *Kardia* is supremely the center in man to which God turns, in which the religious life is rooted, and which determines moral conduct.[49]

Earlier we noted that *lēbh* in the Old Testament is also used to indicate the heart as the seat of sin, the seat of spiritual renewal, and the seat of faith. This is true of *kardia* as well. In addition, we may note that other Christian virtues are ascribed to *kardia*. Love is associated with the heart in 2 Thessalonians 3:5 and 1 Peter 1:22. Obedience is linked to the heart in Romans 6:17 and in Colossians 3:22. Forgiveness is associated with the heart in Matthew 18:35. The heart is linked with lowliness in Matthew 11:29, and is described as the seat of purity in Matthew 5:8 and James 4:8. Thankfulness is associated with the heart in Colossians 3:16, and peace is said to guard the heart in Philippians 4:7.

In a section of his *Dogmatics* in which he deals with "Man as Soul and Body," Karl Barth, speaking of the heart in both Old and New Testaments, puts it this way:

> If we are true to the biblical texts we must say of the heart that it is *in nuce* the whole man himself, and therefore not only the locus of his activity but its essence. . . . Thus the heart is not merely *a* but *the* reality of man, both wholly of soul and wholly of body.[50]

So here again we see the biblical emphasis on the wholeness of man. *Kardia* stands for the whole person in his or her inner essence. In the heart man's basic attitude toward God is determined, whether of faith or unbelief, obedience or rebellion.

Though the Old Testament does not, strictly speaking, have a word for *body*, it does use *bāsār* to describe the physical aspect of man, his *flesh*. In the New Testament there are two words for body: *sarx* and *sōma*. Arndt-Gingrich lists eight meanings for *sarx*, usually translated "flesh"; among the other meanings are: "body," "a human being," "human nature," "physical limitation," "the outward side of life," and "the willing instrument of sin" (particularly in Paul's writings).

---

49. *"Kardia,"* TDNT, 3:611-12.
50. *Church Dogmatics* (Edinburgh: T. & T. Clark, 1960), III/2, p. 436.

*Sarx* in the New Testament, then, has two main meanings: (1) the external, physical aspect of man's existence—in this sense it may be used of man as a whole; and (2) flesh as the tendency within fallen man to disobey God in every area of life.[51] In this second sense, found chiefly in Paul's epistles, we must not restrict the meaning of *sarx* so as to refer only to what we commonly call "fleshly sins" (sins of the body); rather, we should understand it as referring to sins committed by the whole person. In the list of "works of the flesh" (*ta erga tēs sarkos*) found in Galatians 5:19-21, only five out of fifteen concern bodily sins; the rest are what we would call "sins of the spirit"—such as hatred, discord, jealousy, and the like. So even when the word *sarx* is used in the second sense, it looks at the whole person, and not just at a part of him.

Now we look at the word *sōma*, commonly translated "body." Arndt-Gingrich gives five meanings, including the following: "the living body," "the resurrection body," and "the Christian community or church." Clarence B. Bass, in an article on the body in Scripture, also lists five definitions for the word *sōma*: "the whole person as an entity before God," "the locus of the spiritual in man," "the whole man as destined for membership in God's kingdom," "the vehicle for the resurrection," and "the site of spiritual testing in terms of which the judgment will take place."[52] He arrives at the following conclusion:

> Thus, it is clear that the body is used to represent the whole man, and militates against any idea of the biblical view of man as existing apart from bodily manifestation, unless it be during the intermediate state [that is, the state between death and resurrection].[53]

We may summarize our discussion of the biblical words used to describe the various aspects of man as follows: man must be understood as a unitary being. He has a physical side and a mental or spiritual side, but we must not separate these two. The human person must be understood as an embodied soul or a "besouled" body.[54] He or she must be seen in his or her totality, not as a composite of different "parts." This is the clear teaching of both Old and New Testaments.[55]

51. A competent, though older, study of the meaning of *sarx* in Paul's writings is Wm. P. Dickson, *St. Paul's Use of the Terms Flesh and Spirit* (Glasgow: Maclehose, 1883). A more recent study is J. A. T. Robinson, *The Body* (1952).
52. "Body," ISBE, 1:529.
53. Ibid.
54. Barth, *Church Dogmatics*, III/2, p. 350.
55. In addition to the studies of the biblical view of the whole person referred to above, we may note the following: G. C. Berkouwer, "The Whole Man," in *Man*, pp. 194-233; C. A. Van Peursen, *Body, Soul, Spirit: A Survey of the Body-Mind Problem*, trans. H. H.

## PSYCHOSOMATIC UNITY

Though the Bible does see man as a whole, it also recognizes that the human being has two sides: physical and nonphysical. He has a physical body, but he is also a personality. He has a mind with which he thinks but also a brain which is part of his body, and without which he cannot think. When things go wrong with him, sometimes he needs surgery, but at other times he may need counseling. Man is *one* person who can, however, be looked at from *two* sides.

How, now, shall we give expression to this "two-sidedness" of man? We have already noted the difficulties connected with the term *dichotomy*. Some have spoken of *dualism*,[56] while others prefer the term *duality*, as doing greater justice to the unity of man. Berkouwer, for instance, explains that "duality and dualism are not at all identical, and . . . a reference to a dual moment in cosmic reality does not necessarily imply a dualism."[57] Similarly, Anderson says that "we must make a distinction between a 'duality' of being in which a modality of differentiation is constituted as a fundamental unity, and a 'dualism' which works against that unity."[58]

My preference, however, is to speak of man as a *psychosomatic unity*. The advantage of this expression is that it does full justice to the two sides of man, while stressing man's unity.[59]

We can illustrate this by looking at the relationship between the mind and the brain. Recognizing that man should be thought of as a unity with many aspects that constitute an indivisible whole, Donald M. MacKay makes these significant comments about the relation between mind and brain:

Hoskins (London: Oxford Univ. Press, 1966); H. Ridderbos, *Paul: An Outline of His Theology,* trans. John R. De Witt (Grand Rapids: Eerdmans, 1975), pp. 64-68, 114-26; Rudolf Bultmann, *Theology of the New Testament,* trans. K. Grobel, vol. 1 (New York: Scribner, 1951), pp. 190-227; Werner G. Kümmel, *Man in the New Testament,* trans. John J. Vincent, rev. and enl. ed. (London: Epworth, 1963); Robert Jewett, *Paul's Anthropological Terms* (Leiden: E. J. Brill, 1971).

56. John Cooper, "Dualism and the Biblical View of Human Beings," *Reformed Journal* 32, nos. 9 and 10 (Sept. and Oct. 1982).

57. *Man,* p. 211.

58. *On Being Human,* p. 209. See also Robert H. Gundry, *Sōma in Biblical Theology* (Cambridge: Cambridge Univ. Press, 1976), p. 83. Gundry finds "duality" rather than "dualism" taught in both Old and New Testaments, particularly in the writings of Paul.

59. This term is also used by John Murray, "Trichotomy," in *Collected Writings of John Murray,* vol. 2 (Edinburgh: Banner of Truth Trust, 1977), p. 33 ("man is a 'psychosomatic being' "); and by G. W. Bromiley, "Anthropology," ISBE, 1:134 ("man has a physical side and a spiritual side. . . . Both belong together in a psychosomatic unity"). See also Henry Stob, *Ethical Reflections* (Grand Rapids: Eerdmans, 1978), p. 226.

We do not need to picture 'mind' and 'brain' as two kinds of interacting 'substance.' We do not need to think of mental events and brain events as two distinct *sets* of events. . . . It seems to me sufficient rather to describe mental events and their correlated brain events as the 'inside' and 'outside' aspects of one and the same sequence of events, which in their full nature are richer—have more to them—than can be expressed in either mental or physical categories alone.[60]

We are considering them [my conscious experience and the workings of my brain] as two equally real aspects of one and the same mysterious unity. The outside observer sees one aspect, as a physical pattern of brain activity. The agent himself knows another aspect as his conscious experience. . . . What we are saying is that these aspects are complementary.[61]

Man, then, exists in a state of psychosomatic unity. So we were created, so we are now, and so we shall be after the resurrection of the body. For full redemption must include the redemption of the body (Rom. 8:23; 1 Cor. 15:12-57), since man is not complete without the body. The glorious future of human beings in Christ includes both the resurrection of the body and a purified, perfected new earth.[62]

## THE INTERMEDIATE STATE

But now we face an important question. What about the period between death and resurrection, the so-called "intermediate state"? When a person dies, what happens? Since one is not complete without a body, does a person then simply cease to exist until the time of the resurrection? Or does he then "exist" in a totally unconscious state? Or does he immediately after death receive his resurrection body? Or does he receive a kind of intermediate body, later to be replaced by the resurrection body?

The view that man ceases to exist between death and resurrection, held by both Jehovah's Witnesses and Seventh-day Adventists, must be rejected as unbiblical.[63] The idea that immediately after death people will receive "intermediate" bodies also has no scriptural basis. The contrast in the New Testament is always between the present body and the resurrection body (cf. Phil. 3:21; 1 Cor. 15:42-44). Ad-

---

60. Donald M. MacKay, *Brains, Machines and Persons* (Grand Rapids: Eerdmans, 1980), p. 14.

61. Ibid., p. 83. Later in this book (p. 101) MacKay describes the future life of the Christian in a way in which he seems to leave room only for the resurrection of the body and not for the continued existence of the believer in the intermediate state (see below, pp. 218-22). If this is MacKay's position, I would not agree with it. We may still, however, accept the statements made in the above quotations as correct descriptions of the unity of mind and brain during the present life.

62. See my *The Bible and the Future*, chaps. 17 and 20.

63. See my *The Four Major Cults* (Grand Rapids: Eerdmans, 1963), pp. 345-71.

herents of this view sometimes cite 2 Corinthians 5:1 to prove that we shall receive such "intermediate" bodies: "Now we know that if the earthly tent we live in is destroyed, we have a building from God, an eternal house in heaven, not built by human hands." But this passage talks about an *eternal* house in heaven. If we are to understand this "eternal house" as referring to a new body, it would not designate a temporary, "intermediate" body.[64]

Another view, commonly called "soul-sleep," is that man, or his "soul," exists in an unconscious state between death and the resurrection. This view has been held by various Christian groups. John Calvin wrote his first theological book, *Psychopannychia*, to combat the soul-sleep teachings held by the Anabaptists of his day.[65] More recently, this position has been defended by G. Vander Leeuw,[66] Paul Althaus,[67] and Oscar Cullmann.[68]

Herman Dooyeweerd, in rejecting the body-soul dichotomy, affirms a new understanding of the two sides of man: heart and "function-mantle" (*functie-mantel*), the latter term standing for the body, which is the whole of his temporal existence and the entire structure of all of his temporal functions.[69] Heart and function-mantle are not to be understood as two distinct substances within the human being, but rather as describing man in his unitary wholeness.

But this doesn't answer our question as to what happens to the human being between death and resurrection. When Dooyeweerd was asked the question, What kind of functions can still be left over for the "soul" (*anima rationalis separata*, separated rational soul) when it has been torn out of its temporal conjunction with the prepsychical functions[70] (i.e., after death), his answer was: "Nothing!" (*niets!*).[71] In giving this answer, however, Dooyeweerd

> does not deny the continued existence of the soul after death, nor does he represent the state of the disembodied soul as one of unconsciousness. Yet by depriving the soul of its temporal functions, he seems to leave

64. For a different interpretation of the "eternal house in heaven," see *The Bible and the Future*, pp. 104-6.
65. In Calvin, *Tracts and Treatises of the Reformed Faith*, vol. 3, trans. Henry Beveridge (Grand Rapids: Eerdmans, 1958), pp. 413-90.
66. *Onsterfelijkheid of Opstanding*, 2nd ed. (Assen: Van Gorcum, 1936).
67. *Die Letzten Dinge*, 7th ed. (1922; Gütersloh: Bertelsmann, 1957).
68. *Immortality of the Soul or Resurrection of the Dead?* (New York: Macmillan, 1964), pp. 10-11.
69. William S. Young, "The Nature of Man in the Amsterdam Philosophy," *Westminster Theological Journal* 22, no. 1 (Nov. 1959):7.
70. Namely, the arithmetical, spatial, physical, and organic functions.
71. Herman Dooyeweerd, "Kuyper's Wetenschapsleer," *Philosophia Reformata* 4 (1939):204.

only the most shadowy of spectres in the room of the disembodied rational soul.[72]

In the same vein, Berkouwer affirms that we should not conclude from Dooyeweerd's "nothing!" that he rejects the idea of communion with Christ after death.[73]

When Dooyeweerd uttered his "nothing!" he was answering a question about a view of man to which he did not subscribe: that of man as having two separable "parts," an inferior mortal body and a superior indestructible and immortal "rational soul"—the teaching of the ancient Greek philosophers. So we would not be fair to Dooyeweerd if we were to apply his words to his own understanding of the intermediate state. Nevertheless, we must admit that the statement is puzzling. It has led many to raise questions about Dooyeweerd's view of the state of believers between death and resurrection.[74]

The central teaching of the Bible about the future of man is that of the resurrection of the body. But the New Testament does indicate that the state of believers between death and resurrection is one of provisional happiness, one that is "better by far" than the present earthly state (Phil. 1:23). If this is so, the condition of believers during the intermediate state cannot be a state of nonexistence or of unconsciousness.

Sometimes the New Testament simply says that the believer will continue to exist in this state of provisional happiness:

> If I am to go on living in the body, this will mean fruitful labor for me. Yet what shall I choose? I do not know! I am torn between the two: I desire to depart and be with Christ, which is better by far. (Phil. 1:22-23)

> Jesus answered him [the penitent thief], "I tell you the truth, today you will be with me in Paradise." (Luke 23:43)

> Therefore we are always confident and know that as long as we are at home in the body we are away from the Lord. We live by faith, not by sight. We are confident, I say, and would prefer to be away from the body and at home with the Lord. (2 Cor. 5:6-8)

In the Philippians passage Paul contrasts "living in the body" with "departing and being with Christ," clearly implying that it is possible for a person to be no longer living in the present body and yet to be with Christ—a state that is better than the present state. Particularly significant on this point is the passage from 2 Corinthians, where Paul contrasts being "at home in the body" (*endēmountes en tō*

---

72. Young, "The Nature of Man," p. 10.
73. *Man*, p. 256.
74. See Berkouwer's discussion of this matter in *Man*, pp. 255-257.

*sōmati*) with being "away from the body" (*ekdēmēsai ek tou sōmatos*).
If Paul had intended to describe the blessedness of the believer after
the resurrection, he could have used an expression such as "away from
*this* body," implying that believers would then be "inhabiting" a new
body. But he says simply "away from *the* body," telling his readers
that he is thinking of an existence between the present body and the
resurrection body. Note that in both of these passages Paul affirms
that it is possible for believers to be with Christ even when they are
no longer living in their present bodies and before they have received
their resurrection bodies.

At other times, however, the New Testament uses the words "soul"
(*psychē*) or "spirit" (*pneuma*) to refer to believers as they continue to
exist between death and resurrection. The word "soul" is used in the
following passages:

> Do not be afraid of those who kill the body but cannot kill the soul.
> (Matt. 10:28)

> When he opened the fifth seal, I saw under the altar the souls of those
> who had been slain because of the word of God and the testimony they
> had maintained. (Rev. 6:9)

The word "spirit" is used in the following texts:

> But you have come to Mount Zion, to the heavenly Jerusalem, the city
> of the living God. You have come to thousands upon thousands of angels
> in joyful assembly, to the church of the firstborn, whose names are writ-
> ten in heaven. You have come to God, the judge of all men, to the spirits
> of righteous men made perfect. (Heb. 12:22-23)

> He [Christ] was put to death in the body but made alive by the Spirit,
> through whom also he went and preached to the spirits in prison who
> disobeyed long ago when God waited patiently in the days of Noah while
> the ark was being built. (1 Pet. 3:18-20)

So at times the New Testament says that we who are believers
will continue to exist in a provisional state of happiness between death
and resurrection, whereas at other times it says that the "souls" or
"spirits" of believers will still exist during that state. But the Bible
does not use words like "soul" and "spirit" in the same way that we
do; thus, these passages are only intending to tell us that human
beings will continue to exist between death and resurrection, while
awaiting the resurrection of the body. The Bible does not give us
any anthropological description of life in this intermediate state. We
may speculate about it, we may try to imagine what it will be like, but
we can form no clear picture of life between death and resurrection.
The Bible teaches it, but does not describe it. As Berkouwer says,

what the New Testament tells us about the intermediate state is nothing more than a whisper.[75]

Though man now exists in a state of psychosomatic unity, this unity can and will be temporarily disrupted at the time of death. In 2 Corinthians 5:8 Paul clearly teaches that human beings can exist apart from their present bodies. The same point is made in two other New Testament passages:

> May he [Christ] strengthen your hearts so that you will be blameless and holy in the presence of our God and Father when our Lord Jesus comes with all his holy ones [or saints]. (1 Thess. 3:13)

> We believe that Jesus died and rose again and so we believe that God will bring with Jesus those who have fallen asleep in him. (1 Thess. 4:14)

Both of these texts speak about "holy ones" (saints) and "those who have fallen asleep in Jesus" as existing after death and before the resurrection—note that the resurrection of those who have fallen asleep in Christ is mentioned later in 1 Thessalonians 4 (v. 16).[76] It may also be noted that in this verse the expression "the dead in Christ" clearly implies that deceased believers are still in some state of existence before the resurrection.

Man's normal state is one of psychosomatic unity. At the time of the resurrection he or she will be fully restored to that unity and will thus once again be made complete. But we must acknowledge that, according to biblical teaching, believers can exist temporarily in a state of provisional happiness apart from their present bodies during the "time" between death and resurrection. This intermediate state is, however, incomplete and provisional. We look forward to the resurrection of the body and the new earth as the final climax of God's redemptive program.

## PRACTICAL IMPLICATIONS

The understanding of man as a whole person, as developed in this chapter, has important practical implications.

First, the *church* must be concerned about the whole person. In its preaching and teaching the church must address not only the minds of those to whom it ministers, but also their emotions and their wills.

---

75. *De Wederkomst van Christus*, vol. 1 (Kampen: Kok, 1961), p. 79. On the intermediate state, see further Berkouwer, *The Return of Christ*, trans. James Van Oosterom (Grand Rapids: Eerdmans, 1972), pp. 32-64; and *The Bible and the Future*, pp. 92-108.
76. On these two verses, see W. Hendriksen, *I and II Thessalonians*, in the New Testament Commentary (Grand Rapids: Baker, 1955), *ad loc.*; and Leon Morris, *The First and Second Epistles to the Thessalonians*, in the New International Commentary on the New Testament series (Grand Rapids: Eerdmans, 1959), *ad loc.*

Preaching that merely communicates intellectual information about God or the Bible is seriously inadequate; hearers must be stirred in their hearts and moved to praise God. Teachers in church classes must do more than give pupils a rote "knowledge" of Bible verses or doctrinal statements; their teaching should aim at a response that involves all aspects of the person. Church programs for young people should not neglect the body; sports and outdoor activities should be encouraged as an aspect of full-orbed Christian living.

In its evangelistic and missionary task, the church should also remember that it is dealing with the whole person. Though the chief purpose of missions is to confront people with the gospel so that they may repent of their sins and be saved through faith in Christ, yet the church must never forget that the objects of its mission enterprise have bodily as well as spiritual needs. Keeping in mind the fact that man is a unitary being, we should avoid expressions like "soul-saving" to describe the work of the missionary, and we should opt for the *holistic* or *comprehensive* approach in missions. This approach, which is sometimes referred to as "the ministry of word and deed," directs missionaries to be concerned not only about winning converts to Christ but also about improving the living conditions of these converts and their neighbors, working in such areas as agriculture, diet, and health. The establishment of schools for the Christian education of nationals, and the maintenance of clinics and hospitals for both routine and emergency health care should therefore not be considered as outside the province of the mission activity of the church, but as an essential aspect of it. Arthur F. Glasser, former dean of the School of World Mission at Fuller Theological Seminary, says that in the task as Christian missionaries,

> the development of individual and inward faith must be accompanied by a corporate and outward obedience to the cultural mandate broadly detailed in Holy Scripture. The world is to be served, not avoided. Social justice is to be furthered, and the issues of war, racism, poverty and economic imbalance must become the active, participatory concern of those who profess to follow Jesus Christ. It is not enough that the Christian mission be redemptive; it must be prophetic as well.[77]

The *school* should also be concerned about the whole person. Though one of the main purposes of the school is intellectual instruc-

---

77. "Missiology," in *Evangelical Dictionary of Theology,* ed. Walter A. Elwell (Grand Rapids: Baker, 1984), p. 726. See also William A. Dyrness, *Let the Earth Rejoice: A Biblical Theology of Holistic Mission* (Westchester, IL: Crossway Books, 1983); Francis M. Dubose, *God Who Sends: a Fresh Quest for Biblical Mission* (Nashville: Broadman Press, 1983); and J. H. Boer, *Missions: Heralds of Capitalism or Christ?* (Ibadan, Nigeria: Day Star Press, 1984).

tion, the teacher should never forget that the pupil he or she is teaching is a whole person. The school therefore should not just train the mind, but should also appeal to the emotions and the will, since effective teaching should produce in the pupil both a love for the subject and a desire to learn more about it. Schools, further, should evidence a concern for the body as well as for the mind. Spectator sports, at which a few do the playing and a great many merely observe, have their place, but far more important for the student body as a whole is a good physical education program, with an emphasis on intramural sports that will involve all the students.

The concept of the whole person also has implications for *family life*. Christian parents will be concerned to teach their children about God, to train them in Christian living, and to discipline them in love when they fall short. But parents must also be concerned about such matters as wholesome diet and proper care of the body. It is increasingly being recognized today that a regular program of physical exercise is essential to good health; parents therefore should try to teach their children good body care, not only by precept but also by example.

Further, the concept of the whole person has implications for *medicine*. In recognition of the fact that man is a psychosomatic unity, medical science has recently developed an approach called *holistic medicine*.[78] Holistic medicine has been defined as "a system of health care that emphasizes personal responsibility for one's own health and strives for a cooperative relationship among all those involved in providing health care."[79] Holistic health practitioners "emphasize the necessity for looking at the whole person, including physical condition, nutrition, emotional makeup, spiritual state, life-style values, and environment."[80]

In a fascinating book entitled *Anatomy of an Illness*, Norman Cousins makes the comment that one of the most important aspects of recovery from illness is the "will to live": "The will to live is not a theoretical abstraction, but a physiologic reality with therapeutic characteristics."[81] Cousins reports that hundreds of doctors have told him that "no medication they could give their patients was as potent as the state of mind that a patient brings to his or her own illness."[82] According to Cousins, at the graduating exercises of the Johns Hopkins University School of Medicine in 1975, Dr. Jerome D. Frank told

78. The American Holistic Medical Association was founded in May 1978.
79. "Holistic Medicine," *Encyclopedia Americana*, vol. 14 (Danbury, CT: Grolier, 1983), p. 294.
80. Ibid.
81. New York: Norton, 1979, p. 44.
82. Ibid., p. 139.

the graduates "that any treatment of an illness that does not also minister to the human spirit is grossly deficient."[83] The conclusion is clear: Healing and the maintenance of physical health involve the whole person. Physicians, nurses, pastors, and patients must always keep this in mind.[84]

Finally, the concept of the whole person has important implications for *psychology* and *counseling*. Recent psychological studies have laid new emphasis on the wholeness of man—an emphasis that is sometimes called "organismic theory."[85] Hall and Lindzey state that the new stress in psychology on the whole person is a reaction against mind-body dualism, faculty psychology, and behaviorism. This new emphasis, they claim, has been widely accepted:

> Who is there in psychology today who is not a proponent of the main tenets of organismic theory that the whole is something other than the sum of its parts, that what happens to a part happens to the whole, and that there are no separate compartments within the organism?[86]

Counselors must also remember the fact that man is a whole person. They should be trained to recognize problems that require the expertise of others besides themselves, and should be willing to refer their counselees, when necessary, to physicians or psychiatrists. Mental problems should not be thought of as totally distinct from physical problems, because neither type of problem is ever separate from the other. Since antidepressant drugs can cure certain types of depression, a wise counselor will make use of these means. Patients who have deep-seated problems, in fact, can most effectively be healed through the combined efforts of a therapeutic team, consisting, perhaps, of a psychologist, a social worker, a physician, and a psychiatrist.[87]

The counselor ought not to think of spiritual and mental health as somehow totally separable. Since man is a whole person, the spiritual and the mental are aspects of a totality, so that each aspect influences and is influenced by the other. Howard Clinebell puts it this

---

83. Ibid., p. 133.

84. Among the voluminous literature on holistic medicine, the following studies may be noted: David Allen, et al., *Whole Person Medicine* (Downers Grove: InterVarsity Press, 1980); Ed Gaedwag, ed., *Inner Balance: The Power of Holistic Healing* (Englewood Cliffs, NJ: Prentice-Hall, 1979); Jack La Patra, *Healing: The Coming Revolution in Holistic Medicine* (New York: McGraw, 1978); Morton Walker, *Total Health: The Holistic Alternative to Traditional Medicine* (New York: Everest House, 1979).

85. See "Organismic Theory," in Calvin S. Hall and Gardner Lindzey, *Theories of Personality*, 2nd ed. (New York: John Wiley, 1970), pp. 298-337. Note the bibliography at the end of the chapter.

86. Ibid., p. 330.

87. Karl Menninger, et al., *The Vital Balance* (New York: Viking Press, 1963), p. 335.

way: "Spiritual health is an indispensable aspect of mental health. The two can be separated only on a theoretical basis. In live human beings, spiritual and mental health are inextricably interwoven."[88]

Sometimes the pastoral counselor may think that the mere quotation of Bible verses may be all that is necessary to help a parishioner solve a difficult spiritual problem. But an understanding of man as a whole person leads us to realize that such an approach might be quite inadequate. David G. Benner, in an article in which he challenges the common opinion that the human personality can be divided into two parts, a spiritual and a psychological "part," illustrates his point as follows:

> The temptation therefore to label a person's difficulty in accepting God's forgiveness of [his or her] sins as a spiritual problem ought to be resisted in order to leave the counselor maximally open to deal with both psychological and spiritual aspects of that problem. To assume its essential spiritual nature and to proceed by means of an explicit presentation of certain biblical truths is to forget that forgiveness, whether being given or received, is mediated by psychospiritual processes of personality and, therefore, that other psychological factors may also be involved and other techniques be appropriate.[89]

The Christian counselor, therefore, should see the problems of his or her counselee as problems of the whole person. He or she should not only deal with the counselee as a whole person, but should also attempt to restore him or her to the wholeness that is the mark of healthy and godly living.[90]

---

88. *Mental Health Through Christian Community* (Nashville: Abingdon, 1965), p. 20.
89. "What God Hath Joined: The Psychospiritual Unity of Personality," *The Bulletin: Christian Association for Psychological Studies* 5, no. 2 (1979):11.
90. On the whole person, see also Salvatore R. Maddi, *Personality Theories*, 4th ed. (Homewood, IL: Dorsey Press, 1980).

# CHAPTER 12

# The Question of Freedom

The last important problem involved in the Christian doctrine of man that we shall consider is the question of freedom. On this question there has been much discussion. Sometimes this discussion has generated more heat than light because of the ambiguity of the various terms that are used. Words like *free, freedom, liberty, volition,* and *will* may sometimes be used with such diverse meanings that those who are discussing human freedom may be talking past each other even while using the same words.

By way of illustration, let us suppose that someone is trying to get an answer to the question: Does fallen man today have a "free will"? How should we answer this question?

Each of these two words, *free* and *will*, is problematical. To begin with, *will* is not totally clear and can even be misleading. It seems to suggest that within the human being there is a separate kind of "faculty" called "the will," the function of which is to make choices or decisions. Some people are then thought to have a "strong will"—that is, presumably, a strong faculty of willing—whereas others are thought to have a "weak will." When one asks whether the "will" is free, one assumes that the will is a separate agent in a person that may or may not be free in its actions. But such an assumption betrays the acceptance of what has been called "faculty psychology." In "faculty psychology" the various powers, abilities, or capacities of the human being are construed as if they were distinct agents or "persons" within man that perform certain actions. Actually, however, what we call "willing" is simply another name for an activity performed by the whole person; it is the whole person in the process of making decisions.[1] Instead of asking whether the "will" is free, therefore, we should

1. For a perceptive criticism of faculty psychology, see John Locke, *An Essay Concerning Human Understanding* (Oxford: Clarendon Press, 1894), Bk. II, Chap. 21, Secs. 6, 14-17.

ask whether the person is free when he or she makes decisions.[2]

The term *free* is also confusing, since it may mean various things. The questioner referred to above may mean by his question: Is fallen man today still a "creature of option"—one who still can and does make decisions of one sort or another? Or the questioner might mean this: Is fallen man today, apart from God's special grace, still able to live a life that is totally pleasing in God's sight—that is, can he, if he tries hard enough, still live without sin? These two senses of the word *free*, though related, are quite different from each other.

It will be important for us to define our terms carefully, so that we know exactly what is meant when we use them. To avoid confusion, therefore, I shall not use expressions like "the freedom of the will" (though these words may appear occasionally in quotations). Instead, I shall use the words "choice" and "true freedom."

By "choice" or "the ability to choose" I shall mean the capacity of humans to make choices between alternatives—a capacity that implies responsibility for those choices. These choices or decisions may be either good or bad, either God-glorifying or God-defying. By "true freedom" I shall mean the ability of humans, with the help of the Holy Spirit, to think, say, and do what is pleasing to God and in harmony with his revealed will.[3] We must keep these two distinct understandings of the concept of freedom clearly in mind when we ask how our fall into sin and how God's redemptive work have affected our "will" and our "freedom."

## THE ABILITY TO CHOOSE

We now turn our attention to the first of the two expressions, namely, *the ability to choose* (or the capacity for choice). This ability or capacity is an ineradicable aspect of normal human nature. I have made this point earlier. In Chapter 2 we saw that the ability to make choices is presupposed in the fact that the human being is a "created person."[4] I also pointed out that the ability to make choices is an aspect of the image of God in its broader or structural sense.[5] The understanding that human beings have this capacity for choice, and that they retain

2. The word *will* can, of course, be properly understood as meaning the process of choosing or willing something—a process that involves the whole person. Such willing, in fact, is never done apart from rational considerations and emotional drives or appetites. Willing is always a function of the whole person.
3. At times, however, the words "freedom" or "free" will be used in a more general sense, as when they refer to "freedom of speech" or "the free world."
4. See above, pp. 5-10.
5. See above, p. 70.

this capacity even after the Fall, is therefore an essential emphasis in the Christian doctrine of man. The Bible always addresses humans as persons who can make decisions and who are responsible for the decisions they make. God does not deal with the human being as if he or she were a "stick" or a "stone"; he deals with man as with a person who must respond to him, and who is held accountable for the nature of her or his response.[6]

From the Christian perspective, man is and remains, as Leonard Verduin puts it, "a creature of options, one who is constantly confronted with alternatives between which he chooses, saying yes to the one and no to the other."[7] This ability to make choices sets human beings apart from all other creatures on this earth: mountains, plants, and animals. Some animals may indeed seem to be able to make choices, but what appear to be choices on their part are really the result either of instinct (as when the salmon finds a certain stream into which it swims in order to spawn, or when the golden plover migrates from the sunny south back to its previous habitat in the north), or of human training (as when a dog is trained to obey its master by means of rewards and punishments). In possessing the ability to make choices, in fact, human beings reveal a likeness to God. C. S. Lewis makes this point in *The Great Divorce*, where he reproduces an imaginary conversation with his teacher, George Macdonald, who says,

> Time is the very lens through which ye see—small and clear, as men see through the wrong end of a telescope, something that would otherwise be too big for ye to see at all. That thing is Freedom [here meaning the ability to choose]: the gift whereby ye most resemble your Maker.[8]

Needless to say, the ability to make choices is a most important capacity. It is basic to human existence. Apart from it, there can be no responsibility, no dependability, and no planning. Apart from it, there can be no education, no religion, and no worship. Apart from it, there can be no art, no science, and no culture. The ability to choose is a *sine qua non* of all human life.

Unfortunately, however, certain scientific understandings of human nature in our day deny that man has the ability to choose. An example of this is modern psychological behaviorism, especially as exemplified by B. F. Skinner. In his books, *Beyond Freedom and Dig-*

---

6. This thought is particularly emphasized by Emil Brunner (see above, pp. 53-57).
7. *Somewhat Less than God* (Grand Rapids: Eerdmans, 1970), p. 84.
8. *The Great Divorce* (New York: Macmillan, 1963), p. 125. I should like to add, however, that human beings will resemble God most when, in the life to come, they will be able to do God's will perfectly.

*nity*[9] and *About Behaviorism,*[10] Skinner defends the position of environmental determinism. All human behavior, he claims, is completely controlled by genetic and environmental factors. All human "choices" are determined by previous physical causes.[11] To say that the human being is "free" to act as he "wills" is a myth, says Skinner; man's conduct is totally determined by his environment. This view implies, however, that human beings have no responsibility for the decisions they make, and that man really has neither freedom nor dignity.[12]

This view of man has disastrous consequences. One implication would seem to be that, since the criminal is not responsible for his crime, society must coddle him, find excuses for him, and sentence him lightly. Needless to say, the result of such a view of crime and of such a policy toward criminals would probably be an increase in crime.

Another implication is that, on the basis of this view, we cannot build a truly "free" society. If human beings are totally determined by their physical environment, they cannot really make significant choices. Marxism, for example, teaches that what man is, is due to structures and forces outside of himself. The individual, therefore, is not responsible for the deprivations and evils that he or she experiences; but society is. Hence the only way in which such things can be changed is for society to be changed. In countries dominated by Marxism, therefore, all emphasis lies on the collective; the individual must submerge his or her desires to those of the state. The result is a society of people who have been deprived of the "freedoms" most of us hold dear: freedom of speech (including freedom of the press), freedom of assembly, and freedom of religion. In many of these countries there has been a systematic attempt to destroy the Christian church, since the church does not advance the program of the state. In such countries the state is all; the individual does not count.[13]

This denial of human "freedoms," however, is not limited to communistic countries or to countries that, in one way or another, espouse the philosophy of Marxism. Some capitalistic countries are ruled by dictators or dictatorial groups, where people are not allowed to make

9. New York: Alfred A. Knopf, 1972.
10. New York: Alfred A. Knopf, 1974.
11. See Norman Geisler, "Freedom, Free Will, and Determinism," in *Evangelical Dictionary of Theology,* ed. Walter A. Elwell (Grand Rapids: Baker, 1984), p. 428 (reproducing Skinner's position).
12. On Skinner, see above, p. 4. For a discerning critique of Skinner's views, see C. Stephen Evans, *Preserving the Person: A Look at the Human Sciences* (Downers Grove: InterVarsity Press, 1977; repr. Baker, 1982).
13. On Marxism, see also p. 4 above.

their own political choices, where freedom of speech and freedom of assembly are nonexistent, and where dissidents are imprisoned and sometimes executed. In both of these types of repressive regimes, the Marxist and the fascist, the many are controlled by the few. Political decisions are made by those in power: the party, the junta, or the dictator and those who advise him; the people have no choice but to fall in line.

Against this background we see anew the relevance of the Christian view of man for today's world. Only the recognition of the human being as a creature of option and as someone who is entitled to the free exercise of those options (within the limitations of God's ordinances) will make a "free society" possible. And to deny that freedom of option, as is done in communist and fascist countries, is to deny a significant aspect of biblical truth about man. The struggle for political freedom, therefore, must be waged not just in legislative chambers, in oval offices, and on battlefields, but in our homes, our churches, and our schools.

## THE ORIGIN OF TRUE FREEDOM

We need now to consider the higher understanding of freedom, namely, *true freedom*—that is, the ability to do what is pleasing to God.

When human beings were created, they possessed both the capacity for choice and true freedom. In Augustine's well-known words, they were then "able not to sin" (*posse non peccare*). They could have remained standing in their moral integrity, and could have refused to yield to the temptation of the serpent (though even such resistance to temptation would have required God's help).[14]

In the beginning, therefore, man was not a neutral being, neither good nor bad, but a good being who was capable, with God's help, of living a life that was totally pleasing to God. Human beings were created in a "state of integrity." They had the ability not only to make choices, but to make the right choices. So man at that time had true freedom—but it was not yet perfect freedom. He could still fall into sin—and, as a matter of fact, did just that. Our first parents should have advanced to a higher stage where, presumably, their sinlessness would have been unlosable. But, instead, they fell into a lower stage, a stage of sin and depravity.

## TRUE FREEDOM LOST

Though human beings had been created with true freedom, they lost that freedom when they fell into sin. Man then lost, not the capacity

14. On this point see Bavinck, *Dogmatiek*, 2:600.

for choice (which is inseparable from human nature), but true freedom—the ability to live in total obedience to God.

Pelagius, as we recall, denied this teaching.[15] In his view, Adam and Eve were created neutral, neither good nor bad, and human beings today are born in the same condition. Human persons had true freedom before they fell, and they still have true freedom today. People today are just as capable of doing what pleases God as they were before the Fall. The only reason people do wrong today, Pelagius said, is that they are surrounded by bad examples.

Augustine, Pelagius's famous contemporary, strongly opposed these views, especially in his anti-Pelagian writings.[16] Augustine taught that human beings were created good, in a state in which they were "able not to sin." In the beginning, therefore, humans had true freedom. But when they fell into sin, though they did not lose their capacity to make choices, they did lose their ability to serve God without sin—in other words, their true freedom. Man now became a slave to sin; he now entered the state of being "not able not to sin" (*non posse non peccare*).

> For it was by the evil use of his free-will [his ability to do the right—which, however, included the possibility of disobedience] that man destroyed both it and himself. For, as a man who kills himself must, of course, be alive when he kills himself, but after he has killed himself ceases to live, and cannot restore himself to life; so, when man by his own free-will sinned, then sin being victorious over him, the freedom of his will was lost. "For of whom a man is overcome, of the same is he brought in bondage" [2 Pet. 2:19].[17]

The Bible clearly teaches that fallen humankind has lost its true freedom. We have already looked at the biblical evidence that fallen man today cannot in his or her own strength either do what totally meets with God's approval or change the basic direction of his or her life from sinful self-love to love for God.[18] In addition, several New Testament passages directly teach fallen humanity's enslavement to sin. According to John 8:34, Jesus said to some Jews who were disputing with him and claiming that they had never been slaves of anyone, "I tell you the truth, everyone who sins is a slave to sin." The word translated here as "slave" is *doulos*, from the Greek verb *douleuein*, which means "to be enslaved." Whereas in older versions of

---

15. See above, pp. 154-56.
16. These can be found in vol. 5 of *The Nicene and Post-Nicene Fathers*, ed. Philip Schaff, First Series (rpt.; Grand Rapids: Eerdmans, 1971).
17. Augustine, *Enchiridion*, trans. J. F. Shaw, vol. 3 in *Nicene and Post-Nicene Fathers*, First Series (rpt.; Grand Rapids: Eerdmans, 1980), chap. 30.
18. See above, pp. 152-54.

the New Testament, this word was rendered *servant* (KJV) or *bond-servant* (ASV), the newer versions all translate the word as *slave*. Jesus is here saying, therefore, that a person who sins habitually (*poiōn tēn hamartian,* the participle being in the present tense, denoting continuation) is enslaved to sin. And who is there among fallen humankind who does not sin habitually?

In Romans 6 Paul, writing to Christians, indicates that before their conversion they had been slaves of sin, again using either the noun *doulos* or a form of the verb *douleuein*: "Our old self was crucified with him [Christ] . . . that we should no longer be slaves to sin" (v. 6); "you used to be slaves to sin" (v. 17); "you used to offer the parts of your body in slavery to impurity and to ever-increasing wickedness" (v. 19); "you were slaves to sin" (v. 20).

The fact that human beings have now lost true freedom does not mean that they have lost the ability to make choices. They now sin willingly, choosing to do so. They still make choices, but the wrong ones. They are now in bondage to sin.[19]

Both Luther and Calvin stressed the fact that fallen man is now in bondage to sin, and therefore has lost his true freedom. In answer to Erasmus's *Diatribe on Free Will,* Luther wrote, in 1525, *The Bondage of the Will.* In this book he taught that fallen human beings can neither will to turn to God nor play any part in the process that leads to their salvation.[20] Calvin, like Luther, consistently affirmed, in both his commentaries and his *Institutes,* that fallen man is a slave of sin. In the Battles translation of the *Institutes,* the heading of Chapter Two of Book Two reads as follows: "Man Has Now Been . . . Bound Over to Miserable Servitude." Calvin summarizes the main point of this chapter in these words: "The will, because it is inseparable from man's nature, did not perish, but was so bound to wicked desires that it cannot strive after the right."[21]

Both Luther and Calvin also preferred not even to use expressions like "free will" or "the freedom of the will" as descriptions of the state of fallen human beings today. Luther put it this way:

> I wish that the word "free will" had never been invented. It is not in the Scriptures, and it were better to call it "self-will," which profiteth not.[22]

---

19. As I pointed out in Chap. 10, God by his common grace does restrain man's propensity to sin in such a way that unregenerate people can still do certain kinds of good. But this restraint of sin by no means takes away fallen man's enslavement to sin.

20. Carl S. Meyer, "Martin Luther," in *The New International Dictionary of the Christian Church,* ed. J. D. Douglas (Grand Rapids: Zondervan, 1974), p. 610.

21. *Inst.,* II.2.12.

22. Hugh Thomson Kerr, Jr., ed., *A Compend of Luther's Theology* (Philadelphia: Westminster Press, 1943), p. 91.

Free-will is plainly a divine term, and can be applicable to none but the divine Majesty only: for He alone "doth, (as the Psalm sings) what He will in Heaven and earth." (Ps. cxxxv. 6.). . . . Wherefore, it becomes Theologians to refrain from the use of this term altogether, whenever they wish to speak of human ability, and leave it to be applied to God only.[23]

Calvin expressed a similar sentiment:

Then [according to Peter Lombard] man will be said to possess free will in this sense, not that he has an equally free election of good and evil, but because he does evil voluntarily, and not by constraint. That, indeed, is very true; but what end could it answer to decorate a thing so diminutive with a title so superb?[24]

## TRUE FREEDOM RESTORED

Man's true freedom, which he lost in the Fall, is restored in the process of redemption. When the Holy Spirit regenerates a person, renews the image of God in him or her, and begins in him or her the work of sanctification, that person is enabled to turn to God in repentance and faith, and to do what is truly pleasing in God's sight. The state of the regenerated person is now, as Augustine put it, one of "being able not to sin" (*posse non peccare*). Redemption therefore means deliverance from the "bondage of the will"; the regenerated person is no longer a slave of sin.[25]

That true freedom, the freedom to do God's will, is restored to man in the redemptive process is taught in many passages of the New Testament. We turn first to the words of Jesus. After telling the Jews who were arguing with him that everyone who sins is a slave to sin (John 8:34), Jesus went on to say, "Now a slave has no permanent place in the family, but a son belongs to it forever. So if the Son sets you free, you will be free indeed" (vv. 35-36). We may infer from this that the freedom Jesus is talking about is freedom from the enslavement of sin. It is only through Christ that we can receive this freedom.

The thought that Christ has set us free from bondage and enslavement is one of the apostle Paul's favorite themes. In Galatians 5:1 he says, "It is for freedom that Christ has set us free. Stand firm, then, and do not let yourselves be burdened again by a yoke of slavery." In the context of the Epistle to the Galatians, this freedom means not

23. Ibid., p. 88.

24. *Institutes*, trans. John Allen, 7th ed. (Philadelphia: Presbyterian Board of Christian Education, 1936), II.2.7.

25. This point is beautifully made in Q. and A. 8 of the Heidelberg Catechism: "But are we so corrupt that we are wholly incapable of doing any good, and inclined to all evil? Yes, indeed, unless we are regenerated by the Spirit of God" (older trans., Christian Reformed Church).

only freedom from the need to keep God's law in order to earn our salvation, but also freedom to live by the Spirit in such a way as to stop gratifying the desires of the flesh (5:16). Interestingly enough, the most recent Dutch translation of the Bible[26] renders the first part of Galatians 5:1 as follows: "Christ has made us free so that we might become truly free."[27] Though the word *truly* is not found in the original, it conveys a correct understanding of Paul's meaning. Paul also ties in true freedom with the work of the Spirit in 2 Corinthians 3:17, "Now the Lord is the Spirit, and where the Spirit of the Lord is, there is freedom." That freedom, Paul goes on to say, means progressive transformation into the likeness of Christ: "And we, who with unveiled faces all reflect the Lord's glory, are being transformed into his likeness with ever-increasing glory, which comes from the Lord, who is the Spirit" (v. 18).

Paul deals with the question of true freedom particularly in the sixth chapter of Romans. In Romans 3 to 5 Paul has been discussing the blessing of justification—that we are acquitted from the guilt of our sin and clothed with perfect righteousness because of the death and resurrection of Jesus Christ. In chapter 6, however, he begins a discussion of sanctification—that work of God by which he progressively delivers his people from the pollution of sin and enables them to live to his praise. This deliverance and enabling, however, can only take place in union with Christ—that is, with Christ's death and resurrection. In other words, whereas in chapters 3 to 5 Paul teaches that Christ died *for* us and arose *for* us, in chapters 6 to 8 he affirms that we who are God's people have died and arisen *with* Christ.

In chapter 6 Paul shows, in masterful fashion, that oneness with Christ in his death and resurrection means that "just as Christ was raised from the dead through the glory of the Father, we too may live a new life" (v. 4). This new life we now live means deliverance from the enslavement of sin. You who are now in Christ, Paul goes on to say, are no longer slaves to sin (v. 6); "sin shall no longer be your master, because you are no longer under law, but under the grace of God" (v. 14, NEB). He makes the same point in verses 18 and 22: "You have been set free from sin and have become slaves to righteousness" (v. 18); "you have been set free from sin and have become slaves to God" (v. 22). True freedom, therefore, according to Paul, is the freedom of new life in Christ, which implies that we are no longer slaves of sin. This true freedom is, in fact, identical with being new creatures in Christ.

---

26. Amsterdam: Het Nederlandsch Bijbelgenootschap, 1957.
27. "Opdat wij waarlijk vrij zouden zijn, heeft Christus ons vrijgemaakt."

In an earlier chapter I made the point that the Christian should look upon him- or herself as someone who, though not yet perfect, is a new self who is being progressively renewed, and who is therefore *genuinely* new though not yet *totally* new.[28] The same point can be made about the Christian's freedom. As long as he or she is in this present life, the Christian is *genuinely* free but not yet *totally* free. Because of God's redemptive work in him or her, the Christian now has true freedom, but that freedom is not yet perfect. Though no longer a slave of sin, he or she is still tempted to sin and still commits sin. Some day—after the resurrection of the body—the Christian will be perfectly free and totally free.

It follows, then, that this freedom can be abused. Paul warns against such abuse in Galatians 5:13, "For you were called to freedom, brethren; only do not use your freedom as an opportunity for the flesh" (RSV). Peter issues a similar warning: "Live as free men, but do not use your freedom as a cover-up for evil" (1 Pet. 2:16). True freedom is not license; it does not mean doing anything we please. True freedom, as Peter says in the last part of the text just quoted, means to "live as servants of God."

Though it is God who restores our true freedom in the redemptive process, the exercise of that freedom also involves human responsibility. We are not robots or computer-directed machines; we are created persons. As creatures we are totally dependent on God, but as persons we must not only make choices but are held responsible for the choices we make.

To begin with, then, human beings must turn to Christ in faith in order to *receive* true freedom. Though they cannot turn to Christ apart from the enabling power of the Holy Spirit, yet they must so turn. The gospel appeals to man to make a decision for Christ. Paul, describing himself and the other apostles, says, "We are therefore Christ's ambassadors, as though God were making his appeal through us. We implore you on Christ's behalf: be reconciled to God" (2 Cor. 5:20). The biblical emphasis on the sovereignty of God, therefore, does not rule out the need for a personal response to the overtures of the gospel. Neither does the scriptural emphasis on divine election cancel out the necessity of human choice. God saves us as created persons.

The continued *exercise* of our true freedom also involves our responsibility. Though it is true that God sanctifies us by his Holy Spirit, we are called upon to cleanse ourselves from the defilements

---

28. See above, pp. 108-10. See also my *The Christian Looks at Himself*, rev. ed. (Grand Rapids: Eerdmans, 1977), pp. 43, 73-76, 97-98.

of sin: "Since we have these promises, dear friends, let us purify ourselves from everything that contaminates body and spirit, and let us
strive for perfection out of reverence for God" (2 Cor. 7:1). Surely it
is God who brings us to our final perfection; yet here we are told that
it is our duty to be progressively "perfecting holiness in the fear of
God" (NASB). God, to be sure, has freed us from the enslavement of
sin, but we are enjoined to live as free people: "So Christ has made
us free. Now make sure that you stay free and don't get all tied up
again in the chains of slavery" (Gal. 5:1, Living Bible). We cannot
live as free men and women without God's help, but nevertheless we
must do so. Our true freedom is not only a gift; it is also a task.

Calvin describes true freedom as consisting of three aspects:
(1) freedom from the need to keep the law of God in order to earn our
salvation; (2) freedom to obey God's law voluntarily, out of thankfulness; and (3) freedom with respect to external things that in themselves are indifferent.[29] Note that the first and the third of these
freedoms are freedoms *from* certain things, whereas the second is freedom *to* something else. We shall first consider freedoms (1) and (3),
coming back later to freedom (2).

*True freedom is freedom from the need to keep the law in order to
earn our salvation.* This freedom is the main theme of the Epistle to
the Galatians. The churches to whom Paul wrote this letter had evi-
dently been visited by some Judaizers who insisted that, in addition
to having faith in Christ, one had to be circumcised and to conform
in other ways to Jewish law in order to be saved. Paul countered that
no one can be justified or saved by means of the keeping of the law,
since no one can keep God's law perfectly. We are justified through
Christ, who kept the law for us.

> We . . . know that a man is not justified by observing the law, but by faith
> in Jesus Christ. So we, too, have put our faith in Christ Jesus that we
> may be justified by faith in Christ and not by observing the law, because
> by observing the law no one will be justified. (Gal. 2:15-16)

We remember also Paul's memorable message in Romans 3:28, "For
we maintain that a man is justified by faith apart from observing the
law."

This teaching is, in fact, the heart of the gospel. It provides our
basic freedom: freedom from legalistic enslavement to the law as a
means of salvation. This teaching underscores the distinctiveness of
the Christian faith. All non-Christian religions teach that we are saved

29. *Inst.*, III.19.1-9.

by what we do or what we suffer;[30] only Christianity brings the liberating message that we are saved by faith in the perfect obedience of Christ.

*True freedom includes freedom from bondage to rules about "indifferent things."* By "indifferent things" or *adiaphora*, as they are sometimes called, we mean things that are not sinful in themselves since God neither commands nor forbids them. We think, for example, of such matters as moderate smoking, moderate drinking, the use of cosmetics, and the like—practices that, though they may become sinful under certain circumstances, are not sinful in themselves. It sometimes happens, however, that churches make rules about such matters, and compel their members to observe them as a "test of fellowship" or badge of true Christianity.

Calvin's comments on this question are helpful:

> The third part of Christian freedom lies in this: Regarding outward things that are of themselves "indifferent," we are not bound before God by any religious obligation preventing us from sometimes using them and other times not using them, indifferently.[31]

> We should use God's gifts for the purpose for which he gave them to us, with no scruple of conscience, no trouble of mind. With such confidence our minds will be at peace with him, and will recognize his liberality toward us.[32]

Calvin goes on to say that we should exercise our Christian liberty in such matters, using these gifts of God with thanksgiving. But we should not make use of these "indifferent things" if they cause offense to a brother or sister. Quoting 1 Corinthians 10:23 (" 'All things are lawful,' but not all things build up," RSV), Calvin says, "Nothing is plainer than this rule: that we should use our freedom if it results in the edification of our neighbor, but if it does not help our neighbor, then we should forgo it."[33]

The question we face here is the problem of *legalism*. Legalism may mean different things. One type has already been discussed: the claim that we can earn our salvation by keeping God's law. Paul, as we saw, resolutely opposed this claim, since it denied the heart of the gospel. But churches that fully accept Paul's teaching on justification by faith may yet exhibit another kind of legalism: the insistence that

---

30. This is also taught by such well-known cults as Mormons and Jehovah's Witnesses—see my *The Four Major Cults* (Grand Rapids: Eerdmans, 1963), pp. 59-62, 279-85.

31. *Inst.*, III.19.7.

32. Ibid., Sec. 8.

33. Ibid., Sec. 12.

their members abstain from certain practices that are deemed wrong—though they are really "indifferent things."

With respect to the question of which practices are to be put on the list of "forbidden things," there is great variety. In the United States many evangelical churches, particularly those of the fundamentalist type, have rules against smoking, drinking, movies, dancing, and card-playing. Many churches in Europe, however, "whose members readily drink and smoke, recoil in horror at the idea of Christians wearing blue jeans or chewing gum."[34] Some years ago my wife and I heard a sermon on the Parable of the Good Samaritan in a Protestant church in Interlaken, Switzerland. After describing how the Good Samaritan bandaged the injured man, put him on his donkey, and brought him to the inn, the pastor went on to say, "He [the Good Samaritan] gave him a cigarette and a beer, and had a little talk with him." We were greatly amused, and wondered how American fundamentalists might have reacted to this application of present-day Swiss hospitality to the man in the parable!

The danger involved in the type of legalism just described is that abstinence from these "indifferent things" comes to be thought of as the essential mark of a Christian. When this is the case, things that are less important receive greater emphasis than the things that are most important, so that we end up by majoring in minors. When this happens, we are like the Pharisees about whom Jesus said, "You give a tenth of your spices—mint, dill and cummin. But you have neglected the more important matters of the law—justice, mercy and faithfulness" (Matt. 23:23).

Another danger is that such legalism limits the growth of the church "by forming a hard, crusty shell around the accepted group."[35] When we insist that a person is not a true Christian unless he or she abstains from smoking or observes a certain dress code, we may be driving people away from the riches of God's love because of our ideas of what Christian behavior should be like. A similar comment could be made about mission strategy. When on the mission field we identify Christianity with Western culture by insisting on Western music, Western styles of church architecture, or Western types of liturgies, we may offend true Christians in other lands and greatly curtail the influence of the gospel. We must remember that true Christianity is not tied to a specific set of cultural standards. We must continue to stand firm in the freedom for which Christ has set us free.

---

34. Paul Brand and Philip Yancey, *Fearfully and Wonderfully Made* (Grand Rapids: Zondervan, 1980), p. 107.
35. Ibid., p. 108.

*True freedom is freedom to do God's will voluntarily, as a way of showing our thankfulness to him.* If we had to keep God's law in order to earn our salvation, the slightest failure would bring upon us the curse of the law.[36] We would then be constantly afraid of failure, of punishment, of everlasting perdition. But when we know that we do not need to keep the law in order to earn salvation, our fear drops away and we are ready to serve God joyfully and happily. We are then no longer compelled by fear but impelled by gratitude. We then delight in keeping God's law as evidence of our gratitude for his undeserved and unfathomable mercy. This, too, is an aspect of Christian freedom—not just freedom *from* but freedom *for*.

God's law now becomes for us, as the Heidelberg Catechism affirms, a rule of gratitude—a rule we try to keep to the best of our ability "so that in all our living we may show that we are thankful to God for all he has done for us, and so that he may be praised through us."[37] We now do God's will no longer as servants but as sons and daughters. Calvin puts it this way:

> Those bound by the yoke of the law are like servants assigned certain tasks for each day by their masters. These servants think they have accomplished nothing, and dare not appear before their masters unless they have fulfilled the exact measure of their tasks. But sons, who are more generously and candidly treated by their fathers, do not hesitate to offer them incomplete and half-done and even defective works, trusting that their obedience and readiness of mind will be accepted by their fathers, even though they have not quite achieved what their fathers intended. Such children ought we to be, firmly trusting that our services will be approved by our most merciful Father, however small, rude, and imperfect these may be.[38]

What strikes us here is Calvin's insistence that our imperfect obedience will be accepted by God as if it were perfect, since he readily forgives the many imperfections that still cling to our very best deeds. This, too, is what true Christian freedom is all about: freedom to serve God with the trustfulness of a son or daughter, rather than with the craven fear of a servant. As Paul says to the Christians at Rome, "For you did not receive a spirit that makes you a slave again to fear, but you received the Spirit of sonship" (Rom. 8:15).

*True freedom, therefore, is not opposed to law.* Freedom and law are usually thought of as opposites. "Don't fence me in," says the person

36. Cf. Gal. 3:10, "All who rely on observing the law are under a curse, for it is written: 'Cursed is everyone who does not continue to do everything written in the Book of the Law.'"
37. Heidelberg Catechism, Answer 86 (1975 trans., Christian Reformed Church).
38. *Inst.*, III.19.5.

who doesn't want to be bothered by rules or regulations. Actually, however, even in the natural world there is no freedom without limitations. A fish has freedom to swim, but only as long as it stays in the water. A violinist is free to produce luscious string tones and glittering cadenzas only if he or she knows how to do proper fingering and bowing. Only after the rules of voice production have been mastered is a singer free to inspire audiences. All good music is a kind of marriage in which loyalty to the laws of composition is joined to freedom of expression.[39] We speak of the benefits of a "free society," but a community that would have freedom without limitations (such as civil laws, criminal laws, traffic laws, and the like) would breed anarchy.

In the redemptive world it is also true that there is no freedom without limitations. True freedom, in fact, consists in the joyful keeping of God's law. That law, when observed in gratitude, does not bring us into a new bondage, but leads us into a life that is rich, full, and happy, as we try to keep ourselves in the center of God's will. This is why the Old Testament believer delighted in the law of God (Ps. 1:2), and could say about the ordinances of the LORD, "They are more precious than gold . . . they are sweeter than honey, than honey from the comb" (Ps. 19:10). This, too, is why in the New Testament James can speak of the law as "the law that gives freedom" (1:25; 2:12) or "the law that makes us free" (1:25, NEB).

Paul Brand, a medical doctor, in a fascinating book that explores the analogy between the human body and the people of God, compares the law of God with the bones of the human body. Bones are hard and unyielding. But our bones are not there to restrict us; they are there to help us. Since without bones it would be impossible for us to move, our bones free us for action and movement.[40] God's laws are like those bones. Though we tend to think of these laws as the opposite of freedom, this is not really so.

> Are not laws essentially a description of reality by the One who created it? His rules governing human behavior—are they not guidelines meant to enable us to live the very best, most fulfilling life on earth?
> I have discovered . . . that it is possible to see beyond the surface negativism of, for example, the Ten Commandments and to learn some-

---

39. Calvin Stapert, of the Calvin College music faculty, has beautifully illustrated this point in the music of Johann Sebastian Bach: "It seems to me that one of the most beneficial functions Bach's music can perform for our harried, confused generation is to stand as a monumental testimony to the intimate relationship between freedom and law" ("The Statutes of Liberty: Freedom and Law in the Music of Bach," *Reformed Journal* 35, no. 3 [March 1985]:11).
40. Brand and Yancey, *Fearfully and Wonderfully Made*, pp. 81-83.

thing of the true nature of laws. Rules soon seem as liberating in social activity as bones are in physical activity.[41]

We conclude that keeping God's laws in gratitude, as sons and daughters rather than servants, is the pathway of true freedom.

All this further implies that *true freedom is not opposed to service.* Ordinarily we think of freedom and service as opposites; a person who serves, we surmise, is not free. But in the kingdom of God this is not so. From Romans 6 we learn that there is a kind of service that is enslaving—the service of sin. But now, having been delivered from that servitude, we have entered into a new kind of service: we have become slaves or servants to righteousness (v. 18) and to God (v. 22). We now happily live for him "whose service is perfect freedom."[42]

Not only does true freedom mean the service of God; it also means service to others. Paul, in fact, spoke of himself and his fellow apostles in this way: "For we do not preach ourselves, but Jesus Christ as Lord, and ourselves as your servants for Jesus' sake" (2 Cor. 4:5). Paul expresses this same point paradoxically in 1 Corinthians 9:19, "Though I am free and belong to no man, I make myself a slave to everyone, to win as many as possible." Though a free man, he willingly and gladly has become everyone else's servant, in order that he might bring as many as possible to Christ. This kind of service is another aspect of Christian freedom; it is following the example of our Lord, who said to his disciples, "But I am among you as one who serves" (Luke 22:27). Luther expressed this thought most vividly when he said,

> A Christian is a perfectly free lord of all, subject to none.
> A Christian is a perfectly dutiful servant of all, subject to all.[43]

Still another way of putting this thought is this: *true freedom is freedom to love.* In the words of Heinrich Schlier,

> How is the freedom of the Spirit of Jesus Christ seized by us as it is brought to us in the Gospel. . . ? How does this freedom come to realization in us? The decisive answer is in love. It is not in isolation but in life with others that the Christian attains to freedom.[44]

Since true freedom means the joyful keeping of God's law, and since love is the fulfillment of the law (Rom. 13:10), this freedom will express itself in love for God and for others. We may say, in fact, that true freedom, as the fruit of God's redemptive work, is identical with

---

41. Ibid., p. 84.
42. *Book of Common Prayer*, from the "Collect for Peace."
43. From "The Freedom of a Christian," in *Three Treatises* (Philadelphia: Fortress Press, 1960), p. 277.
44. "*Eleutheros*," in TDNT, 2:500.

the renewal of the image of God in us.[45] The more we exercise this freedom, the more our freedom will resemble that of God himself, who is love.

George Matheson has said it unforgettably:

> *Make me a captive, Lord,*
> *And then I shall be free;*
> *Force me to render up my sword*
> *And I shall conqueror be.*

## TRUE FREEDOM PERFECTED

Only in the life to come will our freedom be perfected. Then, as Augustine put it, we shall be in a state of "not able to sin" (*non posse peccare*). After the resurrection of the body we shall no longer be hindered in our obedience to God and love to others by sin and imperfection. Neither shall we then be hindered by such present limitations as disease, weakness, or death (1 Cor. 15:42-43; Rev. 21:4). We shall then have received our "Spiritual bodies"—that is, bodies completely and exclusively ruled by the Holy Spirit (1 Cor. 15:44). Then, finally, we shall be *totally* free.

This freedom will not be mere enjoyment but will involve dedicated service: on the new earth "his [God's] servants will serve him" (Rev. 22:3). Elsewhere in the Book of Revelation John says that the glorified saints "are before the throne of God and serve him day and night in his temple" (7:15).

But that service will also be perfect and final freedom—a freedom for which the whole creation is now longing:

> For the creation was subjected to frustration . . . in hope that the creation itself will be liberated from its bondage to decay and brought into the glorious freedom of the children of God. (Rom. 8:20-21)

So in the end the future of humanity and the future of the universe will come together. On the new earth all of creation will be totally and eternally free from all the results of sin and from all the remnants of the curse, when it will share with all the sons and daughters of God the magnificent freedom that will then be theirs!

And at that electrifying moment the goal of redemption will have been reached. For from that moment on the entire sin-cleansed cosmos and all of glorified humanity will, together with the angels, endlessly serve and praise him who sits on the throne, and the Lamb who has reconciled all things to God by his blood. For when the Son shall set us free, we shall be free indeed.

45. See above, pp. 85-91. On the question of human freedom, see also Berkouwer, *Man*, chap. 9.

# Bibliography

Aalders, G. C. *De Goddelijke Openbaring in de Eerste Drie Hoofdstukken van Genesis*. Kampen: Kok, 1932.

Adams, Jay E. *The Christian Counselor's Manual*. Grand Rapids: Baker, 1973.

Allen, David, et al. *Whole Person Medicine*. Downers Grove: InterVarsity Press, 1980.

Althaus, Paul. *Die Letzten Dinge*. 1922. 7th ed. Gütersloh: Bertelsmann, 1957.

Anderson, Ray S. *On Being Human*. Grand Rapids: Eerdmans, 1982.

Aquinas, Thomas. *Summa Theologica*. Blackfriars trans. New York: McGraw-Hill, 1964-80.

Ayer, Joseph C. *A Source Book for Ancient Church History*. New York: Scribner, 1913.

*Baker's Dictionary of Theology*. Ed. E. F. Harrison. Grand Rapids: Baker, 1960.

Barth, Karl. *Christ and Adam: Man and Humanity in Romans 5*. Trans. T. A. Smail. New York: Harper, 1957.

_____. *Church Dogmatics*, Vols. III/1, III/2, IV/1, IV/2. Edinburgh: T. & T. Clark, 1956-60.

Bass, Clarence B. "Body," ISBE, rev. ed., 1:528-31. Grand Rapids: Eerdmans, 1979.

Bavinck, Herman. *De Algemeene Genade*. Grand Rapids: Eerdmans-Sevensma, 1922.

_____. *Bijbelsche en Religieuze Psychologie*. Kampen: Kok, 1920.

_____. "Calvin and Common Grace." In *Calvin and the Reformation*, ed. Wm. P. Armstrong. New York: Revell, 1909.

_____. *Gereformeerde Dogmatiek* (abbrev. *Dogmatiek*). 3rd ed. 4 vols. Kampen: Kok, 1918.

Beck, J. T. *Outlines of Biblical Psychology*. Trans. from the 3rd German ed. of 1877. Edinburgh: T. & T. Clark, 1877.

Benner, David G. "What God Hath Joined: The Psychospiritual Unity of Personality," *The Bulletin: Christian Association for Psychological Studies* 5, no. 2 (1979): 7-11.

Berkhof, Hendrikus. *Christ the Meaning of History*. Trans. from the 4th ed. by L. Buurman. Grand Rapids: Baker, 1979 (orig. pub. 1962).

_____. *De Mens Onderweg: Een Christelijke Mensbeschouwing.* Tweede druk. The Hague: Boekencentrum, 1962.

Berkhof, Louis. *History of Christian Doctrines.* Grand Rapids: Eerdmans, 1937.

_____. *Systematic Theology.* Rev. and enl. ed. Grand Rapids: Eerdmans, 1941.

Berkouwer, G. C. *Man: The Image of God* (abbrev. *Man*). Trans. Dirk W. Jellema. Grand Rapids: Eerdmans, 1962 (orig. pub. 1957).

_____. *De Mens het Beeld Gods.* Kampen: Kok, 1957.

_____ *The Return of Christ.* Trans. James Van Oosterom. Grand Rapids: Eerdmans, 1972 (orig. pub. 1961-63).

_____. *Sin.* Trans. Philip Holtrop. Grand Rapids: Eerdmans, 1971 (orig. pub. 1958-60).

_____. *The Triumph of Grace in the Theology of Karl Barth.* Trans. Harry Boer. Grand Rapids: Eerdmans, 1956 (orig. pub. 1954).

_____. *De Wederkomst van Christus.* 2 vols. Kampen: Kok, 1961-63.

Boer, John H. *Missions: Heralds of Capitalism or Christ?* Ibadan, Nigeria: Day Star Press, 1984.

Bornkamm, Heinrich, ed. *Imago Dei: Beiträge zur Theologischen Anthropologie.* Giessen: Töpelmann, 1932.

Brand, Paul, and Philip Yancey. *Fearfully and Wonderfully Made.* Grand Rapids: Zondervan, 1980.

Brinsmead, Robert D. "Man as Creature and Person," *Verdict* 1, no. 1 (Aug. 1978): 21-22.

Brockelman, Wilfred. *Gothard, The Man and His Ministry: An Evaluation.* Santa Barbara: Quill Publications, 1976.

Bromiley, Geoffrey W. "Image of God," ISBE, rev. ed., 2:803-5. Grand Rapids: Eerdmans, 1982.

Brown, Francis, S. R. Driver, and Charles Briggs. *Hebrew and English Lexicon of the Old Testament.* New York: Houghton Mifflin, 1907.

Brownback, Paul. *The Danger of Self-Love.* Chicago: Moody Press, 1982.

Brunner, Emil. *The Christian Doctrine of Creation and Redemption.* Trans. Olive Wyon. Philadelphia: Westminster Press, 1953 (orig. pub. 1950).

_____. "Frieden auf Erden," *Grundriss* 6, no. 5 (1944).

_____. *Man in Revolt.* Trans. Olive Wyon. New York: Scribner, 1939 (orig. pub. 1937).

Bultmann, Rudolf. *Theology of the New Testament.* Trans. K. Grobel. 2 vols. New York: Scribner, 1951-55 (orig. pub. 1948-53).

Cairns, David. *The Image of God in Man.* 1953. Rev. ed. London: Collins, 1973.

Calvin, John. *Commentaries on the Old Testament.* Orig. pub. by the Calvin Translation Society, 1843-55. Reprint. Grand Rapids: Eerdmans, 1948-50.

_____. *Institutes of the Christian Religion* (abbrev. *Inst.*). Ed. John T. McNeill. Trans. Ford Lewis Battles. 2 vols. Philadelphia: Westminster Press, 1960.

_____. *New Testament Commentaries.* Ed. David W. Torrance and Thomas F. Torrance. 12 vols. Grand Rapids: Eerdmans, 1963-73.

_____. *Psychopannychia*. Trans. H. Beveridge. In *Tracts and Treatises of the Reformed Faith*, 3:413-90. Grand Rapids: Eerdmans, 1958.

Carey, George. *I Believe in Man*. Grand Rapids: Eerdmans, 1977.

Cassirer, Ernst. *An Essay on Man*. New Haven: Yale University Press, 1967.

Childs, James M., Jr. *Christian Anthropology and Ethics*, esp. chaps. 5 and 6, on the relation between the image of God and ethics. Philadelphia: Fortress, 1978.

Clark, Gordon H. *The Biblical Doctrine of Man*. Jefferson, MD: The Trinity Foundation, 1984.

_____. *A Christian View of Men and Things*. Grand Rapids: Eerdmans, 1952.

Clinebell, Howard. *Mental Health Through Christian Community*. Nashville: Abingdon, 1965.

Cooper, John. "Dualism and the Biblical View of Human Beings," *Reformed Journal* 32, nos. 9 and 10 (Sept. and Oct. 1982).

Counts, William M. "The Nature of Man and the Christian's Self-Esteem," *The Journal of Psychology and Theology* 1, no. 1 (Jan. 1973): 38-44.

Cullmann, Oscar. *Immortality of the Soul or Resurrection of the Dead?* New York: Macmillan, 1964.

Custance, Arthur C. *Man in Adam and Christ*. Grand Rapids: Zondervan, 1975.

Daane, James. "The Fall," ISBE, rev. ed., 2:277-78. Grand Rapids: Eerdmans, 1982.

Dabney, Charles. *Lectures in Systematic Theology*. 1878. Grand Rapids: Zondervan, 1972.

Danhof, H., and H. Hoeksema. *Van Zonde en Genade*. Kalamazoo: Dalm, 1923.

Daniélou, Jean. "The Conception of History in the Christian Tradition," *The Journal of Religion* 30, no. 3 (July 1950): 171-79.

Davidson, A. B. *The Theology of the Old Testament*. New York: Scribner, 1914.

Davis, John Jefferson. "Genesis, Inerrancy, and the Antiquity of Man." In *Inerrancy and Common Sense*, ed. Roger Nicole and J. Ramsey Michaels. Grand Rapids: Baker, 1980.

De Boer, Willis P. *The Imitation of Paul: An Exegetical Study*. Kampen: Kok, 1962.

De Graaff, Arnold, ed. *View of Man and Psychology in Christian Perspective*. Toronto: Institute for Christian Studies, 1977.

De Graaff, Arnold, and James Olthuis, eds. *Toward a Biblical View of Man*. Toronto: Institute for Christian Studies, 1978.

Delitzsch, Franz. *A System of Biblical Psychology*. 2nd ed. Trans. Robert E. Wallis. Edinburgh: T. & T. Clark, 1867.

Demarest, Bruce A. "Fall of Man," *Evangelical Dictionary of Theology*, pp. 403-5. Grand Rapids: Baker, 1984.

Dickson, William P. *St. Paul's Use of the Terms Flesh and Spirit*. Glasgow: Maclehose, 1883.

Dooyeweerd, Herman. "Kuyper's Wetenschapsleer," *Philosophia Reformata* 4 (1939): 193-232.

_____. "What is Man?" In *In the Twilight of Western Thought*. Nutley, NJ: Craig Press, 1968.

_____. *A New Critique of Theoretical Thought* (trans. of *De Wijsbegeerte der Wetsidee*). Trans. David H. Freeman and William S. Young. 4 vols. Philadelphia: Presbyterian and Reformed, 1953-57.

_____. *De Wijsbegeerte der Wetsidee*. 3 vols. Amsterdam: H. J. Paris, 1935.

Dubose, Francis M. *God Who Sends: A Fresh Quest for Biblical Mission*. Nashville: Broadman Press, 1983.

Dyrness, William A. *Let the Earth Rejoice: A Biblical Theology of Holistic Mission*. Westchester, IL: Crossway Books, 1983.

Eichrodt, Walther. *Man in the Old Testament*. Trans. K. and R. Gregor Smith. London: SCM, 1954 (orig. pub. 1951).

Eltester, F. W. *Eikon im Neuen Testament*. Berlin: Töpelmann, 1958.

*Evangelical Dictionary of Theology*. Ed. Walter A. Elwell. Grand Rapids: Baker, 1984.

Evans, C. Stephen. *Preserving the Person: A Look at Human Sciences*. Downers Grove: InterVarsity Press, 1977. Reprint. Grand Rapids: Baker, 1982.

Evans, Robert F. *Pelagius: Inquiries and Reappraisals*. New York: Seabury, 1968.

Ferguson, John. *Pelagius: A Historical and Theological Study*. Cambridge, England: Heffer, 1956.

Fichtner, Joseph. *Man, the Image of God: A Christian Anthropology*. New York: Alba House, 1978.

Gaedwag, Edward, ed. *Inner Balance: The Power of Holistic Healing*. Englewood Cliffs, NJ: Prentice-Hall, 1979.

Geisler, Norman L. "Freedom, Free Will, and Determinism," *Evangelical Dictionary of Theology*, pp. 428-30. Grand Rapids: Baker, 1984.

Gilkey, Langdon. *Shantung Compound*. New York: Harper and Row, 1966.

Glasser, Arthur F. "Missiology," *Evangelical Dictionary of Theology*, pp. 724-27. Grand Rapids: Baker, 1984.

Gregory, Thomas M. "The Presbyterian Doctrine of Total Depravity." In *Soli Deo Gloria*, a festschrift for John H. Gerstner, ed. R. C. Sproul. Philadelphia: Presbyterian and Reformed, 1976.

Greijdanus, S. *Toerekeningsgrond van het Peccatum Originans*. Amsterdam: Van Bottenburg, 1906.

Gundry, Robert H. *Sōma in Biblical Theology*. Cambridge: Cambridge University Press, 1976.

Haag, Herbert. *Is Original Sin in Scripture?* Trans. Dorothy Thompson. New York: Sheed and Ward, 1969 (orig. pub. 1966).

Hall, Calvin S., and Gardner Lindzey. *Theories of Personality*. 2nd ed. New York: John Wiley, 1970.

Heard, J. B. *The Tripartite Nature of Man*. Edinburgh: T. & T. Clark, 1866.

Heidelberg Catechism. 1975 trans. Grand Rapids: Board of Publications of the Christian Reformed Church, 1975.

Henry, Carl F. H. "Image of God," *Evangelical Dictionary of Theology*, pp. 545-48. Grand Rapids: Baker, 1984.

Hodge, Charles. *Systematic Theology*. 1871. 3 vols. Grand Rapids: Eerdmans, 1940.

Hoekema, Anthony A. *The Bible and the Future*. Rev. ed. Grand Rapids: Eerdmans, 1982.

_____. *The Christian Looks at Himself*. Rev. ed. Grand Rapids: Eerdmans, 1977.

_____. *The Four Major Cults*. Grand Rapids: Eerdmans, 1963.

_____. *Herman Bavinck's Doctrine of the Covenant*. Th.D. diss., Princeton Theological Seminary, 1953.

Hoeksema, Herman. *The Protestant Reformed Churches in America*. 1936. Grand Rapids: [the author], 1947.

_____. *Reformed Dogmatics*. Grand Rapids: Reformed Free Publishing Association, 1966.

_____. *A Triple Breach in the Foundation of Reformed Truth*. Grand Rapids: C. J. Doorn, 1924.

"Holistic Medicine," *Encyclopedia Americana*, 14:294. Danbury: Grolier, 1983.

Holwerda, David. "The Historicity of Genesis 1-3," *Reformed Journal* 17, no. 8 (Oct. 1967): 11-15.

Hughes, Philip E. "Another Dogma Falls." Review of *Is Original Sin in Scripture?*, by Herbert Haag. *Christianity Today* 13, no. 17 (May 23, 1969): 13.

_____. *Christianity and the Problem of Origins*. Philadelphia: Presbyterian and Reformed, 1964.

_____. *Scripture and Myth*. London: Tyndale Press, 1956.


Irenaeus, *Against Heresies*. In *Ante-Nicene Fathers*, ed. Alexander Roberts and James Donaldson, 1:315-567. Grand Rapids: Eerdmans, 1953.

*International Standard Bible Encyclopedia* (abbrev. ISBE). Rev. ed. Ed. Geoffrey W. Bromiley. Vols. 1 and 2. Grand Rapids: Eerdmans, 1979-82.


Jacobsen, Marion Leach. *Saints and Snobs*. Wheaton: Tyndale, 1972. Reissued in 1975 as *Crowded Pews and Lonely People*.

Jewett, Paul K. *Emil Brunner's Concept of Revelation*. London: James Clarke, 1954.

_____. *Man as Male and Female*. Grand Rapids: Eerdmans, 1975.

Jewett, Robert. *Paul's Anthropological Terms*. Leiden: E. J. Brill, 1971.


Kantzer, Kenneth S., and Paul W. Fromer. "A Theologian Looks at Schuller," *Christianity Today* 28, no. 11 (Aug. 10, 1984): 22-24.

Kegley, Charles W., ed. *The Theology of Emil Brunner*. New York: Macmillan, 1962.

Kelly, J. N. D. *Early Christian Doctrines*. London: Adam and Charles Black, 1958.

Kerr, Hugh Thomson, Jr., ed. *A Compend of Luther's Theology*. Philadelphia: Westminster Press, 1943.

Kline, Meredith G. *By Oath Consigned.* Grand Rapids: Eerdmans, 1968.
—————. *Images of the Spirit.* Grand Rapids: Baker, 1980.
—————. *Treaty of the Great King.* Grand Rapids: Eerdmans, 1963.
Knutson, F. B. "Flesh," ISBE, rev. ed., 2:313-15. Grand Rapids: Eerdmans, 1982.
Köhler, Ludwig. *Hebrew Man.* Trans. Peter R. Ackroyd. Nashville: Abingdon, 1957.
Koole, J. L. "Het Litterair Genre van Genesis 1-3," *Gereformeerd Theologisch Tijdschrift* 63, no. 2 (May 1963): 81-122.
Kuiper, Herman. *Calvin on Common Grace.* Grand Rapids: Smitter Book Co., 1928.
Kuitert, Harry M. *Do You Understand What You Read?* Trans. Lewis B. Smedes. Grand Rapids: Eerdmans, 1970.
Kümmel, Werner G. *Man in the New Testament.* Trans. John J. Vincent. Rev. and enl. ed. London: Epworth, 1963.
Kuyper, Abraham. *De Gemeene Gratie.* 3 vols. Amsterdam: Höveker en Wormser, 1902-04.

Ladd, George Eldon. *A Theology of the New Testament.* Grand Rapids: Eerdmans, 1974.
Laidlaw, John. *The Bible Doctrine of Man.* Edinburgh: T. & T. Clark, 1905.
Lane, Harlan. *The Wild Boy of Aveyron.* Cambridge: Harvard University Press, 1976.
La Patra, Jack. *Healing: The Coming Revolution in Holistic Medicine.* New York: McGraw, 1978.
Lewis, C. S. *The Great Divorce.* New York: Macmillan, 1963.
—————. *Letters to Malcolm: Chiefly on Prayer.* London: Collins, 1966.
—————. *The Problem of Pain.* New York: Macmillan, 1962.
—————. *The Weight of Glory.* Grand Rapids: Eerdmans, 1966.
Lloyd-Jones, D. Martyn. *The Plight of Man and the Power of God.* Nashville: Abingdon-Cokesbury, 1943.
Locke, John. *An Essay Concerning Human Understanding.* Oxford: Clarendon Press, 1894.
Luther, Martin. *The Freedom of a Christian.* In *Three Treatises.* Philadelphia: Fortress, 1960.
—————. *Lectures on Genesis.* Vol. 1 in *Luther's Works,* ed. Jaroslav Pelikan. St. Louis: Concordia, 1955.

Machen, J. Gresham. *The Christian View of Man.* New York: Macmillan, 1937.
MacKay, Donald M. *Brains, Machines and Persons.* Grand Rapids: Eerdmans, 1980.
—————. *Human Science and Human Dignity.* Downers Grove: InterVarsity Press, 1979.
MacLeod, Donald. "Paul's Use of the Term 'The Old Man,' " *The Banner of Truth* (London), no. 92 (May 1971): 13-19.
Maddi, Salvatore R. *Personality Theories.* 4th ed. Homewood, IL: Dorsey Press, 1980.

"Man—God's Trustee in Creation." *International Reformed Bulletin*, no. 52/53 (Winter/Spring, 1973).

Marsden, George M. *Fundamentalism and American Culture.* New York: Oxford, 1980.

*The Maryknoll Catholic Dictionary,* ed. Albert J. Nevins. New York: Grosset and Dunlap, 1956.

McCarthy, Dennis J. *Treaty and Covenant.* Rome: Pontifical Biblical Institute, 1963.

McDonald, H. D. *The Christian View of Man.* Westchester, IL: Crossway Books, 1981.

—————. "Man, Doctrine of," *Evangelical Dictionary of Theology*, pp. 676-80. Grand Rapids: Baker, 1984.

Mehl, Roger. *Images of Man.* Trans. James H. Farley. Richmond: John Knox, 1965.

Mendenhall, George E. "Ancient Oriental and Biblical Law," *The Biblical Archaeologist* 17, no. 2 (May 1954): 26-46.

—————. "Covenant Forms in Israelite Tradition," *The Biblical Archaeologist* 17, no. 3 (Sept. 1954): 56-57.

Menninger, Karl. *Whatever Became of Sin?* New York: Hawthorne Books, 1973.

Menninger, Karl, et al. *The Vital Balance.* New York: Viking Press, 1963.

Minnema, Theodore. "Reinhold Niebuhr." In *Creative Minds in Contemporary Theology*, ed. Philip Hughes. Grand Rapids: Eerdmans, 1966.

Moberg, David. *The Great Reversal.* Philadelphia: Lippincott, 1972.

Moltmann, Jürgen. *Man: Christian Anthropology in the Conflicts of the Present.* Trans. John Sturdy. Philadelphia: Fortress, 1974.

Moulton, J. H., and G. Milligan. *The Vocabulary of the Greek Testament Illustrated from the Papyri.* Grand Rapids: Eerdmans, 1957.

Mouw, Richard. *When the Kings Come Marching In.* Grand Rapids: Eerdmans, 1983.

Mueller, J. T. *Christian Dogmatics.* St. Louis: Concordia, 1934.

Murray, John. *Collected Writings of John Murray.* Vol. 2. Edinburgh: Banner of Truth Trust, 1977.

—————. "Historicity of Adam," ISBE, rev. ed., 1:50. Grand Rapids: Eerdmans, 1979.

—————. *The Imputation of Adam's Sin.* Grand Rapids: Eerdmans, 1959.

—————. *Principles of Conduct.* Grand Rapids: Eerdmans, 1957.

Nee, Watchman. *The Release of the Spirit.* Indianapolis: Sure Foundation, 1956.

Neve, J. L. *A History of Christian Thought.* Philadelphia: United Lutheran Publication House, 1943.

*A New Catechism (Catholic Faith for Adults).* Trans. Kevin Smyth. New York: Herder and Herder, 1967.

*The New Catholic Peoples' Encyclopedia.* Rev. ed. 3 vols. Chicago: The Catholic Press, 1973.

*The New International Dictionary of the Christian Church.* Ed. J. D. Douglas. Grand Rapids: Zondervan, 1974.

Niebuhr, H. Richard. *Christ and Culture.* New York: Harper and Row, 1951.

Niebuhr, Reinhold. *The Nature and Destiny of Man.* 2 vols. New York: Scribner, 1941-43.

Oehler, G. F. *Theology of the Old Testament.* 1873. Ed. G. E. Day. Grand Rapids: Zondervan, n.d.

Oosterhoff, B. J. *Hoe Lezen Wij Genesis 2 en 3?* Kampen: Kok, 1972.

Orr, James. *God's Image in Man.* 2nd ed. London: Hodder and Stoughton, 1906.

Packer, James I. *Knowing Man.* Westchester, IL: Cornerstone, 1978.

Palmer, Edwin H. "Better Beethoven in Heaven?", *Christianity Today* 23, no. 10 (Feb. 16, 1979): 29.

Pannenberg, Wolfhart. *Human Nature, Election, and History.* Philadelphia: Westminster Press, 1977.

Pearce, E. K. Victor. *Who Was Adam?* Exeter: Paternoster, 1969.

Peck, M. Scott. *The People of the Lie.* New York: Simon and Schuster, 1983.

Pedersen, Johannes. *Israel, its Life and Culture.* Vol. 1. Trans. Mrs. Aslang Moller. London: Oxford, 1954.

Polman, A. D. R. *Woord en Belijdenis.* Vol. 1. Franeker: Wever, 1957.

Popma, K. J. "Het Uitgangspunt van de Wijsbegeerte der Wetsidee en het Calvinisme." In *De Reformatie van het Calvinistisch Denken,* ed. C. P. Boodt. The Hague: Guido de Bres, 1939.

Ramm, Bernard. *The Christian View of Science and Scripture.* Grand Rapids: Eerdmans, 1954.

Ridderbos, Herman. *Paul; An Outline of His Theology.* Trans. John R. De Witt. Grand Rapids: Eerdmans, 1975 (orig. pub. 1966).

Robertson, O. Palmer. *The Christ of the Covenants.* Grand Rapids: Baker, 1980.

Robinson, H. Wheeler. *The Christian Doctrine of Man.* Edinburgh: T. & T. Clark, 1911.

_____. *Inspiration and Revelation in the Old Testament.* Oxford: Clarendon Press, 1946.

Robinson, John A. T. *The Body.* London: SCM Press, 1953.

Rogers, Carl R. "Reinhold Niebuhr's *The Self and the Dramas of History:* A Criticism," *Pastoral Psychology* 9, no. 85 (June 1958): 15-17.

Rowley, H. H. *The Rediscovery of the Old Testament.* Philadelphia: Westminster Press, 1946.

Saucy, Robert L. "Both Depravity and Value," *Journal of Psychology and Theology* 1, no. 1 (Jan. 1973): 45-49.

Schilder, Klaas. *Heidelbergsche Catechismus.* Vol. 1. Goes: Oosterbaan en Le Cointre, 1947.

————. *Is de Term "Algemeene Genade" Wetenschappelijk Verantwoord?* Two lectures delivered in 1942 and 1946. Kampen: Zalsman, 1947.

Schott, Erdmann. *Fleisch und Geist nach Luthers Lehre.* Leipzig: Scholl, 1928.

Schuller, Robert H. *Self-Esteem: The New Reformation.* Waco, TX: Word Books, 1982.

Shedd, William. *Dogmatic Theology.* 3 vols. 1888-94. Grand Rapids: Zondervan, n.d.

Skinner, B. F. *About Behaviorism.* New York: Alfred A. Knopf, 1974.

————. *Beyond Freedom and Dignity.* New York: Alfred A. Knopf, 1972.

Smalley, William, and Marie Fetzer. *Modern Science and Christian Faith.* Wheaton: Van Kampen, 1950.

Smedes, Lewis B. *Mere Morality.* Grand Rapids: Eerdmans, 1983.

Solomon, Charles R. *The Handbook of Happiness.* Denver: Heritage House Publications, 1971.

Stacey, W. David. *The Pauline View of Man.* London: Macmillan, 1956.

Stange, Carl. "Luther und das Sittliche Ideal." In *Studien zur Theologie Luthers.* Gütersloh: Bertelsmann, 1928.

Stob, Henry. *Ethical Reflections.* Grand Rapids: Eerdmans, 1978.

Strong, A. H. *Systematic Theology.* 3 vols. Philadelphia: Griffith and Rowland, 1907-09.


Tennant, F. R. *The Origin and Propagation of Sin.* Cambridge: Cambridge University Press, 1902.

*Theological Dictionary of the New Testament* (abbrev. TDNT). Ed. G. Kittel and G. Friedrich. Trans. G. W. Bromiley. 10 vols. Grand Rapids: Eerdmans, 1964-76.

*Theological Dictionary of the Old Testament.* Ed. G. Johannes Botterweck and Helmer Ringgren. Trans. John T. Willis. Rev. ed. Vols. 1 and 2. Grand Rapids: Eerdmans, 1977.

Thiessen, H. C. *Introductory Lectures in Systematic Theology.* Grand Rapids: Eerdmans, 1949.

Tinsley, E. J. *The Imitation of God in Christ.* Philadelphia: Westminster Press, 1960.

Torrance, Thomas F. *Calvin's Doctrine of Man.* London: Lutterworth, 1949.

Trooster, S. *Evolution and the Doctrine of Original Sin.* Trans. John A. Ter Haar. Glen Rock: Newman Press, 1968 (orig. pub. 1965).


Vander Leeuw, G. *Onsterfelijkheid of Opstanding.* 2nd ed. Assen: Van Gorcum, 1936.

Vander Velde, George. *Original Sin.* Amsterdam: Rodopi, 1975.

Van der Zanden, L. *De Mens als Beeld Gods.* Kampen: Kok, 1939.

Van Peursen, C. A. *Body, Soul, Spirit: A Survey of the Body-Mind Problem.* Trans. H. H. Hoskins. London: Oxford, 1966.

Verduin, Leonard. *Somewhat less than God.* Grand Rapids: Eerdmans, 1970.

Versteeg, J. P. *Is Adam a "Teaching Model" in the New Testament?* Trans. Richard B. Gaffin, Jr. Nutley, NJ: Presbyterian and Reformed, 1978.

Vine, W. E. *An Expository Dictionary of New Testament Words.* Old Tappan, NJ: Fleming H. Revell, 1940.

Vitz, Paul C. *Psychology as Religion: The Cult of Self-Worship.* Grand Rapids: Eerdmans, 1977.

Vollenhoven, D. H. Th. *Het Calvinisme en de Reformatie van de Wijsbegeerte.* Amsterdam: H. J. Paris, 1933.

Von Meyenfeldt, F. H. *Het Hart (Leb, Lebab) in het Oude Testament.* Leiden: E. J. Brill, 1950.

Vos, Geerhardus. *Biblical Theology.* Grand Rapids: Eerdmans, 1948.

_____. *Dogmatiek.* 3 vols. Grand Rapids, 1910 (mimeographed).

Vos, Louis A. "Calvin and the Christian Self-Image." In *Exploring the Heritage of John Calvin,* ed. David E. Holwerda. Grand Rapids: Baker, 1976.

Voskuil, Dennis. *Mountains into Goldmines: Robert Schuller and the Gospel of Success.* Grand Rapids: Eerdmans, 1983.

Walker, Morton. *Total Health: The Holistic Alternative to Traditional Medicine.* New York: Everest House, 1979.

Wallace, Ronald S. *Calvin's Doctrine of the Christian Life.* Grand Rapids: Eerdmans, 1961.

Warfield, Benjamin B. "Augustine and the Pelagian Controversy." In *Studies in Tertullian and Augustine.* New York: Oxford, 1930.

_____. *Two Studies in the History of Dogma.* New York: Christian Literature Co., 1897.

Weber, Otto. *Foundations of Dogmatics.* Vol. 1. Trans. Darrell L. Guder. Grand Rapids: Eerdmans, 1981 (orig. pub. 1955).

Weinfeld, M. "The Covenant of Grant in the Old Testament and in the Ancient Near East," *Journal of the American Oriental Society* 90 (1970): 184-203.

*What, Then, is Man? A Symposium of Theology, Psychology, and Psychiatry.* St. Louis: Concordia, 1958.

White, William L. *The Image of Man in C. S. Lewis.* Nashville: Abingdon, 1969.

Whiteley, D. E. H. *The Theology of St. Paul.* Philadelphia: Fortress, 1964.

Wilkinson, Loren, ed. *Earthkeeping: Christian Stewardship of Natural Resources.* Grand Rapids: Eerdmans, 1980.

Wolff, Hans Walter. *Anthropologie des Alten Testaments.* Munich: Christian Kaiser, 1973.

Young, Edward J. *Genesis 3.* London: Banner of Truth, 1966.

_____. *In the Beginning.* Edinburgh: Banner of Truth, 1976.

Young, William S. "The Nature of Man in the Amsterdam Philosophy," *Westminster Theological Journal* 22, no. 1 (Nov. 1959): 1-12.

# Index of Subjects

Ability to choose, 228-32
Actual sin, 143, 172, 173
Adam and Christ, headship of, 115, 117, 118, 121, 148-49, 160, 164, 167
Adam: as first and last, 30, 114-17, 121, 149; as head and representative of human race, 115, 117, 121, 143, 148-49, 159-60, 161, 164, 166-67; historicity of, 112-17; as type of Christ, 115, 121, 149, 164
'Ādām, 12-13
Age of man, 147
Angels, fall of, 121-23
Anthropology: deterministic, 6-7; idealistic, 2-3; scholastic, 4, 36-42
Anthropomorphisms, 126-27

Bāsār, 212-13

Cathedral, 175
Choice, 228
Christ: as perfect image of God, 20-22, 73-75; as our second head, 115, 117, 118, 121
Christian: as lord and servant, 242; as captive and free, 243
Church as image of God, 89, 101
Common grace: biblical basis for, 194-96; distinguished from saving grace, 189; doctrine of, 63-64, 189-94; the three points of, 192; as means by which sin is restrained, 196-99; value of, 199-202
Condemnation, 157, 161, 164-65, 167
Continuity and discontinuity between this life and the life to come, 94-95, 201-2
Covenant of grace, 9-10
Covenant of works, 118-21, 161 n.65
Covenant with Noah, 121 n.25
Created person, 5-10
Cultural mandate, 14, 79-80, 94

Culture, 100
Cursing of the ground, 136-37

Death, 137-39; infant, 165
Depravity, pervasive, 150-52
Destiny, 96-97
Dignity of human life, 2
Direct imputation, 160-62
Dispensationalism, 200 n.29
Dominion, 14, 43, 61, 78-80, 95
Donum superadditum, 38, 40, 46
Dualism and duality, 217

Epitelountes, 90
Eschatology: and our cultural task, 201-2; and the image of God, 30-31, 47-48, 91-95
Evangelism and missions, 98-99
Existentialism, 1

"Faculty psychology," 227
Fall, historicity of, 50, 52-53, 57-58, 113-17, 132
Fallen man, 46; as image-bearer, 15-20, 61
Flesh as the instrument of sin, 108-9, 151, 215-16
Forgiveness of sin, 107
Free will, 227-28, 233-34

Garden of Eden, 139-49
General revelation, 196-98
Guilt, 148-49, 173; transmission of, 156-62, 164-66

Health, spiritual and mental, 225-26
Heart, scriptural understanding of, 171-72
Holistic medicine, 224-25
Human nature, 187-88
Human values, 2

255

# Index of Proper Names

# Index of Scriptures

**261**